CHINA'S FOREIGN RELATIONS

New Perspectives

Edited by

Chün-tu Hsüeh

薛君度 編著

中國外交關係新論

PRAEGER SPECIAL STUDIES • PRAEGER SCIENTIFIC

Library of Congress Cataloging in Publication Data

Main entry under title:
China's foreign relations.

   Includes index.
   Contents: China and the super powers /
Chün-tu Hsüeh and Robert C. North — China
nd Japan / Herbert S. Yee — Korea in China's
foreign policy/ Chün-tu Hsüeh — [etc.]
   1. China — Foreign relations — 1976-
I. Hsüeh, Chün-tu,
DS779.27.C52   327.51   81-22670
ISBN 0-03-060239-4 (hb)   AACR2
ISBN 0-03-061699-9 (pbk.)

Published in 1982 by Praeger Publishers
CBS Educational and Professional Publishing
A Division of CBS, Inc.
521 Fifth Avenue, New York, New York 10175 U.S.A.

© 1982 Chün-tu Hsüeh

23456789 145 987654321
Printed in the United States of America

To friendship:
Personal, professional, and international

PREFACE

The studies contained in this volume examine China's foreign relations from the security and geopolitical perspective as well as interaction of perception and policymaking. Special attention is given to China's grand strategy of the international united front, which has evolved from the profound changes in domestic politics and international environments in recent years.

Chapters 2 and 4 are revised and updated versions of two articles published originally in *Dimensions of China's Foreign Relations*, which I edited (Praeger, 1977), and Chapter 6 is a revised seminar paper of an international conference. The remaining chapters are new and original contributions. It may be mentioned that the articles in *Dimensions of China's Foreign Relations* seem to have withstood the test of time and that the book remains a useful complement to this present volume for the understanding of China's foreign relations.

Again, as in the past, my thanks go to the contributors without whose support and cooperation this book could not have been published. Needless to say, the contributors themselves are solely responsible for the facts and interpretations of their own chapters. Betsy N. Brown, our editor at Praeger Publishers, has been very helpful and inspirational.

An explanation is necessary concerning the spelling of Chinese names and places in this volume. On January 1, 1979, the *pinyin*, or Chinese phonetic alphabet, was officially adopted in the People's Republic of China (PRC) to replace the Wade-Giles and conventional systems that have been used for over a century to transliterate Chinese names and places. The rest of the world rushed to follow suit. Thus, Mao Tse-tung became Mao Zedong, and Chou En-lai, Zhou Enlai. Traditional anglicized spelling of some geographical names such as Peking and Canton became Beijing and Guangzhou, respectively, and Hong Kong became Xianggang. Fortunately, China is still China, not Zhongguo. Similarly, spelling of the names of some well-known historical figures remains unchanged. Thus, consistency was wisely sacrificed for practical considerations.

During this "transition period" of confusion, I have decided to use both the *pinyin* and the Wade-Giles romanization, which is still prevalent in academic institutions and scholarly publications, both in the United States and abroad. The criterion depends on which usage is better known. Some well-anglicized place names and the names of Mao Tse-tung and Chou En-lai, who died in 1976, remain unchanged; otherwise there would be unnecessary confusion with their spellings in the sources cited in the footnotes. For all the current PRC leaders, the *pinyin* system is used.

Generally speaking, the *pinyin* method of transliterating Chinese characters to Roman letters is closer to the actual pronunciation in "Mandarin." But changing the spelling of my name from "*Hsüeh* Chün-tu" to "*Xue* Jundu" is not helpful at all to Americans in pronouncing my family name!

C.T.H.

CONTENTS

1

INTRODUCTION

Chün-tu Hsüeh

A FRAMEWORK FOR ANALYSIS

China's foreign relations are dictated by its foreign policy and interactions with other states. Since the founding of the People's Republic of China (PRC) in 1949, one of China's consistent objectives in its foreign policy has been security, and the Chinese leaders have shown a capacity for adaptation to changing conditions and for employing various tactics to achieve the goal. The perception of threats to its security varied from the 1950s to the 1980s, but the concern has been consistent.

The other factor that has influenced China's foreign policy is domestic needs and politics. In the 1980s, the most important of all the domestic programs is modernization. Hence, it is necessary for China to have peace and advanced science and technology. The two basic external and internal factors (security and modernization) may account for the importance of the "American connection" to China as a long-term stretegy and policy, which is supplemented by seeking closer relations with Japan, Western Europe, and the third world countries to form an international united front against Soviet hegemonism.

In addition to policy goals and domestic factors, China's foreign policy and foreign relations are influenced by national interest, ideology, nationalism, international environment, perception and interaction, the balance of power, historical experience and cultural values, leadership and decision making, revolutionary strategy, the theory of contradictions, and the theory of the three worlds: the first world of the superpowers; the third world of underdeveloped nations in Asia, Africa, and Latin America; and the second world juxtaposed between the two primarily made up of Japan and Western Europe.[1]

However, China's foreign policy and foreign relations have actually and largely hinged on its relations with the two superpowers. When its relations with one or two of them changed, its relations with many other countries invariably changed accordingly. The chapters in this volume illustrate this framework of analysis, which can describe and explain much of the dramatic changes in China's foreign policy and foreign relations in the past, and it may very well be able to predict its foreign policy and foreign relations in the future.

CHINA AND THE FIRST WORLD

In the 1950s, the Peking government followed a policy of "leaning to one side" because of the U.S. hostility and the need for Soviet support for its socialist construction. Ideology, of course, also played an important role. China signed a 30-year military alliance with the Soviet Union in 1950 (which was formally terminated in 1980) to cope with the possible threat from Japan or any other power allied with Japan (i.e., the United States), oriented its foreign trade and cultural exchanges toward the socialist camp, and opposed the nonaligned position taken by some countries. There were also active party-to-party and people-to-people activities among the socialist countries.

As a result of the Sino-Soviet split in the 1960s, however, "antirevisionism" became one of Peking's cardinal policies. Influenced by the ultra-Leftist Party line of the time, the foreign policy platform enunciated in the Constitution of the Chinese Communist Party of April 1969 was anti-American imperialism, anti-Soviet revisionism, and antireactionaries of all countries! Isolated and enraged by international denial (headed by the United States) of its legitimacy, Peking actively supported insurgencies and national liberation movements in the third world as a countermove to the "collusions" of the two superpowers.

The Sino-Soviet dispute originated from Khrushchev's denunciation of Stalin in the Twentieth Congress of the Communist Party of the Soviet Union in 1956, gradually developed, and broke into the open when the Soviet government suddenly recalled its advisers from China in 1960. One of the main issues of the dispute was the different views of the strategy against the United States. Although the dispute was characterized by ideological and policy differences, its fundamental cause was the conflict of national interests. There is no need to go into the details of the developments; suffice it to say that in 1958 the Soviet leaders put forward what the Chinese considered "unreasonable demands" designed to bring China under military control.

The Chinese government has never officially published these demands, which, nevertheless, have long been surmised to a great extent by Western analysts. In essence, the demands were: the permanent stationing of Soviet forces in Luda (Dairen and Port Arthur) in the northeast (Manchuria); the establishment of a joint Pacific fleet under the Soviet command; establishment of a Soviet sphere of influence for the development of resources in the northeast provinces and Xinjiang (Sinkiang) Uygur Autonomour Region in the northwest; establishment of a powerful longwave radio station for naval communication in China under Soviet control; and the institution of a division of labor between the two socialist states — China would be responsible for agricultural products and the Soviet Union industrial development and supplies.*

The Chinese rejected these demands. In June 1959 the Soviet government unilaterally tore up the 1957 agreement on new technology and national defense, and refused to provide China with a sample of an atomic bomb and technical data concerning its manufacture. In 1969 Sino-Soviet relations deteriorated into border conflicts. With the Soviet invasion of Czechoslovakia in the previous year still fresh in Chinese minds, Peking realized that the primary threat to China's security was from the Soviet Union while contradictions with the United States became secondary, and that it was necessary to improve Sino-American relations.

U.S.-Chinese relations took a dramatic turn with the "ping pong diplomacy" in April 1971 and President Nixon's visit to China in February 1972. By the end of the 1970s the two countries had developed "parallel interests," and 1979 saw the establishment of formal diplomatic relations. As the world entered the 1980s, the two governments discussed "complementary actions" against the Soviet intervention of Afghanistan. In U.S. military circles, there began even some talk of forming an alliance with China and other Pacific countries, similar to that of NATO in the Atlantic. Admittedly, this is only a minority view, and it is unlikely to be realized in the foreseeable future. Nevertheless, closer military relations short of formal alliance between China and the United States are expected to develop in time.† Secretary of State Alexander M. Haig's announcement in Peking (June 16, 1981) that the United States would sell arms to China was another step in this direction.**

---

*A talk given by Geng Biao, vice premier of the State Council and secretary-general of the Military Commission of the Central Committee of the Chinese Communist Party, in the Chinese Embassy, Washington, D.C., May 29, 1980, 6:00 P.M., less than two hours after he had successfully concluded negotiations with U.S. Defense Secretary Harold Brown. To the best of my knowledge, this was the first time a Chinese leader openly revealed the Soviet terms, some of which confirmed what had generally been known in the West. However, I am solely responsible for any misrepresentation or inaccuracy of these five demands, because I have not submitted my notes to the vice premier for confirmation or verification. Geng Biao was subsequently appointed defense minister in March 1981.

†My conversations with former Secretary of Defense James R. Schlesinger, June 12, 1981.

**However, some of the military hardware that the Chinese were interested in was considered too advanced and sophisticated to be useful for the present technological level of the Chinese military establishment. My conversations with former Secretary of Defense Melvin R. Laird, April 6, 1981.

Chapter 2 by Robert C. North and myself deals with the developments of China's relations with the two superpowers. It examines the role of ideology and national interests in the making of China's foreign policy. This chapter is a study of how a changing environment has affected Peking's perception of Soviet-American relations, how changing perceptions have affected basic policy and interaction patterns among all three countries, and how the change of policy has in turn altered China's views of the two superpowers. Finally, it analyzes the prospects for Sino-Soviet relations, and discusses Sino-American relations after normalization.[2]

CHINA AND THE SECOND WORLD

Sino-American rapprochement has brought a decisive change in China's position in the world. China (and the United States as well) had downplayed ideology and shifted its emphasis in the direction of trade, economic, cultural, and technological cooperation with other countries. Much of Sino-Japanese relations has developed along these lines since the establishment of diplomatic relations between the two countries in September 1972, particularly after the signing of the Treaty of Peace and Friendship in August 1978. Since then the two countries have entered a new stage of cooperation. Although the "China boom" was temporarily upset by the cancellation of several giant contracts because of Chinese economic retrenchments in 1980-81, the Japanese fully understood that it was not due to the change of Chinese policy. It is expected that the two countries will forge ahead to maintain and continue to improve their good relations.*

Japan is not only important to China's modernization programs, strategically she is also a crucial factor in China's united front strategy against Soviet hegemonism. China no longer issues charges, as she did before normalization of relations, against the threat of renewed Japanese militarism, and has dropped her opposition to the U.S.-Japanese security treaty. In fact, China has now acknowledged the stabilizing role of the treaty in Asia and the Pacific, and encouraged the Japanese to strengthen their military establishment. The change of China's policy toward Japan may be explained to a great extent by China's changing relations with the two superpowers. Chapter 3 by Herbert Yee analyzes the bilateral relations of China and Japan, taking into account considerations of the American and Soviet factors. He also presents the interesting aspects of images, myths, and emotion that have affected Sino-Japanese relations.

Western Europe also belongs to the second world. China's foreign policy toward Europe has also been influenced by its relations with the two superpowers. In the 1950s Peking considered Western Europe as part of the capitalist

---

*My conversations with Saburo Okita, former Japanese foreign minister (1979-80), June 12, 1981.

camp headed by the United States. In the 1960s, Peking encouraged Western European countries to assert their independence from both superpowers. The establishment of diplomatic relations between China and France in 1964 was a major move for both countries. It was China's first successful step to break up U.S. diplomatic containment on the European front. Unlike the British, who had resigned themselves to their loss of influence after World War II, the French have not lost their historic sense of grandeur. However, as illustrated by Jean-Luc Domenach in Chapter 6, Sino-French relations are inevitably limited and secondary in comparison with China's relations with the two superpowers.

Since the 1970s Peking has considered Western European unity as an effective instrument against Soviet hegemonism and a crucial factor in the united front strategy. Consequently, trade between China and the European Community has greatly increased in recent years. In 1980, the total two-way trade amounted to more than US$4.9 billion, or 13.4 percent of China's foreign trade. The European Community has become China's third most important trading partner, next only to Japan and the United States.[3] There have been frequent exchange visits between the PRC leaders and those of the Western European countries, including a visit to Belgium, France, and Great Britain by the chief of the general staff of the Chinese People's Liberation Army in July 1981.

In Chapter 7 Raymond Wylie argues that Chinese-West European relations are gradually emerging as an important factor on the international scene. In particular, the Chinese see Western Europe as a key area of attention in their search for greater strategic security, economic development, and regional and global influence. The Europeans are also aware of the commercial and security value of China. To the extent that both sides share common interests in their quest for a greater voice in an increasingly multipolar world, they can be regarded as "objective allies."

After the Sino-Soviet split, the Chinese classified the East European countries into two categories. One consisted of Albania, later Rumania in the early 1960s, and Yugoslavia in 1977. China recognized the socialist character of these countries, and consequently classified them as members of the third world. Sino-Albanian relations, however, have greatly deteriorated since the death of Mao Tse-tung in 1976.

The remaining five countries — Bulgaria, Czechoslovakia, the German Democratic Republic (GDR), Hungary, and Poland — have been much closer to the Soviet Union, and China has considered them members of the second world. They are the subject of Chapter 8 by Karel Kovanda. As indicated in this chapter, China's attitude toward them changed considerably in the wake of the Soviet invasion of Czechoslovakia in 1968. These countries had hitherto been viewed as mere appendages of the Soviet Union. After the invasion, China started playing up the contradictions between them and the Soviet Union. In the first stage, the Chinese expressed support for *popular struggles*, notably in Czechoslovakia and Poland. In the second stage, the support broadened to include *regimes* as well, especially national and economic issues of discord between the Soviet Union and these countries.

It may be noted that China has not only improved state-to-state and party-to-party relations with Yugoslavia, but with Italian and other Communist Parties in Western Europe. China has maintained correct and normal state-to-state relations with the East European countries that are close to the Soviet Union, but little party-to-party relations. For the past several years, however, China has refrained from criticizing the Communist Parties of these countries. But it is difficult to improve their party-to-party relations unless the leaders of these countries are also inclined to do so.

CHINA AND THE THIRD WORLD

China considers herself a developing country belonging to the third world. The Democratic People's Republic of Korea (DPRK) and the Republic of Korea (ROK) also belong to the third world; the former, however, is a socialist country having close ties with China, while the latter is not. In Chapter 4 on the divided Korea I analyze China's policy in a framework of several basic factors, interaction variables, and Korea's response to a changing international environment. It underscores Sino-American rapprochement as an underlying factor in the initiation of the dialogue and subsequent negotiation gestures of the two parts of Korea. China's anxiety over South Korea being supported by the United States has been greatly reduced after the normalization and improvement of relations with the United States, although officially Peking's position toward Korean unification seems to have remained the same. The chapter also discusses at some length traditional Chinese-Korean relations in the context of the international system of East Asia before the coming of the Western powers.

Of all the third world regions, South and Southwest Asia, like Korea, are special to China for geographical and security reasons. In South Asia, China has had close ties with Pakistan for a number of years. In June 1981, Peking made two major moves in this area. Premier Zhao Ziyang paid a friendly visit to Pakistan, Nepal, and Bangladesh, and Vice Premier and Foreign Minister Huang Hua's visit to India to discuss the long-standing border dispute and other issues reflects a new Chinese posture of attempting to improve relations with other states wherever possible. It was the first time a high-ranking Chinese official went to visit India since Chou En-lai called on Jawaharlal Nehru in 1960. The visit was particularly significant in view of the fact that India had been linked to the Soviet Union through a 1971 friendship treaty, and since then the two countries have maintained close trade, defense supplies, and industrial ties.

In Southeast Asia, China and Vietnam are neighboring countries with very close ties in history, geography, and culture. For ideological and security reasons, China gave all-out support to the Vietnamese revolution, first against the French, and then against the United States. A few examples will suffice to understand the magnitude of the support. In 1954, the Vietnamese won the battle of Dien Bien Phu with the artillery sent by China, whose generals participated personally in the front-line command. In 1962, China supplied over 900,000 rifles and machine guns to South Vietnam for unfolding guerrilla warfare. Beginning from October 1965 more than 300,000 Chinese air defense forces, engineers, railway builders, logistic and other personnel were sent to work in North Vietnam until they were withdrawn by July 1970. It cost the Chinese US$20 billion to support the Vietnamese between 1950 and 1978, a great sacrifice for the country and the people.[4]

However, Sino-Vietnamese relations deteriorated after the Vietnam War because China could no longer give Vietnam massive aid in peace time as requested. Furthermore, instead of setting a high priority on economic reconstruction, the Vietnamese leaders took advantage of a momentum to assert an aggressive policy. But China was opposed to Vietnamese ambition of ruling a unified Indochina. Consequently, Vietnam turned against China with Soviet support. As a result of Vietnam's invasion of Kampuchea, not to mention Vietnam's border incursions and persecution of "overseas Chinese," China launched a punitive attack to "teach the Vietnamese a lesson" in February-March 1979. The aggression against Kampuchea by the "Cuba of Asia" with Soviet support is considered by Peking as an important part of the Soviet global strategy for world hegemonism.[5] Thus, the Sino-Vietnamese relationship has become a factor of the Sino-Soviet conflict.

Chapter 5 by Shee Poon Kim deals with China's relations with the Association of Southeast Asian Nations (ASEAN) in the region. It analyzes the interaction process between China and the ASEAN states. ASEAN is a regional organization formed by Indonesia, Malaysia, the Philippines, Singapore, and Thailand in 1967 for promoting their common interests of economic growth, social progress, and cultural development, but avoiding political issues and military dimensions. China's attitude toward ASEAN has changed from hostility to cultivation as a result of the changes of Peking's relations with the United States and, in addition, since 1978, Soviet-Vietnamese collusion. As elsewhere, the overriding determinant of China's policy toward ASEAN is security and strategic calculation, especially the concern for encirclement by a superpower.

ASEAN relations with China have also been influenced by similar variables. The collapse of the Thieu regime in South Vietnam in April 1975 created a new sense of urgency. Indeed, the Communist victory in Vietnam in 1975 and the Vietnamese invasion of Kampuchea in 1978 brought about an entirely new power configuration in Southeast Asia. China, the United States, and the ASEAN states share a common interest of containing Soviet-Vietnamese expansion in the region and dealing with the Vietnamese refugee problem. Premier Zhao Ziyang declared at a press conference in Bangkok in February 1981 that if Vietnam invades Thailand, China would "resolutely stand on the side of Thailand and support the Thai people's struggle against aggression."[6] He visited the Philippines, Malaysia, and Singapore in August, seeking closer relations with the

ASEAN states to solve the Kampuchean problem. Secretary Alexander M. Haig's visit to the Philippines after Peking in June reaffirmed U.S. concern and interest in the area.

In international relations, no two nations, not even allies, can have completely identical national interests without contradictions. The PRC-ASEAN relations are no exception. The ASEAN states are particularly sensitive to two issues: China's relations with the local communist movements and the ethnic factor of the so-called "overseas Chinese," not to mention other policy objectives and resolution of conflicts. The ASEAN states cannot but continue to have misgivings when China refuses to forego its support of local Communists, although the Chinese leaders have openly and repeatedly assured them that China's relations with the Communist Parties of the ASEAN countries are mainly political and moral, that China does not approve of exportation of revolution, and that the party-to-party relations will not affect the state-to-state relations.[7]

It may be mentioned that it is difficult, if not theoretically impossible, for China to declare that it would not support the cause of communism elsewhere. Furthermore, if the Chinese did in fact openly declare not to support the Communist Parties in the ASEAN states, the local Communists would inevitably turn to the Soviet Union and Vietnam. It is significant to note that the level of Chinese support has been very low in recent years, and in the case of the Philippines, it has been almost nil.*

The other delicate problem between China and the ASEAN states is the "overseas Chinese." Ethnic Chinese constitute about 75 percent of Singapore's population, 37 percent in Malaysia, 8 percent in Thailand, 1.5 percent in the Philippines, and 2 percent in Indonesia. It is a unique dimension of China's foreign relations. In most cases, the so-called overseas Chinese are actually citizens of foreign countries, i.e., ethnic minorities, but they are frequently regarded as "aliens" by their governments and fellow citizens alike.

Overseas Chinese have increasingly identified themselves with the country of their residence since the end of World War II, although several stereotyped concepts concerning them still persist. One is that they are sojourners, even though they may have in fact lived abroad for several generations, and no longer consider China as their country. The other criticism is that they are not assimilated with the society; in this regard the critics often ignore the fact that the policy of the colonial governments in the past was designed to prevent assimilation. The third misconception pertains to the question of their loyalty. But the truth is that the overwhelming majority are loyal citizens of their adopted or native-born countries, although some did become involved in insurgency or communist movements in these countries.

---

*My interview with Ambassador Eduardo Z. Romualdez in the Philippine Embassy, Washington, D.C., July 23, 1975. There is no evidence to indicate that the situation has changed since the interview.

One may wonder whether the persistence of these misconceptions is actually a rationalization or excuse for racial discrimination and persecution. But discrimination, legal or not, against their own citizens of Chinese descent in some of the ASEAN states is hardly conducive to "nation building," state identity, and emotional loyalty for ethnic Chinese there.

For many years, particularly during the Cultural Revolution, overseas Chinese and Chinese with overseas connections in China were looked upon with suspicion, if not downright persecution, by the Chinese authorities. Since 1978 the Chinese government has stressed once again the positive role they can play in China's economic progress and modernization. As a move to attract their investment and expertise for the development of China as well as their support for the reunification of Taiwan, Peking has appealed to their patriotism and offered them material incentives.[8] It has also rehabilitated the Overseas Chinese Affairs Office in the State Council, and revitalized the All-China Federation of Returned Overseas Chinese and other united front organizations and activities.

However, the basic policy that had been formulated in the 1950s has remained the same. China does not recognize dual nationality. It has consistently favored and encouraged the overseas Chinese to become law-abiding citizens of the country of their residence on a voluntary basis, while opposing efforts of foreign governments to force them to change their nationality.[9]

It may be mentioned that although ASEAN is a unitary regional "actor" in international relations, it is an organization composed of five members of diversified political systems with different national interests. The development of China's relations with the ASEAN states has been uneven and will continue to be uneven. For example, diplomatic relations were established between the PRC and Malaysia, the Philippines, and Thailand in 1974-75, but there are no diplomatic relations between China and Singapore (trade missions were exchanged in 1981). On the other hand, Indonesia, which suspended diplomatic relations with China in October 1967, has not been inclined to resume relations. There has not even been direct trade between the two countries.*

Chapter 9 by Robert L. Worden deals with another third world region — Latin America. The crux of China's interest in Latin America has been her attempts to offset, initially, the U.S. influence and, second, the increasing presence of the Soviet Union. The change of Sino-Soviet relations has inevitably altered China's relations with Latin American countries, particularly Cuba.

---

*According to "China: International Trade," published by the National Foreign Assessment Center, Washington, D.C., May 1981, China exported some $161 million of goods to Indonesia in 1980. There is no indication whether it was indirect trade. In any event, there has been a great increase of trade between China and the other four ASEAN states since the 1970s. According to the same source, the total two-way trade betweeen Malaysia and China increased from $321 million in 1978 to $533 million in 1980. For the same period, trade between China and the Philippines increased from $160 million to $277 million; Singapore, $384 million to $862 million; and Thailand, $157 million to $598 million.

The major foreign policy issues that China has considered in formulating its Latin American relations include Peking's long-term moral support of wars of national liberation, the 200-nautical-mile maritime zone, economic independence, and the nuclear-weapon-free zone. This last chapter analyzes China's post-Mao perspective on Latin America as a part of its third world policy. It briefly discusses the evolution of that policy since 1949 and relates it to Latin America in terms of China's strategic view of and relations with the region. The description of the strategic view includes analysis of superpower contention and the role of Cuba in the third world. Bilateral relations are discussed in terms of diplomatic exchanges and economic interests. The concluding section projects Latin America as a "last frontier" in Chinese foreign affairs and as an area of mutual concern in Sino-American relations.

CONCLUDING REMARKS

In the 1960s China was a nation in self-inflicted chaos. It advocated revolution, and actively supported insurgencies in many parts of the world. It was vulnerable to outisde intervention, isolated and enraged by international denial of its legitimacy. The 1970s witnessed significant changes as a result of Sino-American rapprochement. As the world entered the 1980s, China had finally reached the stage of maturity in its foreign relations. The chapters in this book, which deal almost exclusively with state-to-state relations, reflect China's new perspectives and outlook in foreign affairs. The salient features of China's new posture may be summarized as follows:

• The Soviet hegemonism is considered the most dangerous threat to China and world peace.
• China is turning toward the West, and seeks a united front primarily with the United States, Japan, and Western Europe as well as the third world countries against the Soviet hegemonism; however, China intends to maintain an independent and nonalignment policy.
• China has downplayed ideology and world revolution while emphasizing security and national interest.
• China has shifted its emphasis from supporting people's wars of national liberation to developing state-to-state relations with the countries with which Peking has established diplomatic relations, and it generally refrains from encouraging forces seeking to destabilize nonrecognized governments.
• China is increasingly and constructively participating in the international system.

In analyzing China's foreign policy, it is difficult to discern conflicting and competitive factional perceptions in that country. Therefore, the prevailing views of the dominant group as expressed by the government and mass media at any given time are considered China's perceptions. It is also always difficult to judge whether a government means what it says or says what it means. Henry Kissinger recalls that during his October 1971 visit to China, Chou En-lai told him that the United States "should observe Peking's actions, not its rhetoric."[10] And during President Nixon's meeting with Chairman Mao in the following year, Mao "laughed uproariously at the proposition that anyone might take seriously a decades-old slogan scrawled on every public poster in China."[11]

China's foreign policy is made by its leaders. There is little information on the decision-making process other than the routine bureaucratic procedure common to all countries. Apparently there is little input from the masses, the media, the general public, or the "pressure groups." In recent years, increasing attention has been paid to methodology for the study of China's foreign policy. Each approach, be it traditional or innovative, has its merits and shortcomings. It may be judged by how much insight it can really yield in terms of effort — the question of "cost and benefit" or "claim and performance." No approach is perfect, but one certainly can complement the other.[12]

NOTES

1. The theory of the three worlds was put forward by Mao in 1974, and expounded by Deng Xiaoping in his speech at the Special Session of the U.N. General Assembly on April 10, 1974. See *Peking Review*, April 19, 1974, pp. 6-11. The evolution of the three-world theory may be traced to Mao's talk with the American correspondent Anna Louise Strong, August 1946. See *Selected Works of Mao Tse-tung*, vol. 4 (Peking: Foreign Languages Press, 1969), pp. 97-101. For an English version of a major article on the subject by the editorial department of the *Renmin Ribao* [People's Daily], "Chairman Mao's Theory of the Differentiation of the Three Worlds is a Major Contribution to Marxism-Leninism," see *Peking Review*, November 4, 1977, pp. 10-41.

2. For historical background and contemporary evolution of the triangular relations, see Steven I. Levine, "Soviet-American Rivalry in Manchuria and the Cold War," in *Dimensions of China's Foreign Relations*, ed. Chün-tu Hsüeh (New York: Praeger, 1977), chap. 2; and "The Superpowers in Chinese Global Policy," in *China in the Global Community*, ed. James C. Hsiung (New York: Praeger, 1980), chap. 3.

3. *Shichang* [Market], Peking, April 18, 1981.

4. An article by a prominent Vietnamese leader Hoang Van Hoan, who defected to China in 1979, in *Beijing Review*, December 7, 1979, pp. 12, 15, 17. The $20 billion cost was revealed earlier by Deng Xiaoping during his interview by Italian journalist Oriana Fallaci, August 1978.

5. *Hongqi* [Red Flag], no. 1 (1979), pp. 79-81. See also *Beijing Review*, January 19, 1979, pp. 13-16; and "Soviet Strategy in East Asia," ibid., March 23, 1981, pp. 19-21.

6. *Beijing Review*, February 9, 1981, p. 15.

7. Ibid., August 17, 1981, p. 8; also the *China Daily* (Peking), August 13, 1981.

8. The overseas Chinese policy of the post-Mao leadership may be seen from the *Renmin Ribao* [People's Daily] editorial of January 4, 1978; *Peking Review*, January 20, 1978, pp. 15-16; also May 26, 1978, pp. 16-17.

9. For a discussion of various aspects of the overseas Chinese policy, see Shao-chuan Leng, "The PRC's Policy of Protecting Chinese Nationals Abroad," in *Dimensions of China's Foreign Relations*, ed. Chün-tu Hsüeh (New York: Praeger, 1977), chap. 9.

10. Henry Kissinger, *White House Years* (Boston: Little, Brown, 1979), p. 778.

11. Ibid., p. 1062.

12. For discussions of methodology, see James C. Hsiung, "The Study of Chinese Foreign Policy: An Essay on Methodology," in *China in the Global Community*, ed. James C. Hsiung and Samuel S. Kim (New York: Praeger, 1980), pp. 1-15; and Davis B. Bobrow, et al., *Understanding Foreign Policy Decisions: The Chinese Case* (New York: Free Press, 1979), chap. 3.

2

CHINA AND THE SUPERPOWERS: PERCEPTION AND POLICY

Chün-tu Hsüeh
Robert C. North

INTRODUCTION

During the 1950s and early 1960s, combinations of political, economic, and military power were viewed as critical variables in the foreign relations of the People's Republic of China (PRC); but ideology was widely accepted as the prime motivator of Peking's foreign policies, the overriding determinant of world bipolarity, and China's relations with both the Soviet Union and the United States. The course of events since the 1960s has seriously challenged this view. Changes in relationships among China, the Soviet Union, the United States, Japan, India, Pakistan, and other countries suggest that power and related considerations have overridden ideological determinants in a number of critical circumstances.

For Marxist-Leninist proponents, whether in Moscow or Peking, the state has been viewed as the instrument of the ruling class, and its leaders articulate the national interest.[1] If the ruling class is bourgeois, the state, its values, its purposes, its interests, and its behavior will be shaped accordingly. If, on the other hand, the ruling class is proletarian, the state will serve as an instrument of the working class and its behavior will be shaped by working-class interests.

In line with these fundamental assumptions, the world view of the Chinese Communist leadership centered originally on the two-camp theory, which seemed to be consistent with the realities of the world situation and the policies of the two superpowers in the 1950s. For practical as well as ideological reasons, Chairman Mao decided to "lean to one side." The validity of both his perception and policy was reinforced by the apparent reality of Sino-Soviet solidarity

13

at the time. Under these circumstances, the imperatives of ideology seemed to serve realpolitik quite effectively, but once China and the Soviet Union were in open conflict, how were their disputes to be accommodated and accounted for within a theory that forced antagonists into one of two carefully defined camps? What, in fact, happened to ideology as world politics moved from bipolarism to polycentrism?

Clearly, as assumptions behind the two-camp theory were increasingly violated, something had to give. In part, Chinese Communist theoreticians solved the ideological impasse by denouncing Soviet leaders as revisionists, or even by casting doubt on the proletarian nature of the Russian Revolution itself, just as ideologues in Moscow dismissed the Chinese Communist revolution as essentially peasant in its character. But then, as ideology and reality became more and more at odds, the two-camp theory itself was conveniently shelved in the 1960s and subsequently discarded by the Chinese.[2] Reacting to the hostility of the two superpowers toward them, the Chinese adopted a domestic policy of self-reliance. Influenced by extreme internal revolutionary fervor during the Cultural Revolution, China took a hard-line position against "imperialism," "revisionism," and "reactionaries" all over the world.

In the meantime, U.S. perceptions of monolithic communism and of Peking's intentions and capabilities had also changed. On both sides, however, there was a tendency to assimilate the new perceptions with the old ones, and unconsciously, perhaps, to distort what was seen in such a way as to minimize any conflict with previous expectations. The "straining toward consistency," a phenomenon well known to psychologists, persisted. Eventually, Chinese Communist leaders, perhaps rudely prodded by reality, became convinced of U.S. sincerity in wanting to end the Vietnam War and to improve Sino-American relations. These changes in reality and perception made it possible for President Richard Nixon to visit Peking in February 1972. In July Mao reportedly told French Foreign Minister Maurice Schumann that the world was no longer divided into blocs. In April 1974, Peking leaders declared that the socialist camp was "no longer in existence," and that the world today actually consisted of three parts, or three worlds, which were "both interconnected and in contradiction to one another."[3] As a result of these developments, there have been some corresponding alterations in Chinese views of U.S.-Soviet relations. Such changes raise questions about the extent of conflicts between ideology and national interest.[4]

In the 1970s Peking identified itself with the third world, with special emphasis against the two superpowers and their hegemonies. By the end of the decade and the beginning of the 1980s, Soviet hegemonism was singled out for opposition. This chapter examines against the background of a changing environment some important alterations in how China has tended to perceive Soviet-American relations and how changing perceptions have affected basic interaction patterns among all three countries. It analyzes some pertinent variables and their interaction in order to understand several of the changes that have taken place, or are likely to take place, in China's foreign relations.

IDEOLOGY AND "REALITY"

A major weakness of ideology as a useful concept for the social sciences stems from the variety of meanings assigned to it.[5] In a broad sense, ideology is the science that deals with the evolution of human ideas. In terms of a more specialized definition, ideologies are "characterized by a high degree of explicitness of formulation over a very wide range of the objects with which they deal," and for their adherents, "there is an authoritative and explicit promulgation." As compared with other patterns of beliefs, they are "relatively highly systematized or integrated around one or a few pre-eminent values, such as salvation, equality or ethnic purity." Consensus and complete individual subservience to the ideology are normally demanded from those who accept it.[6]

According to another definition, ideology consists of "selected or distorted ideas about a social system or a class of social systems when these ideas purport to be factual, and also carry a more or less explicit evaluation of the 'facts.' "[7] A difficulty with such a definition for purposes of disciplined analysis is the problem of subjective bias and the inability of human beings to establish among themselves, beyond any shadow of doubt or controversy, what "true reality" is. By whom are the pertinent ideas perceived as "selected or distorted," and according to whose criteria?

The word "ideology" is often employed disparagingly to characterize an opponent's belief system. As used by Marx and Engels, ideology referred to elaborate beliefs promulgated by the capitalist class in order to justify its favored position in society. Later, the term was frequently used with reference to a set of values determined by irrational or quasi-rational considerations.[8] In the United States and elsewhere, ideology is used with reference to nazism, facism, Marxism-Leninism, or the thoughts of Mao.

In this chapter the term "ideology" is presumed to mean "a pattern of beliefs and concepts (both factual and normative) that purport to explain complex social phenomena with a view to directing and simplifying sociopolitical choices facing individuals and groups."[9] An ideology might thus refer to any widely shared and socially or legally sanctioned body of assumptions, expectations, or other perceptions, as well as values and imperatives, about the universe, man's role and purpose in it, and man's proper relations with his fellowman. As thus defined, almost any society may be said to possess an ideology, but in some countries, particularly in those inspired and organized by Marxist-Leninist doctrine, the ideology tends to be more highly rationalized and cohesive than in others. It is regularly interpreted, reviewed, and reinterpreted by persons in authority, and adherence to its major imperatives is often enforced by Party or government sanctions.

Any given ideology must be fundamentally dependent upon and shaped by a wide range of human perceptions about the nature of man and the workings of the universe. Without perceptions of the past, the present, and various possible futures, ideology could not exist. Indeed, no human being, beggar or king, has informational contact with his environment at all, or even with himself, except through his nervous system. This is true of leaders and citizenry in any country. In these terms, prevailing assumptions, expectations, values and impera- tives – the foundations of any ideology – are dependent upon and shaped by a wide range of perceptions about the nature and workings of human beings and of the larger universe.

What human beings perceive as "reality" appears to be so solid and unmis- takable that it is difficult for national leaders and others to recognize the extent to which that "reality" is inferred by them and their advisers and "may not match the reality which future events reveal."[10] Thus, in many ways, national leaders, like all other human beings, construct the reality in which, day by day, they actually operate.[11] There are, as a result, as many subjective realities as there are individual perceivers, although many such constructs may overlap suffi- ciently to permit broad consensus and collective action.[12]

Human perceptions are notoriously fallible. Indeed, a perception may be viewed as a "choice" or a "guess" about the true nature of whatever is per- ceived.[13] A person's accuracy of guess or choice may be influenced by idiosyn- cratic experience, faulty memory, "false" belief based on past experience or indoctrination, fatigue, anxiety, fear, uncertainty, expectation, hope, and a wide range of other considerations. Normally, "The perception that actually occurs is the one that requires the least reorganization of the person's other ideas." But if an environmental change is sufficiently unmistakable and its implications sufficiently overwhelming, a considerable and possibly quite painful reorganiza- tion of belief may be difficult to resist. Because of the mediating function of perception, it follows, therefore, that as ideology may affect events, so also events may affect ideology. The two tend to be intensely interactive.[14]

As long as the assumptions, expectations, and other perceptions embodied in a prevailing belief system and acted upon by the national leadership are not critically at variance with reality, that ideology may be expected to exert a strong influence upon policy and behavior. To the extent that conditions and events of the objective environment persistently challenge a prevailing ideology, on the other hand, disturbing tensions and uncertainties are likely to be gener- ated, and if the discrepancies increase in frequency and importance, at least some elements of the belief system will tend to be reinterpreted, modified, or replaced – especially if the implications of the environmental alterations are too pressing to be ignored.[15] Under such circumstances, however, there is likely to be a lag of months or perhaps years between the point where the first discrep- ancies become evident to the leadership and the time when major ideological reinterpretations, modifications, or replacements are undertaken. During this period, changes in policy and behavior that are considered indispensable may be rationalized as temporary measures or in other ways until such time as the leaders and/or their constituents are psychologically ready for the needed ideological adjustments. Thus, radical changes in the environment, critical alter- ations in the international configuration of power, for example, can so widen the gap between reality and belief as to render prevailing ideologies obsolete and force policy changes that may run counter to the most fundamental ideological assumptions and tenets.

TWO VIEWS OF THE TWO-CAMP THEORY

The standard theme in Marxist-Leninist doctrine, that the world is divided into two hostile and irreconcilable camps — the socialist camp and the capitalist or imperialist camp — was shared by the Soviet and the Chinese Communists for a long time. Until the end of the 1950s, the Chinese supported the Soviets in opposing the capitalist camp, headed by the United States, and they consistently backed the Soviet Union in its dealings with the other Communist states and parties. The policy of "leaning to one side" declared by Mao in July 1949 and the 1950 Sino-Soviet treaty of military alliance were, in considerable part, the outcome of this Chinese world view, but it may have been derived also from the attitudes and policies of other countries, especially the United States, where many people tended to share the fundamental perception that the world was indeed divided into two camps.

During World War II, however, and even immediately after, views on both sides had been much more flexible. Some American observers have suggested that if Mao or Chou En-lai had been invited to visit the United States in early 1945, or if John Leighton Stuart, United States ambassador to the Nationalist government, had gone to Peking in June 1949,[16] the People's Republic of China might have leaned somewhat differently, or possibly walked upright between the two sides. Under such circumstances, it would have been difficult to conceive of the Peking regime, whether in a geopolitical context or in terms of economic and military power, as a realistic threat to the United States.

To argue the "if's" of history is often a useless pastime, but is it conceivable that Chinese Communist foreign policy may have been influenced by Washington, above, beyond, or aside from the proclaimed Marxist-Leninist-Maoist ideology? Admittedly, the friendly gestures of the Chinese Communists toward the United States in 1944-45 were made when they were engaged in a power struggle with the Nationalists, and according to Mao himself, Stalin did not begin to trust him until after the outbreak of the Korean War.[17]

It would have been to the advantage of the Chinese Communist leaders if they could have gained contact with or support from the United States during 1944-45 because of "political effects on the Kuomintang."[18] Given the situation of the United States in World War II, one might not have expected Washington to shift its support from a recognized, legitimate, allied government to encompass the Communist movement. Yet the United States did go out of its way to endorse the Communist demand for a coalition government in China — a fact that many liberal critics of U.S. policy seem to have forgotten.[19] One may argue, perhaps, that if President Harry Truman had approved Ambassador Stuart's proposed trip to Peking, relations between the two countries in subsequent years might have been different. Against this background, it is worth speculating on the extent of the influence of the attitude of the United States in May and June 1949 on Mao's policy of "leaning to one side," which he expounded in July.

Even as late as August 22, 1949, the National Security Council accepted the view that Chinese Communist success in surmounting their internal difficulties — overpopulation, undeveloped natural resources, technical backwardness, and social and political lag — might well lessen rather than intensify their subservience to the Kremlin. Similarly, a Chinese Communist failure to achieve a viable economy might force the Peking government to depend more, rather than less, on the USSR.[20] The National Security Council also conceded that any attempt on the part of the United States "openly" to deny Chinese territory such as Taiwan to the Communists would probably react to the benefit of the Communists by rallying all the antiforeign sentiments to their side.[21]

Four months later, on the other hand, after Communist power had been established on the Chinese mainland, the joint chiefs of staff informed the National Security Council that "a modest, well-directed and closely supervised program of military advice and assistance to the anti-Communist government in Formosa would be in the security interests of the United States."[22] This partial and still somewhat tentative shift in position was an early indicator of what became, with the outbreak of the Korean War, a generally consistent and hostile policy toward the People's Republic and a broad containment policy which, in Asia at least, leaned heavily upon an assumption of Sino-Soviet collaboration.

The fundamental shifts in U.S. perceptions, assumptions, and policies are documented in the Government Printing Office edition of the (so-called) Pentagon Papers. Essentially, during the early 1950s, policymakers in Washington were apprehensive lest the United States find itself confronted with an alignment of the USSR, Communist China, and a rehabilitated Japan. In the weeks that immediately followed the close of World War II, the USSR, as viewed by the National Security Council, had become an Asian power of the first magnitude "with expanding influence and interests throughout continental Asia and into the Pacific."[23] As perceived from Washington, however, the Soviet Union could not build "a powerful, self-sufficient, war-making complex in Asia without access to and control over Japan."[24] Many eminent scholars have been reluctant to accept this explanation of U.S. policies in Asia, and undoubtedly there were other considerations involved. But these documents from the National Security Council reveal the importance of the interdependency of resources and strategy in the influencing of U.S. policy.

With the outbreak of the Korean War in June 1950, U.S. leaders feared that Communist expansion on the Asian mainland, by denying Western-Japanese access to rice, tin, iron ore, rubber, oil, tungsten, fibers, and other vital resources of Asia, would drive Japan into the Soviet-Chinese bloc.[25] For without such vital raw materials and markets, acquired under one guarantee or another, Japan could not maintain a tolerable living standard, let alone thrive and grow. The denial of Soviet — and by extension, Chinese and other Communist countries — access to Southeast Asia and other parts of the Asian mainland thus became an indispensable prerequisite for the successful barring of Soviet influence and control over a potentially revitalized and highly productive Japan.

In this way, the resource requirements of Japan and the strategic interests of the United States (as both were perceived in the National Security Council) became powerful elements in the complex blend of motivations that drove the concerns and activities of the United States deeper and deeper into eastern and Southeast Asia. These considerations also contributed to the American version of the two-camp theory in that the United States required a rationalization and public justification for its Asian policy and activities.[26]

In its Communist and non-Communist versions of the two-camp theory, each side was thus provided with a persuasive explanation of events as they unfolded in Asia during the 1950s and provided the leadership concerned with convenient rationalizations for their policies and actions. In effect, each bloc acted like the mirror image of the other. On the one hand, China and the United States were at war in Korea, and at times it looked as though U.S. forces might cross the Yalu River to overthrow the new regime on the Chinese mainland. On the other hand, the Peking government had a pressing need for Russian economic and military aid, and there was at least an appearance of Sino-Soviet solidarity. Reciprocating Peking's hostility, the United States denounced the PRC as aggressive and expansionist and as an instrument of the Soviet Union. After the Korean armistice in 1953, Washington continued to deny the legitimacy of the Peking government, maintained an isolation and containment policy against it, and blocked it from taking its seat in the United Nations. As late as 1957, Secretary of State John Foster Dulles still asserted that communism in China was a passing phase.[27] Misinterpretations of the intentions of leaders in Peking and overestimation of China's capability even prompted discussion in the United States of the possibility and desirability of allying with the Soviet Union against the Chinese, a subject with an undertone of racism.[28] Through their stubborn adherence to a set of basic assumptions and to the respective policies that seemed to flow from them, the cold war partisans on both sides tended to create their own outcomes almost in defiance of underling "reality."

Just as the United States persisted in denying legitimacy to the Peking government for more than a decade after the Sino-Soviet conflict became publicly manifest, so China clung to the idea of two camps long after it ceased to approximate world realities. Although the Sino-Soviet dispute had its beginnings in Nikita Khrushchev's secret speech denouncing Stalin at the Twentieth Party Congress in February 1956, the two-camp theory was reaffirmed by Mao when he talked to the Chinese students in Moscow in November 1957.[29] As late as spring 1959, Chinese leaders and writers were still discussing international politics in terms of "two worlds."[30] Yet the doctrine of two hostile and irreconcilable camps had already come into question.

The uncertainty stemmed from the interaction of a number of factors. The turning point was Khrushchev's visit to the United States for talks with President Dwight D. Eisenhower in September 1959, which took place shortly after the Soviet government had abrogated unilaterally the 1957 Sino-Soviet agreement on new technology for national defense and refused to provide the Chinese with a sample atomic bomb or technical data concerning its manufacture. The Chinese perceived the Soviet action as a gift to the United States, and the latter reciprocated by an invitation to the Soviet premier to visit the country.[31]

Under such circumstances, the Chinese may have concluded that the two camps were not really as irreconcilable as had originally been thought. The theory became even more untenable as the Sino-Soviet dispute intensified and the U.S.-Soviet detente further developed in the 1960s. As a theoretical basis for the new situation, the Chinese hurled charges of Soviet revisionism. The argument was that the rise to power of revisionism signals the rise to power of the bourgeoisie and the emergence of common interests between that privileged class and U.S. capitalists.[32]

CHINESE VIEWS OF SOVIET-U.S. RELATIONS

During the 1960s, Chinese views of Soviet-American relations centered on the following themes: collaboration, collusion, alliance, encirclement of China, superpowers, nuclear plot, struggle for hegemony, capitulation on the part of the Soviet Union, the superpowers colluding and at the same time contending with each other, and the Soviet Union as an accomplice of U.S. policies. Some of these themes were briefly mentioned in the early 1960s when the Chinese Communist Party and the Communist Party of the Soviet Union began to engage in polemics. During the most active period of the Cultural Revolution (1966-69), the Chinese elaborated on all of them.

In the celebrated Nine Articles (September 1963-July 1964), commenting on the Open Letter of the Central Committee of the Communist Party of the Soviet Union, the Chinese began to attack explicitly Khrushchev's line of "Soviet-U.S. cooperation for the settlement of world problems." They criticized Soviet leaders for being "intoxicated with the idea of the two 'superpowers' establishing spheres of influence throughout the world." The Soviet leadership was accused of being "increasingly anxious to strike political bargains" with the United States at the expense of the interests of the socialist camp and the international communist movement. The Cuban missile crisis was cited as an outstanding example of the Soviet "error of capitulationism."

Chinese Communist apprehensions about Soviet-American relations were exacerbated by the escalation of the Vietnam War, by the increasingly hostile and militant Soviet attitude toward Peking, and by insecurities, frustrations, and suspicions generated by the Cultural Revolution.[33] Encirclement and collusion became the themes most frequently mentioned in the Chinese press and by the Peking leaders.[34] As viewed from Peking, the United States already had many military bases around mainland China — in Taiwan, Japan, South Vietnam, and the SEATO countries, such as Thailand and the Philippines. Now the United States was seen as shifting the emphasis of its global strategy step by step from Europe to Asia in order to complete its "arc of encirclement."[35] At the same time, the Soviet Union was not only going out of its way to bring about detente in Europe but was also vigorously encouraging and supporting the resurgence of Japanese militarism.[36]

Since there remained some cracks and breaches in the "cordon," Soviet leaders came forward to patch them up, making India, Mongolia, and other countries the flanks in the encirclement of China. Vice-President Hubert Humphrey's meeting with Alexei Kosygin in New Delhi in January 1966 was viewed by the Chinese as a Soviet-U.S.-Indian "united front against China."[37]

Soviet Foreign Minister A. A. Gromyko's visit to Japan in July 1966 "close on the heels" of Secretary of State Dean Rusk was seen by Peking as a "new counter-revolutionary 'Holy Alliance' " of the United States, Japan, and the Soviet Union.[38] One writer considered that the "Soviet-Japanese collusion" was "the extension of U.S.-Japanese collusion, a variation of U.S.-Soviet collaboration, and a product of America's imperialist policy of containment of China."[39] And the Japan-U.S. joint communique after the Sato-Nixon meeting in November 1969 was denounced by Premier Chou En-lai as a "new stage" in the "military collusion" between the United States and Japan.[40]

Soviet activities in Southeast Asia — shipping munitions to Rangoon, increasing Soviet naval strength in the Indian Ocean, supporting the Suharto government in Indonesia, establishing diplomatic relations with Singapore and Malaysia, encouraging the Vietnam peace talks, and bringing about the Indo-Pakistan rapprochement — were all perceived as part of Moscow's efforts to organize an anti-China ring in collaboration with the United States. The Chinese concluded that the United States no longer regarded the Soviet Union as an enemy, but looked upon it as a friend.[41] The Soviet leadership had ceased to support the world revolution and had become an accomplice of the United States in suppressing peoples' revolutions the world over.[42]

Closely associated with the development of the cordon, as Peking saw it, was a network of specific Soviet-American collaborative undertakings and collusions. Specific charges within the framework of the collusion theme were often repeated by the Chinese press throughout 1967 and 1968.[43] In regard to Vietnam, Soviet leaders were accused of placing the Vietnam question within the framework of Soviet-American cooperation and of easing the European situation so that the United States could transfer more of its troops to Vietnam. Soviet policy toward North Vietnam was "sham support and real betrayal," plotting and peddling various kinds of "peace talk frauds," and scheming to use so-called "united action" to control North Vietnam and to sow dissension between the Chinese and Vietnamese peoples in order to undermine their military unity.[44]

Soviet leaders were charged with carrying out a "policy of three-fold assistance": to help the United States promote the "peace fraud," escalate the war, and encourage "anti-China madness" in the United States. The Chinese interpreted the Soviet occupation of Czechoslovakia as a "political dirty deal" between the superpowers. According to a Chinese commentary, the occupation of Czechoslovakia was carried out "with tacit U.S. consent" in return for "the tacit consent and support" of America's war in Vietnam.[45]

Chinese views of the United States and the Soviet Union in the Middle East reflected the idea that the two superpowers apparently had agreed to work toward preventing a direct military confrontation, but otherwise they remained in conflict in that area. The various proposals the two countries submitted in 1967-69 to settle Middle East issues were considered by the Chinese as the basis for "collusion and bargaining between imperialism and social imperialism."[46] The Chinese accused the Soviet Union of forcing the Arab countries to seek peace with Israel by giving up territories and stamping out the flames of the Palestinian people's armed struggle,[47] thus directly serving "U.S. imperialism and its tool of aggression, Israel."[48]

Until the Peking government represented China in the United Nations, the world organization was often treated by Peking with scorn. It was frequently considered to be an instrument of the United States, an organ "in the service of old and new colonialism," "a vile place for a few powers to share the spoils,"[49] and a "U.S.-Soviet political stock market."[50] The Chinese accused the Soviet representative at the U.N. General Assembly of "attempting to bring the Korean question into the orbit of Soviet-U.S. collaboration for world domination."[51] At one time the Peking leaders even suggested the establishment of a "revolutionary United Nations."[52]

Two of the main reasons for the Sino-Soviet split was the Soviet attempt to control China, and the Soviet failure to live up to its commitments to assist China's nuclear development.[53] The late Foreign Minister Chen Yi reportedly said that China must have atomic bombs even if the Chinese people do not have pants to wear. Peking viewed the Soviet agreement with the United States on the prevention of nuclear proliferation as a plot to monopolize nuclear weapons and collusion in the conspiracy against China's security. The partial nuclear test ban was denounced as "nuclear blackmail"[54] and a "big fraud,"[55] aimed at "tying China's hands."[56] The 1967 draft treaty on the nonproliferation of nuclear weapons was attacked by Peking as a "major step" in Soviet-American "collaboration on a worldwide scale" and "another treacherous crime" committed to contain China's influence abroad.[57]

China refused to sign the 1968 Nuclear Non-Proliferation Treaty. In the first public Chinese reaction to the strategic arms limitation treaties (SALT), signed between the United States and the Soviet Union during President Nixon's visit to Moscow in May 1972, Premier Chou En-lai reportedly argued that the treaties actually marked the beginning of a new stage of the arms race between the two superpowers.[58]

INTERACTION OF PERCEPTION, REALITY, AND POLICY

To what extent did Chinese views correspond to the realities of Soviet-American relations in the 1960s? How did Peking leaders respond to world events as they perceived them? How did their perception, the real-world situation, and Chinese foreign policy interact?

It is not necessary to examine each Chinese allegation of Soviet-U.S. collusion, nor is it possible, in view of the limited information available, to discuss the private beliefs of leaders in Peking as opposed to their official views, the differing opinions on crucial issues, or the variance between public statements and those expressed in secret channels. But public statements provide useful indicators, however rough, of Chinese official views at any given time.

An examination of public statements from Peking suggests that some were rationally calculated to create particular impressions at home or abroad; some were based on misperceptions, the outcome of self-isolation; and some were not much more than ideological rhetoric. But even when careful allowance is made for considerations of this kind, it seems evident that many of the views held by Chinese leaders were not unfounded. From the perspective of an observer in Peking, China was indeed being encircled — by U.S. forces in Japan, Taiwan, Southeast Asia, and South Asia, and by the USSR along a vast perimeter from Sakhalin to Western Siberia and to some extent from Afghanistan to the Indian Ocean and even North Vietnam. And Chinese fears of attack, including a possible Soviet preemptive strike, were not entirely unjustified.

Against the background of the Sino-Soviet controversy, overtures of the USSR toward Japan could only deepen Chinese anxieties. Japan had always been considered by the Chinese as the core of the U.S. military alliance in Asia and the hub of its ring of encirclement of China. Thus, it was not until Prime Minister Kakuei Tanaka's visit to the People's Republic and the establishment of diplomatic relations between the two countries in September 1972 that Peking changed its attitude toward the Japanese government. Shortly afterwards, the Chinese press's attacks on Japanese militarism were conspicuously absent — an illustration of how perceptions of national leaders, reality, and the policies of other countries can interact.

However misconceived the Chinese collusion theory may have appeared from the perspective of Washington or Moscow, there was an element of reality in it. Both superpowers had been in favor of maintaining the status quo in the world, and each had given up attempting to interfere in the other's sphere of influence. In the Taiwan Straits crisis in 1958 and in the Sino-Indian conflicts in 1959 and 1962, Washington and Moscow had a parallel interest in preventing a deterioration of those conflicts into direct confrontations; at times, they even found themselves on the same side of the barricade, with Peking on the other side. This policy of restraint held through the later 1960s (for example, West Berlin, the Wall, Cuba, Czechoslovakia). Even some Europeans have harbored misgivings similar to those of the Chinese. In his April 1969 press conference,

President Nixon mentioned that he had found concern on the part of European countries about the possibility of a "U.S.-Soviet condominium" in which, at the highest level, the two superpowers would make decisions affecting Europe's future. One European statesman used the term "Yalta" in his conversation with the president.[59]

During the Cultural Revolution, some of the anxieties and hard-line policies of the Chinese Communists were outcomes of the country's domestic struggle. But three major events that took place at that time undoubtedly reinforced Chinese attitudes: the U.S. escalation of the Vietnam War, dating from 1965; the Soviet invasion of Czechoslovakia in August 1968; and the Sino-Soviet border clashes of March and August 1969.

Chinese leaders were concerned that the Vietnam War might lead to a military confrontation between China and the United States. A strategic response to such an eventuality was indicated by Chou En-Lai. In an interview given to a Pakistani correspondent in April 1966, Chou made it quite clear that China would not take the initiative to provoke a war with the United States. But once war broke out, it would not be contained or limited.[60]

With regard to the role of the USSR in Vietnam, Soviet leaders were virtually compelled to support North Vietnam and oppose the United States for reasons of solidarity with a Communist state and of competition with China.[61] But apparently they wanted to avoid an open-ended involvement that would endanger basic Soviet-American relations and their global interests. In his press conference on March 4, 1969, President Nixon asserted that the USSR was in a very delicate position, that the Soviet government had been helpful in terms of getting the Paris peace talks started, and that the Russians would like to use what influence they appropriately could to help bring the war to a conclusion.[62]

As to the nuclear issue, it was apparent to the Chinese that the United States and the Soviet Union were engaged in a nuclear arms race while at the same time sharing a common interest in maintaining nuclear superiority. To break the nuclear monopoly of the two superpowers, China assigned a high priority to the production of its own nuclear weapons through self-reliance. Until the Sino-Soviet controversy, Peking had consistently supported Moscow's position on nuclear negotiations. The dispute was intensified when the Soviet Union proceeded to negotiate the partial nuclear test ban treaty with the United States.

Through the development of limited nuclear capability, the Peking government greatly altered its position in the international configuration of power with the result that it no longer felt the need, as it did in the mid-1950s, for the protection of another country's nuclear umbrella.

After China's successful nuclear development in 1964, the nuclear policy of the USSR has increasingly taken China into account (along with the United States). With improvements in Chinese-U.S. relations, on the other hand, U.S. nuclear policy has become far less concerned with China, whereas its concern with the USSR has remained central. As compared with the nuclear policies of the other two powers, however, that of China has remained relatively consistent. While some of the Chinese proposals — total prohibition of nuclear weapons and the dismantling of nuclear bases on foreign soil — may be considered unrealistic and rhetorical, to date China is the only nuclear power that has declared that it will never, at any time or under any circumstances, be the first to use nuclear bombs.[63]

The word "collusion" suggests an explicit intention that is difficult to identify in the documentation available. In many respects the Soviet-American detente had little to do with China, but undoubtedly the Soviet Union and the United States had parallel interests, as well as the common interest in keeping China at arm's length.[64] As viewed from Peking, however, parallel actions of the two superpowers amounted to collusion. Irrespective of either side's intention, U.S.-Soviet collusion — or, at any rate, parallelism — took shape whenever the vital interests of the two countries demanded it.

Given the perceptions maintained by Chinese leaders of a "new Holy Alliance" against China, their belief that revolution was the main trend in the world, and their assumption that all political forces were undergoing a process of upheaval, division, and reorganization, their response to this perceived situation took the form of opposing simultaneously the United States, the Soviet Union, and "reactionaries" all over the world.[65] The Peking leadership also actively supported national liberation movements in Asia, the Middle East, Africa, and Latin America — the "storm center" and "first intermediate zone" separating the United States from socialist countries.[66]

A NEW REALITY

"When the extreme is reached, the reverse will set in." During the early 1970s, this old Chinese saying proved applicable even to Communist dialectics. Peking's extreme and inflexible policy could not long be sustained after consolidation of the domestic struggle and in the midst of other changes that were taking place. The policy violated the most elementary rules of diplomacy.

After the Sino-American rapprochement and changes in Peking's attitude toward the Vietnam War, the Chinese no longer accused the Soviet Union of being America's accomplice in the war. In fact, during 1972, Chinese comments on the war hardly mentioned the Soviet Union. On the other hand, by the end of the 1960s the United States had abandoned, in part at least, its previous justification of the war in terms of containing Chinese expansion. Instead, ironically enough, President Nixon's trip to Peking was partially rationalized in terms of seeking Peking's support for ending the war. When an agreement was finally signed in January 1973, both Peking and Moscow endorsed it.

For generations classic writers in the field of diplomacy have maintained with considerable consistency that the foreign policies and external activities of any country, but especially those of a great power, are likely to be explained best in terms of the struggle for survival, the maximizing of power, and the defense of national interests.[67] For two decades after World War II, the international configuration of power did not seem to change significantly: the world remained essentially bipolar. Then the entire system underwent rapid alterations in the direction of multipolarity. To some extent this new trend was the result of a decline of United States power, nationalism, and the emergence of many new nations and to some extent it was attributable to the remarkable rise of Japan. But developments inside the People's Republic of China, new needs and problems within the Soviet Union, and outcomes of competitions and conflicts between Peking and Moscow were probably of even greater importance.

Although General Eisenhower had told President-elect John F. Kennedy that any change in China policy by the incoming administration would bring him out of retirement fighting, Washington began to show signs of flexibility toward the People's Republic under the Kennedy administration.[68] The various friendly, if sporadic, gestures by the United States toward Peking during the 1960s are so well known that there is no need to retell them here. Suffice it to say that at first the Chinese were suspicious of the new signals from Washington;[69] but by the end of 1970 they finally were convinced of U.S. sincerity in wanting to end the Vietnam War, to avoid taking sides in the Sino-Soviet dispute, and to improve Sino-American relations. Mao decided to welcome President Nixon to visit China.[70]

The alteration of the world configuration that began in the late 1960s and early 1970s also can be explained in considerable part by such objective factors as the increased need within China of new equipment, replacement parts, and specialized technologies, especially as time passed after the disruption of Soviet technical assistance programs; the achievement and continuing development of a Chinese nuclear capability; the erosion of U.S. efforts in Vietnam and elsewhere as a result of fatigue, frustration, and competing domestic requirements; Soviet failures in agriculture and the growing Soviet need for new, highly refined technologies; and the rapid growth of Japan in terms of industry, commerce, and specialized, refined technologies that, along with those of the United States, West Germany, and elsewhere, were in demand by the USSR and increasingly by China. All of these factors seem to have contributed to an alteration in relative capabilities and power among the countries, the generation of new demands, and a groping toward new relationships.

For much of the nineteenth century and well into the twentieth, China had been characterized by a population that was large (relative to readily available resources) and growing; a technology that lagged in comparison with the West; and vulnerability to economic, political, and military penetration by Western powers and later by Japan. In order to rectify these weaknesses, the society somehow had to accumulate capital, mobilize labor and resources, and develop new capabilities. During the early 1950s, the Peking government, with considerable reliance upon Soviet technical assistance, developed a program along these lines that involved tight government control of production, minimal consumer consumption, and strict regulation of priorities. There were serious weaknesses in the Chinese Communist program, but over the long run it was sufficiently successful, even after the Great Leap Forward and the withdrawal of large-scale Soviet assistance, to place the People's Republic in the running as a major world power.[71]

The basic assumptions underlying U.S. attitudes toward China and much of the rest of Asia during the late 1940s and early 1950s have been touched upon earlier. Once these assumptions had been made explicit in top echelons of the government, the reasoning behind the domino theory and the justification for the expansion of U.S. power and influence on the Asian mainland became difficult to refute. The Sino-Soviet conflict, the rapid growth of a Western-Oriental Japan, the Chinese Communist achievement of nuclear weaponry, and the failure of the United States to force a decisive outcome anywhere on the Asian continent combined to cast doubt upon the underlying premises, however, and by the late 1960s, the cost of American involvement was beginning to erode public support. It was no longer clear what the country's purpose was, and there were growing anxieties about where it might lead.

The Soviet antagonist, meanwhile, was suffering difficulties of its own. The Chinese had largely repudiated Moscow's leadership of the Communist world and were competing for influence over many local movements. And, viewed from Moscow, Chinese progress in the development of nuclear weaponry posed a new threat to the USSR along its eastern borders. The consideration that, in view of the superior military power of the Soviet Union, it is difficult for outsiders to understand this "threat" does not decrease its potency. Perhaps it is akin to the "threat" that Japan felt about a regenerate China in the 1930s and the United States about the PRC for two decades after World War II. Aggressive, stronger powers often feel that they are being threatened while overlooking the fact that they are actually threatening others.

There were further difficulties. Confronted by new failures in the agricultural sector and by a rapidly growing need for highly specialized Western (and Japanese) technologies, the Soviet Union was reaching toward the United States, Japan, West Germany, and elsewhere on the basis of increased trade and technical exchange agreements.

As an outcome of its remarkable postwar recovery and its spectacular economic growth during the late 1950s and early 1960s, Japan has begun to play a pivotal role, being in a position to supply both the USSR and the PRC with technology, machinery, and parts in exchange for basic resources. At the same time, however, the dependence of Japan upon raw materials and markets beyond its borders makes the country deeply dependent upon unbroken trade access and favorable exchange in many parts of the world. In this sense, the economic well-being of Japan depends to a large extent upon the skill of the Japanese in maintaining viable relations not only with the United States but also with the USSR and the People's Republic of China — a difficult feat in the best of circumstances.

The infrastructural changes that have come about in relations among the PRC, the United States, the USSR, Japan, and other countries are suggested by the sharp change in trade patterns during the 1960s and early 1970s. In 1957, Communist countries were receiving 72 percent of China's exports, and their own goods accounted for 66 percent of Chinese imports. These relationships contrasted sharply with the 28 percent of Chinese exports received by non-Communist countries and the 34 percent of Chinese imports accounted for by non-Communist countries. By 1966, these patterns had been sharply reversed, however, and they have continued to be so since. Thus, in 1970, only 25 percent of China's exports were being received by Communist countries, as opposed to 75 percent by non-Communist nations. And a mere 15 percent of China's imports were supplied by Communist countries as contrasted with 85 percent supplied by non-Communist nations.[72]

Amidst these many changes leaders in Peking began to realize that neither their perceptions nor the policy based on them conformed entirely to reality on the world scene. Some major reassessments were required. Presumably, a dramatic change in relations with the United States was not the only option available to the Chinese Communists. Peking might have sought an accommodation with the USSR and the reestablishment of comradely relations. But Mao no longer trusted the Soviet leadership. Moreover, in historic, geopolitical, and other terms, the Soviet threat to China appeared both more real and more imminent than that of the United States. In addition, a Sino-Soviet rapprochement would not have enabled Peking to solve the Taiwan problem, which remained an important issue in the unification of China. Solution of that problem is dependent upon reaching an understanding with the United States.[73]

The ping-pong diplomacy of April 1971 opened a new trend in Sino-American relations. Many Western commentators have inferred that the Chinese may have viewed the Nixon visit as analogous to the payment of tribute by foreign barbarians to the court of the Middle Kingdom. This comparison amounts to one of those farfetched and misleading attempts at explanation made by those who tend to account for the China of today almost wholly in terms of the past. Perhaps Mao's meeting with Chiang Kai-shek in Chungking for peace negotiations after World War II is a more appropriate analogy, except that in the case of Nixon's visit it was a president of the United States who made the journey to negotiate. In any case, the Nixon visit to Peking undercut the Chinese charge of Soviet-U.S. collusion in the encirclement of China. Peking kept silent on President Nixon's summit conference in Moscow in May 1972,* and Chou En-lai

---

*However, on the day of Nixon's departure for the Soviet Union on May 20, 1972, the *People's Daily* prominently carried an article written by a group of workers condemning the two powers as the "arch-criminals" in modern time. While the commentary made no mention of Nixon's trip, it reiterated the theme that the two superpowers were colluding and at the same time contending with each other for world domination, and that the third world had formed a united front against the two "paper tigers."

made only a passing remark about Leonid Brezhnev's visit to the United States in June 1973.[74]

The collusion charge made a brief reappearance in November,[75] and again in Chou's report to the Tenth Party Congress in August 1973. Chou's major theme was that the two superpowers were colluding and at the same time contending with each other for world hegemony. However, "contention is absolute and protracted, whereas collusion is relative and temporary."[76] He also introduced for the first time the theme that the Soviet Union was "making a feint to the East while attacking in the West."[77] Thus the perceived Soviet threat was shifted from China to Europe, which has been considered by the Chinese as the "focus of superpower contention."

A content analysis of the *Peking Review* for 1974-76 suggests that Peking virtually has abandoned the collusion theme. However, Chou En-lai's other themes were subsequently reiterated on numerous occasions. Beginning with the 1974 New Year's Message, Peking has stressed the contending aspect of Soviet-American relations, repeatedly attempted to expose the falsehood and myth of detente, and linked superpowers with hegemony.[78] In the view of the Peking leaders, "detente is a superficial phenomenon," used by the Soviet Union to "hoodwink the people, lull the vigilance of the adversary, divide Western Europe and dominate the world." It lulls the West by creating a false sense of security. However, the "stark reality is not that detente has developed to a new stage, but that the danger of a new world war is mounting." Detente "in words is designed to camouflage intense rivalry for hegemony in deeds," and the fierce contention makes "the outbreak of war hard to avoid."[79] Deng Xiaoping pointed out at the banquet in honor of President Ford in December 1975: "Rhetoric about 'detente' cannot cover up the stark reality of the growing danger of war," and he exhorted the United States not to fear Soviet "hegemonism" but to form a broad international front and wage "tit-for-tat struggle."[80] It is significant to note that many Americans have also criticized detente as a one-way street, and that in the spring of 1976 President Ford deemed it necessary, for domestic political purposes, to abandon the use of the term.

After the public rapprochement, the first practical convergence of views and policy between the United States and China occurred during the Bangladesh conflict in late 1971. The Chinese considered that the treaty of "peace, friendship and cooperation" concluded between India and the Soviet Union in August 1971 was not only in substance a "treaty of military alliance" and made India's war against Pakistan possible,[81] but it also represented another step on the part of the Soviet Union to "expand its sphere of influence so as to contend with another superpower for world hegemony."[82] China thus joined with the United States in lending support to Pakistan, while the Soviet Union supported India.

A review of articles dealing with Soviet-American relations in the *Peking Review* and the *Beijing Review* for the years 1977-81 indicates that China's perception of U.S.-Soviet relations have undergone a further shift as China's relations with the United States greatly improved, particularly after the establishment of diplomatic relations in January 1979. In 1977 and early 1978, emphasis was still given to the Soviet-U.S. contention for hegemony as the "root of the unrest in the world, and their scramble" would "eventually lead to war," but the Soviet "social-imperialism" was considered "the most dangerous source of world war."[83] Furthermore, a distinction was made between the two rivals: "One superpower is bent on expansion; the other has its vested interests to protect."[84] As Deng Xiaoping remarked in Washington during his visit in January 1979, "for quite some time now, the Soviet Union is on the offensive, whereas the United States is on the defensive."[85]

Since 1978, a series of internal and international events has further changed China's perception and policy. Internally, Peking has dramatically reversed the ultraleftist Party line that prevailed intermittently for two decades until the death of Mao in September 1976 and the arrest of the "Gang of Four" a month later. Since then the Peking leaders have adopted various popular rational and practical measures to provide a conducive environment for carrying out the program of "four modernizations."[86] Externally, the Soviet-Vietnamese friendship treaty of November 1978 was followed by the Vietnamese invasion of Kampuchea (Cambodia), and the Soviet-Afghan "friendship treaty" of December 1978 was followed by the massive Soviet military intervention in Afghanistan in December 1979. The United States reacted strongly to the Soviet move in Afghanistan,[87] which seems to have vindicated Peking's persistent views of the Soviet Union and detente.

INTERNATIONAL UNITED FRONT

In order to meet the continuing challenge of the two superpowers, and influenced by the internal political climate of the Cultural Revolution, Peking perceived the 1960s and the early 1970s as an age of world revolution and people's wars.[88] It saw an increasing number of medium-sized and small countries joining forces to oppose the hegemony and power politics of the superpowers.[89] This appraisal was the basis of the international united front policy that has been facilitated by Peking's representation in the United Nations since the fall of 1971.[90]

For a decade starting in 1956, the People's Republic of China extended aid on a fairly sustained basis to less developed non-Communist countries in Africa, East Asia, South Asia, and the Middle East. Then, in 1967, this aid began to taper off. In the early 1970s, China again increased its aid programs for third world countries. After 1973, however, the annual amount of aid extended to the developing countries decreased; and the decreases continued in the immediate post-Mao period.[91] Against a background of common experience, sympathy, and interest, the Chinese began to identify themselves genuinely with the peoples of Asia, the Middle East, Africa, and Latin America. Peking has stressed repeatedly that it belongs to the third world,[92] and that the Chinese people have suffered too much from foreign oppression for them to want to become a super-power, bullying smaller countries.[93] Mao reportedly told French Foreign Minister Maurice Schumann in July 1972 that despite its possession of nuclear weapons China is not a superpower.[94] That remark may be considered as a revelation of intention as well as a realistic self-assessment of power.

The third world comprises over 100 developing countries, in Asia, Africa, Latin America, and other regions, constituting more than 70 percent of the world's population.[95] The medium-sized and small countries, if they all work in concert, may yet tip the scales of the balance of power. This assertion may seem less extravagant if placed within the context not only of the energy crisis but also of predicted scarcities in many other resources critical to the functioning of a highly industrialized society. According to Leninist theses, colonies and semicolonies have always been the foundation and lifeline of imperialism. In any event, the growth of the ranks of the third world has changed the makeup of the United Nations.

When the United Nations was founded in 1945, there were only 51 member states. Since then the membership has increased to 154 and 5 observers in June 1981, and the states of Africa and Asia constitute about two-thirds of the membership. Of more than 100 countries that joined the world organization after its founding, the overwhelming majority have achieved independence after World War II. Their role in the United Nations has been steadily growing, and they have become a force that cannot be ignored.[96]

Contrary to many observers' misgivings in the past on seating Peking in the United Nations, the People's Republic of China has played a constructive rather than a disruptive role in the world organization. At the same time, the Chinese delegates have consistently backed the claims of many Afro-Asian and Latin American countries. They supported, for example, the draft resolution put forward by Sri Lanka and 12 other countries on declaring the Indian Ocean to be a peace zone.[97] In line with the claims of several Latin American nations, they also have insisted that those countries should have jurisdiction over the seas within 200 nautical miles, as opposed to the 12 nautical miles advocated by the United States and the Soviet Union.[98] It is expected that China will continue using the United Nations to implement its third world policy.

In order to unite all the forces that can be united, Peking has sought out also the second world, the developed capitalist countries that have been subjected to superpower pressure. China thus has encouraged Japan to oppose hegemony (especially Soviet hegemony) and to increase its defense spending, supported Western Europe, and encouraged Eastern Europe to resist Soviet domination. As one European scholar put it, there is an objective geopolitical link between China and Europe in that both are the principal neighbors of an expansionist Soviet Union.[99] Having reversed its earlier views on the enlarged European Economic Community, Peking now considered that a Common Market of ten countries might be a serious obstacle to U.S.-Soviet hegemony, and that the "Western European unity against hegemonism is a historical necessity and the need of our time."[100] In May 1975, Peking decided to accredit a representative to the European Economic Community, and in recent years there have been more and more exchanges of visits between Chinese and European leaders, including Hua Quofeng's visits to Rumania, Yugoslavia, and Iran in August 1978, and Western Europe in the fall of 1979. As for Eastern Europe, the PRC has always enjoyed a reservoir of goodwill there despite their differences. Peking's championship of equality among the socialist countries cannot but favorably impress many people in that area, although some of the countries there cannot openly express their views contrary to the Kremlin line.

Although China originally adopted a policy of forming an international united front of small and medium-sized countries against the two superpowers, Peking's adversarial relationship with the United States began to change into a somewhat lower level of conflict in the 1970s. According to Mao, "There are many contradictions in the process of development of a complex thing, and one of them is necessarily the principal contradiction whose existence and development determine or influence the existence and development of the other contradictions."[101] The relationship between China and the Soviet Union clearly had developed into the principal contradiction by the end of the 1960s, while the contradiction between China and the United States became a secondary one. In the early 1970s, Peking might still have applied to the United States its domestic revolutionary formula of "uniting and at the same time struggling." China's policy of the international united front, now directed almost exclusively against the Soviet Union, includes, in addition to the third world countries, the United States, Western Europe, and Japan.[102] Referring to the international situation and the 1980s as "a decade of troubles," Deng Xiaoping pointed out "the need" for China, the United States, and other countries "to unite and deal seriously with Soviet hegemonism."[103]

THE PROSPECTS FOR SINO-SOVIET RELATIONS

Sino-Soviet relations have three dimensions: party-to-party, state-to-state, and people-to-people. There have been no party-to-party or people-to-people relations for the past 20 years, and there will not be any until governmental relations are improved.

Some of the original disagreements between the two countries are no longer issues: for example, the denunciation of Stalin, ideological dispute, views on the national liberation movement and world revolution, policy toward the United States in the context of the 1960s, and the Soviet cancellation of the Sino-Soviet technology and defense agreement. Furthermore, if personality were also a factor, the leaders who were deeply involved with the dispute — Khrushchev and Mao — are no longer alive. However, there are still some major differences between the two countries.

First, the ideology. The ideological dispute of the 1960s is no longer a factor, but ideological differences still exist in the 1980s. While the Chinese

Communist authorities have repudiated the ultraleftist Party line, Chinese communism is not reverting to the Soviet model. To what direction — Yugoslavia, Eurocommunism, and what not — it will develop remains to be seen. In all probability it will be "Communism, Chinese style," a model with distinctive Chinese characteristics. In any event, the ideological factor is not as crucial as that in the past.

Second, the difference of world view. From the Chinese viewpoint, the main problem is Soviet hegemonism, which manifests itself in global expansions: Africa, the Middle East, the Indian Ocean, Afghanistan, and, above all, support of the Vietnamese aggression in Kampuchea.

In bilateral relations, there are a border dispute and the stationing of one million or several hundred thousand Soviet troops on the Chinese border, not to mention the Soviet missile threat. The border dispute, however, was never a major issue. It was, and still is, primarily a by-product or symptom of the Sino-Soviet dispute rather than the main cause of the conflict. It is simply not true that the difficulty arose because the Chinese wanted to recover the lost territory of the past century.

So it comes to the third, and the most important difference of all: the irreconcilable conflict of national interests. The Chinese maintain that if only the Soviets could abandon hegemonism, reduce its troops from the border, withdraw its army from Mongolia, and no longer support the Vietnamese aggression in Indochina, Sino-Soviet relations would be improved. But it is unlikely that the Soviets will do anything of this sort, nor that Vietnam will withdraw its troops from Kampuchea in the foreseeable future.

The economic condition in Vietnam now is much worse than that during the Vietnam War. But the Vietnamese have enormous capacity to endure hardship, and they have not reached the end of the road. With the exception of direct military action and participation, the Chinese will use every means to support the Kampuchea resistance. This is one of China's cardinal policies. It is expected that the strength of the Kampuchea guerrilla forces will grow, however slowly. It will probably take at least four or five years, if not more, before the situation is favorable for a settlement. In this connection, it may be said that any premature establishment of U.S.-Vietnamese relations will not help solve the problem, nor would it lure Vietnam away from Soviet influence.

For the reasons just analyzed, it is unlikely that there will be a Sino-Soviet reconciliation in the foreseeable future. However, we must not rule out the possibility. After all, Sino-Soviet relations have already deteriorated for 20 years, but the hostilities cannot go on forever. In fact, there were indications in the past that both sides wished to improve relations, but as an old Chinese expression states, "The tree wants to be quiet but the wind does not stop."

It may be mentioned that after Sino-American rapprochement and the opening up of China, there is little that the Soviet Union can offer to the People's Republic that Peking cannot obtain elsewhere.

What the Soviets expect the Chinese to do as a quid pro quo for improving the relations is unclear. In any event, it is extremely unlikely that Sino-Soviet relations would be able to return to the "solidarity" of the 1950s. The Soviet Union had attempted to control China. The Chinese have learned a lesson from, and paid a heavy price for, "leaning to one side." But limited improvement of relations is not impossible, and it is not necessarily against the interests of the United States, because it would be beneficial to all the parties concerned to have some release of global and regional tensions.

SINO-AMERICAN RELATIONS AFTER NORMALIZATION

Sino-Soviet relations cannot be discussed without taking into consideration the "American connection." China and the United States have considerably strengthened their relations since the normalization on January 1, 1979. There have been frequent exchanged visits between Chinese and U.S. high-ranking officials and leaders, including Deng Xiaoping (January 1979)* and Vice-President Walter Mondale (August 1979), not to mention numerous delegations of various kinds. In 1979, 308 official Chinese delegations came to the United States, while 40,000 American tourists and numerous American delegations visited China.[104] The two countries signed more than 15 bilateral agreements concerning, among other things, trade, culture, science and technology, claims/assets, and consular relations. Chinese consulates general were opened in Houston and San Francisco, and American consulates general in Canton and Shanghai. About 700 Chinese students and visiting scholars came to the United States to study or do research in 1979.

In 1980, more than 70,000 Americans visited China, while almost 10,000 Chinese came to the United States. Chinese commercial and scientific delegations to the United States averaged nearly 130 per month by late 1980. As of December 1980, there were 342 American teachers — many hired directly by the Chinese government — and almost 100 private students, scholars, and advanced trainees in China, almost double the number 12 months earlier. By January 1981, the Chinese had established their largest overseas study program in 20 years by placing 2,100 officially sponsored scholars in American institutions. In addition, at least 2,900 privately sponsored mainland Chinese scholars and students were enrolled at American schools, bringing the total in the United States to more than 5,000.[105]

The total U.S.-China trade in two-way turnover increased from $96 million in 1972 to more than $2 billion in 1979, $4.8 billion in 1980, and approximately $5.8 billion in 1981. In January 1980, the United States granted "most-favored-nation" status to China without according the same privilege to the Soviet Union. Secretary of Defense Harold Brown's visit to Peking in the midst of the Afghan crisis resulted in a further understanding of the need for taking

---

*In June 1981, Premier Zhao Ziyang accepted President Reagan's invitation to visit the United States "at a convenient time."

parallel actions and consultations. In May, in the wake of China's successfully launching an intercontinental ballistic missile (ICBM), a Chinese military delegation headed by Vice Premier Geng Biao returned the visit and concluded agreements with the United States by which Washington would sell to China certain kinds of equipment that could be used for military purposes. A major step for establishing military relations was taken when Secretary of State Alexander M. Haig, Jr., announced during his visit in Peking (June 16, 1981) that the United States would sell arms to China. In fact, the two countries for months had been using two electronic intelligence-gathering stations in northwest China to monitor Soviet missile tests.

It should be noted, however, that China is considered by the United States as a "friend," not as an "ally." The fact that the United States has slightly tilted to China in the triangular relations was not a result of Chinese manipulation, but rather the outcome of Soviet behavior and expansionist policy. After Afghanistan, the Chinese might very well be justified in saying to Washington, "I have told you so." Those who have misgivings about what happens after China has become more powerful may very well take note of the fact that China will be preoccupied with enormous economic problems and modernization programs in many years to come.

In spite of fundamental differences in ideology, social values, and political and economic systems, the United States and China have grave common concern for the Soviet military buildup, the Kremlin's use of Cubans in Africa, Soviet support of the Vietnamese regional hegemonism in Southeast Asia, and Soviet strategic ambitions in Afghanistan and the Persian Gulf. The "American connection" has become a cornerstone of China's long-range foreign policy,[106] and the "Chinese connection has become a factor of increasing importance to Washington's global strategy and security."[107] The relationship between the two countries, in the words of Secretary Haig, is a "fundamental strategic reality and a strategic imperative. It is of overriding importance to international stability and world peace."[108]

America's China policy under the Reagan administration was "clearly and definitively outlined" in his statement of August 24, 1980, before the election. It is based on adherence to the communique associated with the normalization agreement with the PRC and to the 1979 Taiwan Relations Act, which established a nonofficial status with the people of Taiwan. Washington does not view these — an international agreement and a domestic law — "as mutually exclusive."[109] Peking, however, has strongly opposed the act as interference in domestic politics, particularly arms sales to Taiwan.[110] It is significant to note that, in May 1981, China downgraded Sino-Dutch diplomatic relations because the Dutch government approved the sale of submarines to Taiwan.

In spite of President Reagan's personal views and sentiments on Taiwan, he has to accept reality. It is unlikely that he will be able to change the basic course and direction of the relationship between China and the United States that had been mapped out by three American presidents, although there may be a change of style and scope with regard to Washington's nonofficial relations with Taiwan. However, if Washington does not pay due attention to China's sensitivity on the issue, there is a danger of making incalculable and unnecessary damage to U.S.-Chinese relations, and of creating a possible renewal of tensions on the Taiwan Strait in the future. To what extent this might affect Sino-Soviet relations is difficult to assess. The result of Haig's visit to China in June 1981 demonstrated once again that the two countries were willing to seek closer relations despite the Taiwan issue. It is significant to note, however, that within hours after the three-day conference in Peking, the *People's Daily* published a long and conciliatory article calling for negotiations with Moscow to settle the border dispute, and that Haig's departure from Peking was marred by the absence of Foreign Minister Huang Hua at the airport because of President Reagan's remarks about Taiwan during a press conference in Washington.

While China's options may be limited, her role in U.S. global security can be crucial. Furthermore, U.S.-Chinese relations should not be viewed entirely in terms of a "China card" in Soviet-American relations. They have merits of their own, and it is mutually beneficial for the two countries to improve their bilateral relations.[111]

NOTES

1. According to a Russian view, "Foreign policy is a combination of the aims and interests pursued and defended by the given state and its ruling class in its relations with other states, and the methods and means used by it for the achievement and defense of these purposes and interests." Furthermore, it is "closely bound up with character of the social and state system of the states in question, and it is a direct continuation of domestic policy." V. I. Lenin, *Diplomaticheskii Immunitet* (Moscow, 1949), pp. 4-5, quoted by Vernon V. Aspaturian, "International Politics and Foreign Policy in the Soviet System," in *Approaches to Comparative and International Politics*, ed. R. Barry Farrell (Evanston, Ill.: Northwestern University Press, 1966), p. 213.

2. For a discussion of the revised doctrine of the two camps, see an article by a Soviet analyst. According to the Soviet writer, there is no possibility of a "convergence" between the two social systems. However, the criterion for membership in the socialist camp is adherence to Marxist-Leninist ideology as interpreted by the Communist Party of the Soviet Union (CPSU). Third world political systems that lean in this direction may be provisionally included. All others are objectively aligned with the capitalist camp. It may be recalled that the two-camp doctrine of Stalin's day was intimately connected with the concept of "capitalist encirclement." In 1959, Khrushchev declared that the capitalist encirclement had come to an end because of the change in the world balance of power. He introduced the concept of "three camps." The third camp was formed by newly liberated and independent nations after World War II. *International Affairs*, August 1970. See also R. Judson Mitchell, "The Revised 'Two-Camps' Doctrine in Soviet Foreign Policy," *Orbis* 16, no. 1 (Spring 1972).

3. Teng Hsiao-p'ing, speech at a special session of the U.N. General Assembly, April 10, 1974; *Peking Reivew*, Supplement, April 12, 1974.

4. It should be stressed that as a tactical move, it has been permissible for Communists to ally with internal bourgeois elements and compromise with the capitalist states. As Lenin put it, "One must be able to analyse the situation and the concrete conditions of each compromise, or of each variety of compromise." In his report to the Tenth National Congress of the Chinese Communist Party in August 1973, Chou En-lai pointed out that

"in both international and domestic struggles," one must not forget "necessary struggles" when there is "an alliance with the bourgeoisie," and that one should not forget the "possibility of alliance under given conditions" when "there is a split with the bourgeoisie." Vladimir I. Lenin, *Left-Wing Communism: An Infantile Disorder* (New York: International Publishers, 1940). See also Chou En-lai, *Peking Review*, September 7, 1973, p. 21.

5. Cf. Edward Shils, "The Concept and Function of Ideology," and Harry M. Johnson, "Ideology and the Social System," both in the *International Encyclopedia of the Social Sciences* (1968), vol. 7, pp. 66, 76-77.

6. Shils, "The Concept and Function of Ideology," p. 66.

7. Johnson, "Ideology and the Social System," p. 77.

8. Gordon W. Allport, "The Historical Background of Modern Social Psychology," in *The Handbook of Social Psychology*, ed. Gardner Lindzey and Elliot Aronson, 2d ed. (Reading, Mass.: Addison-Wesley, 1968), p. 21.

9. Julius Gould, "Ideology," in *A Dictionary of the Social Sciences*, ed. Julius Gould and William L. Kolb (New York: The Free Press, 1964), pp. 315-17.

10. Joseph de Rivera, *The Psychological Dimension of Foreign Policy* (Columbus, Ohio: Charles E. Merrill, 1968), p. 21.

11. Ibid.

12. Richard A. Brody, "Cognition and Behavior: A Model of International Relations," in *Experience, Structure and Adaptability*, ed. O. J. Harvey (New York: Springer, 1966), pp. 334-39.

13. de Rivera, *The Psychological Dimension of Foreign Policy*, p. 20.

14. Ibid., p. 22.

15. See Karl W. Deutsch, *The Nerves of Government* (New York: The Free Press, 1963), pp. 94-97.

16. For an account of the episode, see Seymour Topping, *Journey Between Two Chinas* (New York: Harper & Row, 1972), pp. 83-84, 89. See also U.S. Senate, Committee on Foreign Relations, *The United States and Communist China in 1949 and 1950* (Washington, D.C.: U.S. Government Printing Office, 1973), pp. 10-17.

17. Mao Tse-tung, speech to the Tenth Plenary Session of the Eighth Central Committee, September 24, 1962, "Excerpts from Confidential Speeches, Directives and Letters of Mao Tse-tung," New York *Times*, March 1, 1970.

18. Mao Tse-tung, remarks to John Service in August 1944, in John S. Service, *The Amerasia Papers* (Berkeley, Calif.: Center for Chinese Studies, University of California, 1971), p. 171.

19. Cf. Barbara W. Tuchman, "If Mao Had Come to Washington: An Essay in Alternatives," *Foreign Affairs* (October 1972): 44-64.

20. "Draft Report by the National Security Council on the Position of the United States with Respect to Asia," *United States-Vietnam Relations, 1945-1967*, Book 8 (Washington, D.C.: U.S. Government Printing Office, 1971), p. 243.

21. Ibid., p. 244.

22. Ibid., p. 245.

23. Ibid., p. 228.

24. Ibid., p. 255.

25. In these terms, Indochina was of much greater strategic importance than Korea — and critical to U.S. security interests. See "National Security Council Staff Study on United States Objectives and Courses of Action with Respect to Communist Aggression in Southeast Asia," ibid., pp. 468-76.

26. This latter consideration does not mean that leaders in Washington merely "invented" an ideology to deceive the public and cover up their concern for strategic, resource, and other critical factors. Nor does it necessarily deny the reality of Soviet ambitions in Asia. Rather, it documents the intense interconnections between ideological and other, more pragmatic factors. Given the world situation, the assumptions, expectations,

perceptions, and other elements of the "ideology" came easily to many of the leaders themselves and it seems quite probable that few of them ever fully distinguished in their own minds between the various factors contributing to their motivations. See Ole R. Holsti, "Cognitive Dynamics and Images of the Enemy: Dulles and Russia," in *Enemies in Politics*, ed. David J. Finlay, Ole R. Holsti, and Richard R. Fagen (Chicago: Rand McNally, 1967), pp. 25-96, for an appreciation of some of the implications and complexities of the cognitive dynamics of a national leader. Note references to China on pp. 69n, 74, 75, 81, 83-85.

27. See John Foster Dulles, "Our Policies Toward Communism in China" (Address before the International Convention of Lions International, San Francisco, June 28, 1957), in *State Department Bulletin*, July 15, 1957, pp. 91, 95; also quoted in Dean Acheson, *Power and Diplomacy* (New York: Atheneum, 1963), p. 132.

28. Morton A. Kaplan, "Bipolarity in a Revolutionary Age," in *The Revolution in World Politics*, ed. Morton A. Kaplan (New York: Wiley, 1962), p. 259.

29. Mao Tse-tung, *Mao Chu-hsi tsai Su-lien ti yen-lun* [Chairman Mao's Statements in the Soviet Union] (Peking, 1957), pp. 14-15; also quoted in Stuart R. Schram, *The Political Thought of Mao Tse-tung*, rev. ed. (New York: Praeger, 1969), pp. 407-8.

30. See, for example, an article on economic competition in two worlds, *Shih-chieh chih-shih* [World Knowledge] (Peking), January 5, 1959, pp. 16-17; see also Chou En-lai, *Report on the Work of the Government* (Peking: Foreign Languages Press, 1959), pp. 56-72.

31. "Statement by the Spokesman of the Chinese Government," *Hongqi* [Red Flag], August 15, 1963; *Peking Review*, August 16, 1963.

32. *Red Flag* Commentator, "Confessions Concerning the Line of Soviet-U.S. Collaboration Pursued by the New Leaders of the C.P.S.U.," *Hongqi* [Red Flag], February 11, 1966; English translation in *Peking Review*, February 18, 1966, p. 10. See also the editorial departments of *People's Daily* and *Red Flag*, *On Khrushchev's Phoney Communism and Its Historical Lessons for the World: Comment on the Open Letter of the Central Committee of the CPSU* (9th article), July 14, 1964 (Peking: Foreign Languages Press, 1964); and the editorial departments of *People's Daily*, *Red Flag*, and *Liberation Army Daily*, "Leninism or Social-Imperialism?," *Peking Review*, April 24, 1970, p. 7. For the Chinese view that the CPSU has become an instrument of bourgeois dictatorship in the name of the Party of the entire people, see *Peking Review*, December 8, 1967, pp. 32-34.

33. For the origin and early development of the Cultural Revolution, see Chün-tu Hsüeh, "The Cultural Revolution and the Leadership Crisis in Communist China," *Political Science Quarterly* (New York: June 1967), pp. 169-90.

34. For the Chinese perception of American threat and encirclement, see the map showing "American imperialism's military encirclement of China" in the *People's Daily*, January 29, 1966, reproduced in Arthur Huck, *The Security of China* (New York: Columbia University Press, 1970), p. 12. The theme of encirclement was often expressed by Peking leaders. See, for example, Premier Chou En-lai's speech at the reception celebrating the twentieth anniversary of the founding of the PRC, *Peking Review*, October 3, 1969, p. 18.

35. *Peking Review*, January 29, 1966.

36. "Kremlin's New Tsars Rig up Anti-China Encirclement," *Peking Review*, April 4, 1969, pp. 25-27.

37. *Peking Review*, February 18, 1966, p. 10.

38. In the words of the Observer of the *People's Daily*, "The Soviet Union is not only going out of its way to bring about a 'detente' in Europe but is also vigorously supporting and encouraging the all-round resurgence of Japanese militarism and its ambitions for overseas expansion in Asia." *Peking Review*, August 5, 1966, p. 18.

39. *Shih-chieh chih-shih*, February 25, 1966, pp. 5-8.

40. Chou En-lai, speech at the banquet given by Premier Kim Il Sung at Pyongyang, April 5, 1970; *Peking Review*, April 10, 1970, p. 13.

41. The Observer, "Confession of Worldwide U.S.-Soviet Collusion on a Big Scale," *People's Daily*, October 16, 1966; *Peking Review*, October 21, 1966, pp. 20-21.

42. In his speech at the reception given in Peking by the Albanian ambassador to China on November 29, 1966, marking the twenty-second anniversary of Albanian liberation, Premier Chou En-lai accused the Soviet Union of being an accomplice of U.S. imperialism. On more than one occasion, Chou ridiculed the Soviet leadership as "busy running errands" for the United States. A detailed analysis of American global strategy in February 1968 condemned the Soviet's "notorious activities as the No. 1 accomplice of U.S. imperialism." This theme had been stated by Foreign Minister Chen Yi in his speech to the Peking masses. See *People's Daily*, November 30, 1966; English translation in *Peking Review*, December 2, 1966; also *People's Daily*, June 22, 1967; for a slightly different wording, see *Peking Review*, June 20, 1967. See also New China News Agency, February 29, 1968; and *People's Daily*, July 11, 1966, reprinted in *Shih-shih ts'ung-shu* [Current Event Series], no. 6 (Hong Kong: San-lien, 1966), pp. 24-25.

43. For example, see *Peking Review*, August 25, 1967, pp. 19-20; July 5, 1968, p. 33; and July 19, 1968, p. 29.

44. *Peking Review*, January 7, 1966; June 13, 1966; June 23, 1966; July 8, 1966, p. 22. In the month between September 24 and October 24, 1966, the *People's Daily* published two editorials and three articles signed by "The Observer," condemning U.S.-Soviet collusion on the Vietnam War in and out of the United Nations. In addition, it published four New China News Agency dispatches and reprinted one article each from Albania and Australia dealing with the same theme. For a collection of these articles, see *Shih-shih ts'ung-shu*, no. 16 (Hong Kong: San-lien, 1966).

45. *Peking Review*, August 30, 1968, pp. 19-20; see also "Communique of the Enlarged Twelfth Plenary Session of the CPC Eighth Central Committee," adopted on October 31, 1968, *Peking Review*, Supplement, November 1, 1968.

46. *Peking Review*, May 30, 1969, pp. 20-21.

47. Ibid.; *Peking Review*, May 23, 1969, p. 30.

48. *Peking Review*, July 19, 1968, p. 29.

49. *People's Daily*, January 6, 1965; quoted in "Blueprint for a House Divided," *Current Scene* 3, no. 27 (September 17, 1965).

50. *Shih-chieh chih-shih*, December 10, 1965, pp. 5-8.

51. *Peking Review*, January 1, 1967.

52. Chou En-lai, remarks, *People's Daily*, January 24, 1965.

53. Spokesman of the Chinese government, statement, August 15, 1963, *Peking Review*, August 16, 1963.

54. Editorial, *People's Daily*, July 19, 1963; English translation in *Peking Review*, July 26, 1963; see also The Observer, "Why the Tripartite Treaty Does Only Harm and Brings No Benefits," *People's Daily*, August 10, 1963; *Peking Review*, August 16, 1963.

55. *Red Flag*, August 1, 1963; *Peking Review*, August 2, 1963.

56. Editorial, *People's Daily*, August 3, 1963; see also *Peking Review*, August 9, 1963.

57. *People's Daily*, September 3, 1967; *Peking Review*, September 8, 1967, p. 34.

58. Washington *Post*, July 18, 1972.

59. "A Report on Our Foreign Relations," *Department of State Publication*, no. 8445 (March 1969), p. 4.

60. *Peking Review*, May 13, 1966, p. 5. Chen Yi had also made a similar remark at a press conference in the fall of 1965, *Peking Review*, October 8, 1965.

61. Harrison E. Salisbury, *To Peking and Beyond* (New York: Quadrangle, 1973), p. 226.

62. "A Report on Our Foreign Relations," pp. 13-15.

63. For Peking's policy statements on nuclear weapons, see the following issues of *Peking Review*: July 16, 1963, pp. 47-48; August 2, 1963, pp. 7-8; Special Supplement,

October 28, 1966; and December 3, 1971, pp. 14-16. China has consistently adhered to the stand declared on the above occasions, with a possible exception that China has not proposed an Asian-Pacific nuclear-free zone since the end of 1964 (the proposal was made in August 1960). See William J. Cunningham, *Arms Controls in Northeast Asia* (Washington, D.C.: Senior Seminar in Foreign Policy, Department of State, May 1972), p. 15.

64. Michael Tatu, *The Great Power Triangle* (Paris: Atlantic Institute, 1970), reprinted in U.S. Senate, Subcommittee on National Security and International Operations, Committee on Government Operations, *International Negotiation* (Washington, D.C.: U.S. Government Printing Office, 1971), pp. 211-12.

65. This "three-anti" policy was written down in the Chinese Communist Party's constitution adopted in April 1969. See also the joint editorial of the *People's Daily*, *Red Flag*, and the *Liberation Army Daily*, August 1, 1969; *Peking Review*, August 6, 1969, p. 6. It was reiterated in the Party's constitution adopted in August 1973.

66. The concept of the "intermediate zone" was originally applied to the international scene by Mao in his talk with Anna Louise Strong in August 1946: "The United States and the Soviet Union are separated by a vast zone which includes many capitalist, colonial and semi-colonial countries in Europe, Asia and Africa." It was revived in 1964 in the context of an attempt to build the "Third Force" in world politics, based on antiimperialism and Gaullism. The first intermediate zone is the third world. Mao Tse-tung, *Selected Works*, vol. 2 (Peking: Foreign Languages Press, 1961), p. 99.

67. Cf. Stanley Hoffman, "International Systems and International Law," in *Power, Action and Interaction*, ed. George H. Quester (Boston: Little, Brown, 1971), p. 371; Hans J. Morgenthau, "Another 'Great Debate': The National Interest," ibid., p. 56; Arnold Wolfers, "The Pole of Power and the Pole of Indifference," ibid., pp. 149-50; Glenn H. Snyder, "Balance of Power in the Missile Age," ibid., p. 461; and Inis L. Claude, Jr., "International Law and Organization," in *American National Security: A Study in Theory and Policy*, ed. Morton Berkowitz and P. G. Bock (New York: The Free Press, 1965), p. 290.

68. James C. Thomson, Jr., "On the Making of U.S. China Policy, 1961-9," *China Quarterly*, no. 50 (April/June 1972), p. 221.

69. "The Chinese," remarked the *People's Daily* editorial of April 6, 1966, "are not taken in." *Peking Review*, April 8, 1966, p. 7.

70. Edgar Snow, *The Long Revolution* (New York: Random House, 1972), p. 172.

71. U.S., Arms Control and Disarmament Agency, *World Military Expenditures, 1971* (Washington, D.C.: U.S. Government Printing Office, 1972), pp. 22-23, 50. For an elaborate and different assessment of national power, see Ray S. Cline, *World Power Assessment: A Calculus of Strategic Drift* (Washington, D.C.: Center for Strategic and International Studies, Georgetown University, 1975).

72. Audrey Donmithorne, "China as a Trading Nation," *Current Scene*, February 7, 1972, pp. 1-4.

73. Cf. Aldo Beckman et al., *The China Trip – Now What* (Chicago: University of Chicago Center for Policy Study, 1972), p. 12.

74. *Peking Review*, September 7, 1973, p. 23.

75. Yeh Chien-ying, speech, *Peking Review*, November 10, 1972, p. 3; and Li Teh-sheng, speech, *Peking Review*, November 17, 1972, p. 3.

76. Chou En-lai, "Report to the Tenth National Congress of the Communist Party of China," *Peking Review*, September 7, 1973, p. 22. The theme was reiterated by Deng Xiaoping in his address to a special session of the U.N. General Assembly, April 10, 1974. *Peking Review*, April 12, 1974, Supplement. The first major comment on the contending-colluding subject in the 1970s appeared in the *Peking Review* of March 20, 1970, on the occasion of U.S.-Soviet agreement on cultural exchange, which began in 1958 and renewed negotiation every other year. The theme subsequently has been reiterated on many occasions. The origin of the superpower theme may be traced to Liao Ch'eng-chih's remarks on December 1961, *Peking Review*, December 22, 1961, pp. 12-14. See also an article written by the

editorial departments of *People's Daily* and *Red Flag*, March 31, 1964; and *The Proletarian Revolution and Khrushchev's Revisionism* (Peking: Foreign Languages Press, 1964).

77. The theme was reiterated by Deng Xiaoping in his banquet speech welcoming former British Prime Minister Edward Heath. *Peking Review*, May 31, 1974, p. 8.

78. For example, *Peking Review*, October 11, 1974, pp. 9-10; September 26, 1975; October 3, 1975, p. 10; October 24, 1975, p. 8; December 8, 1975, p. 8. For an earlier view of detente, see *Peking Review*, October 3, 1973, pp. 12-13. See also "Third World Struggle Against Hegemony," *Peking Review*, September 21, 1973, pp. 13-15.

79. *Peking Review*, January 18, 1974, pp. 7-11; February 15, 1974, pp. 16-18; March 29, 1974, p. 7; October 25, 1974, p. 8; January 17, 1975, pp. 6-8.

80. *Peking Review*, December 5, 1975, p. 8.

81. Chinese government, statement, December 16, 1971, *Peking Review*, December 17, 1971. On this point, see M. R. Masani, "Is India a Soviet Ally?" *Asian Affairs*, January 1974, pp. 121-35, especially 125-26. The former Indian ambassador to Brazil concluded that the Indo-Soviet Treaty was a "treaty of alliance."

82. Huang Hua, then permanent representative of the People's Republic of China to the U.N. Security Council, statement, at an urgent meeting of December 5, 1971, *Peking Review*, December 10, 1971, p. 9; see also *Peking Review*, December 17, 1971, p. 12; and January 28, 1972, pp. 14-15.

83. "Soviet Social-Imperialism — Most Dangerous Source of World War," by the Institute of World Economy of the Chinese Academy of Social Science, *Hongqi* [Red Flag], no. 7, 1977; English translation in *Peking Review*, July 15, 1977, pp. 4-10. See also reports on the work of the government by Premier Hua Guofeng (Hua Kuo-feng) to the National People's Congress in February 1978 and June 1979 in *Peking Review*, March 10, 1978, p. 36, and *Beijing Review*, July 6, 1979, pp. 27-31, respectively.

84. Speech by Foreign Minister Huang Hua, Chairman of the Chinese Delegation at the U.N. General Assembly Special Session on Disarmament, May 23, 1978; *Peking Review*, June 2, 1978, pp. 5-16.

85. *Beijing Review*, February 16, 1979, p. 18.

86. For a discussion of China's modernization and its implications for Sino-American relations, see Chün-tu Hsüeh's paper, "Modernization and Revolution in China," presented at an international seminar sponsored by the Chinese University of Hong Kong, December 5-7, 1979.

87. Strobe Talbott, "U.S.-Soviet Relations: From Bad to Worse," in *Foreign Affairs: America and the World 1979* (New York, 1980), pp. 515-39.

88. For a discussion of Chinese foreign policy and the united front policy, See J. D. Armstrong, *Revolutionary Diplomacy* (Berkeley: University of California Press, 1977).

89. *Peking Review*, January 6, 1972, p. 9; and *Peking Review*, January 28, 1972, p. 14.

90. For China's performance in the United Nations, see Samuel S. Kim, *China, the United Nations, and World Order* (Princeton: Princeton University Press, 1979).

91. For a study of economic aid of the Soviet Union, China, and East Europe, see "Communists Fall to Third in Economic Aid to Developing Nations," *International Policy Report* 2, no. 1 (Washington, D.C., April 1976). During 1970-71, China extended nearly $1.2 billion in economic aid to the developing countries — total commitments amount to almost 55 percent of all such extensions of aid by the Peking government since 1956. Leo Tansky, "China's Foreign Aid: The Record," *Current Scene* 10, no. 9 (September 1972): 2. However, U.S. Central Intelligence Agency, *Handbook of Economic Statistics, 1979*, ER79-10274, August 1979, Table 74-76, lists China's economic aid to the developing countries as $781 million and $563 million for the years 1970 and 1971 respectively. The amount was dropped to $185 million for 1978. See also U.S. Central Intelligence Agency, *Communist Aid Activities in Non-Communist Less Developed Countries*, 1978, ER79-10412U, September 1979, Table 5. It may be noted, as revealed by former Secretary of

State Cyrus Vance in his address at Harvard University and cited by an article in the Washington *Post*, June 12, 1980, the United States ranked only thirteenth among the world's 17 largest industrial nations in the percentage of gross national product it devotes to development assistance, which accounted for only about 1.5 percent of the federal budget.

92. *Peking Review*, November 19, 1971, p. 8.

93. Chinese government, statement, October 29, 1971, on the United Nations resolution seating the Peking government in the U.N. Similar statements have been made on a number of occasions, for example, the 1971 New Year's Day joint editorial of the *People's Daily*, *Red Flag*, and *Liberation Army Daily* and remarks made by Chou En-lai to a Canadian delegation, July 28, 1971. See also a speech by Deng Xiaoping (Teng Hsiao-p'ing) at a special session of the U.N. General Assembly, April 10, 1974, *Peking Review*, April 12, 1974, p. 5.

94. Washington *Post*, July 12, 1972.

95. *Peking Review*, April 12, 1974, p. 8. See also "Rise of Third World and Decline of Hegemonism," *Peking Review*, January 10, 1975, pp. 6-8. For the impact of the proliferation of small independent states on world politics, see Elmer Plischke, *Microstates in World Affairs: Policy Problems and Options* (Washington, D.C.: American Enterprise Institute for Public Policy Research, 1977).

96. Jen Ku-ping, "The Third World: Great Motive Force in Advancing World History," *Peking Review*, November 1, 1974, p. 6.

97. *Peking Review*, December 17, 1971, p. 19.

98. For China's stand at the U.N., see *Peking Review*, March 31, 1972, p. 17.

99. Alain Bouc, "Peking Now Wants a United Europe," *European Community*, no. 154 (March 1972): 85; New China News Agency, June 29, 1971; Vladmir Reisky de Dubnic, "Europe and the New U.S. Policy Toward China," *Orbis* 16, no. 1 (Spring 1972): 87.

100. An article by the *People's Daily* Commentator, February 21, 1978; *Peking Review*, March 3, 1978, p. 22.

101. Mao Tse-tung, *Selected Works*, vol. 1 (Peking: Foreign Languages Press, 1955), p. 331.

102. Television interview of Deng Xiaoping, Washington, January 31, 1979, in *Beijing Review*, February 16, 1979, p. 17. On January 5, 1979, Deng also said in an interview with 27 American journalists in Peking that there was "no question of alliance" among China, Japan, and the United States as reportedly accused by the Soviet Union, but there was "much common between us on matters of global strategy and on political questions." *Beijing Review*, January 12, 1979, p. 18.

103. Deng's remark during his meeting with the Chinese and U.S. delegations attending the first meeting of the Sino-American Joint Commission on Cooperation in Science and Technology, *Beijing Review*, February 4, 1980, p. 3. Similar statements were made by Deng to a group of American newspaper editorial writers in Peking. the Washington *Post*, June 6, 1980, p. A18.

104. The Washington *Post*, January 21, 1980.

105. U.S. Department of State, Bureau of Public Affairs, *Gist* (March 1981).

106. In his major speech at the annual meeting of the National Committee on United States-China Relations, New York, September 17, 1979, Chinese ambassador Chai Zemin had this remark: "The situation today requires us to view and approach Sino-U.S. relations with a politico-strategic perspective. In so doing, we will find a common basis for strengthening the cooperation between our two countries, both in the general aspect and in our bilateral relations. This basis will be a reliable and durable one, and not a transient expediency."

107. As Vice-President Walter Mondale remarked during his visit to Peking in August 1979: "A secure and modern China is as much in America's interests as a strong and prospering U.S. is in the interests of China." *Wall Street Journal*, August 29, 1979. The theme was reiterated by Richard C. Holbrooks, then assistant secretary of state for East Asian and Pacific affairs, Department of State, in his speech at the annual meeting of the

National Council for U.S.-China Trade, June 4, 1980. Secretary of State Alexander Haig, in an interview for *Time* magazine (New York), referred to the U.S.-China policy as a "fundamental strategic reality and a strategic imperative." *Time*, March 16, 1981, p. 24.

108. An interview with Secretary of State Alexander Haig, *Time* (New York), March 16, 1981, p. 24.

109. Ibid.

110. For a major Chinese article commenting on the Taiwan Relations Act, see *Guangming Daily* (Peking), May 31, 1981; see also the Xinhua commentary on Sino-American relations, June 18, 1981.

111. For a discussion of various aspects of Sino-American relations by a number of specialists, see Richard H. Solomon, ed., *The China Factor: Sino-American Relations and the Global Scene* (Englewood Cliffs, N.J.: Prentice-Hall, 1981); see also Richard H. Solomon, *Choices for Coalition-Building: The Soviet Presence in Asia and American Policy Alternatives* (Santa Monica: Rand Paper Series, P-6572, April 1981). For a Chinese view, see Huan Xiang, "On Sino-U.S. Relations," *Foreign Affairs* (Fall 1981), pp. 35-53.

3

CHINA AND JAPAN:
A NEW ERA OF COOPERATION

Herbert S. Yee

When China's Foreign Minister Huang Hua and his Japanese counterpart Sunao Sonoda signed the Treaty of Peace and Friendship on August 12, 1978, at the People's Great Hall in Peking the world witnessed one of the most dramatic breakthroughs in modern diplomacy. The PRC accomplished remarkably its chief objective of incorporating an "antihegemony" clause in the treaty. It thus signaled a clear Japanese tilt toward the Chinese and the abandonment of Japan's equidistance diplomacy. These strategic and diplomatic gains were won by China, of course, not overnight. After the turmoil of the Cultural Revolution had subsided in the late 1960s and in the wake of serious border clashes with the Soviets in 1969, Peking began its diplomatic offensive to counterweigh the military threat from the north. Naturally, the United States, the other superpower, was regarded as an ideal counterbalance to the Soviet Union by the Chinese leaders. The PRC amazed the world by its swiftness and flexibility in inviting President Nixon to visit China in February 1972.

Peking, however, was fully aware of the limitations of its American card. Even before the U.S. withdrawal from Vietnam in the mid-1970s the Chinese had already foreseen America's declining military presence in Asia. The Soviet ascendency in the region, on the other hand, had become more apparent after the unification of the two Vietnams and Hanoi's subsequent tilt toward China's archrival. Fearing the Soviet encirclement, the Peking leaders reinforced promptly the noncommital American connection by courting the second world industrial countries including Western and Eastern European states and Japan. As a major American ally, with a security treaty that obliged the United States to protect its islands in the event of an attack, Japan occupied a pivotal position in China's global strategy. A strong tie with Tokyo, in Peking's calculations, would certainly enhance the solidarity of an anti-Soviet united front.

The Soviet intervention in Afghanistan, however, alerted the PRC of the necessity of reassessing its global strategy. Peking warned the U.S. and its allies that the Russians would continue to expand and would strike, if unchecked, the southern front and threaten the oil-rich Persian Gulf area because of the stalemate at the two other fronts in Europe and Asia. The whole world, the PRC reiterated, must therefore be united and stand firm against the relentless "Polar Bear." Yet in private the Peking leaders realized that China must rely on its own efforts to defend its lengthy border against threats from its northern neighbor.

To China's leaders, however, the Soviet invasion of Afghanistan had also exposed its hidden vulnerability. The Russians were obviously overstretched, burdened with heavy military and economic commitments in Eastern Europe, Cuba, Vietnam, Afghanistan, and other parts of the world. The Soviet global expansion thus seriously impeded its own plans to revive the faltering economy. Furthermore, as viewed from Peking, the Kremlin leaders were also troubled by internal ethnic instability and increasing resentment and unrest from Eastern European allies. This allegedly inherent Soviet weakness apparently convinced some Chinese leaders that the Russians may not be in a position to launch any nuclear or large-scale conventional attack against China for some time to come. Indeed, the Peking leaders felt so confident of their assessment of Soviet vulnerability that they even lowered the priority of modernizing China's obsolete defense systems. The Chinese leaders apparently believed that China had some respite in concentrating its efforts to build up an economically strong and technologically advanced socialist state despite the menacing Soviet threats.

This does not suggest that the PRC has neglected or undermined its antihegemony global strategy. As far as Peking is concerned, the united front scheme remains the most effective operational strategy to curb the Soviet expansion. The Peking leaders are apparently feeling the way of forming an integrated foreign policy by linking the antihegemony strategy to China's modernization drive. How has China's global strategy affected its bilateral relations with Japan? There is no simple answer, though it is clear that the two have been closely connected in Peking's calculations. This chapter will first examine briefly China's relationship with Japan from a historical and cultural perspective and then evaluate the developments and prospects of bilateral Sino-Japanese relations in the context of China's overall foreign policy strategy.

IMAGES, MYTHS, AND REALITIES

"If Japan and China cooperate, they can support half the Heavens," said Deng Xiaoping.[1] Indeed, the prospect of a partnership between the world's second largest capitalist economy and the most populous and steadily modernizing socialist China is awesome. The diplomatic, economic, and military implications are bound to be profound and far-reaching in regional and global politics. However, never before had either country considered the other as viable partner. Imperial China apparently felt self-sufficient and was too arrogant to consider Japan as a country of equal status. Japan after the Meiji restoration likewise looked down at the Chinese and never took the weak and disarrayed China seriously. Can the current leaderships in Peking and Tokyo shake off the unhappy memories of the past century and start a genuine partnership based on mutual trust and benefit? There is little doubt about the Chinese eagerness and sincerity to learn from Japan's successful modernization experience and to cooperate with the Japanese in developing China's backward economy. Cooperation between Japan and China, therefore, depends to a large degree on Japanese attitudes.

Because of history, cultural and ethnical affinity, the Japanese had long developed some kind of emotional attachment to China. Many regarded China as their "half-brother." These feelings of intimacy were reinforced by a strong sense of postwar guilt toward the Chinese. Many Japanese regretted the tremendous damages the imperial Japanese armies had caused in China and felt that their country should repay this debt. Yet the Japanese attitudes toward their neighbor, based primarily on their perceptions or images of China, have undergone several crucial turnarounds since 1949. When Mao declared the establishment of the People's Republic in 1949, Japan faced the first time in more than a century a unified and rigorous China promising one day to become a major actor in world politics. Meanwhile, Japan was struggling for economic survival from the shambles of the war. The emergence of a strong socialist China thus revived some of the old inferior feelings toward China among the Japanese. The Japanese intellectuals in particular were awed by the prospect of a revolutionary socialist China endowed with Marxist-Leninist ideology. Some suggested that Japan may once again learn from the Chinese model as it has done for more than one thousand years prior to the Meiji era.

These admirations for a new socialist China, however, were soon evaporated after the radical leftists had led China into political chaos and economic disasters. The Japanese watched unbelievably the policy blunders of the Great Leap Forward and the political anarchy, especially the rebellious Red Guards, of the Cultural Revolution. What happened inside the PRC seemed to confirm the old Japanese saying that China was just too big a country and the Chinese people too disorganized to be effectively ruled by any government. Moreover, the downfall of the Gang of Four, who were regarded by some Japanese as true revolutionaries, shattered any lingering illusions or images of a revolutionary China. The usually biased Japanese press toned down markedly favorable reports from China.[2] The increase of Japanese visitors including government officials and private delegations to China after the establishment of formal diplomatic relations between the two countries in 1972 also helped to dispel the myths about socialist China. More and more Japanese have begun to see and understand a real China — a huge country encountering similar problems like other developing states in finding its way toward economic prosperity and political stability.

As pointed out by one keen observer of Japan's foreign relations, past Japanese patronizing attitudes toward the Chinese were based primarily on sympathetic concerns about a feeble and backward China.[3] It is thus conceivable that a strong and modernized China would wipe out any remaining sentimental linkage between the two peoples. To many Japanese, the PRC has no doubt already achieved the great power status and scored impressive accomplishments in its 30-year history. It is also true, however, that China's progress in the last three decades fell far behind Japan's miraculous economic growth. After all, China is still a poor and technologically backward country. Many Japanese have inclined to believe that Japan, because of history and cultural affinity to China and its presumptuous understanding of Chinese conditions, should have the responsibility to assist the Chinese in their modernization drive.

On many occasions when assisting the Chinese, the Japanese were unusually frank and direct in their advice and criticism. Some Japanese officials went so far as to lecture their Chinese counterparts on economic management.[4] They were at times impatient with the low efficiency and appalled by the erratic planning of China's cumbersome bureaucracies. Most Japanese, nevertheless, realized that the conditions in China are very different from those in Japan. Unlike Japan, more than 80 percent of China's manpower is tied to the agriculture sector, which constitutes less than one-third of China's total production values. It may take China a long time, many Japanese believe, to restructure its economy and develop the full potential of its apparently inexhaustible human resources. Most Japanese have friendly feelings toward the Chinese. According to a public opinion poll conducted by the prime minister's office in 1980, 79 percent of respondents felt "friendly toward China," an increase of 8 percent over an identical poll in 1979; those answering "I don't" decreased from 20 percent to 14 percent. Eighty percent of the respondents from the 1980 poll also believed that "friendly relations have developed" between China and Japan.[5]

The Chinese are also eager to have better relations with the Japanese. At a press conference held in Tokyo, October 1978, Deng Xiaoping appealed to the two peoples to forget the unfortunate past and to forge ahead with more friendly contacts.[6] The Chinese government urged its people to erase the deep-rooted hatred against the Japanese and stressed the importance of Japan's valuable experience to China's modernization programs by presenting the Chinese people a highly favorable Japanese society — blessed with economic prosperity, political stability, and low crime rates.

EMOTIONAL LINKAGE AND CULTURAL EXCHANGES

Exchanges of visits were greatly promoted as Peking launched its cultural diplomacy. The Chinese government arranged, with the cooperation of the

Japanese government, the visit of a group of Japanese nationals born in China during the war years to Japan in the autumn of 1980. The dramatic television scene showing the reunions of China-born Japanese and their parents touched the hearts of millions of Japanese and highlighted the emotional linkage between the two peoples. Japanese parents were also invited to China searching for their lost sons and daughters. Moreover Japanese television networks were granted access to China making documentary films, featuring the mystique of China's society and its gorgeous historical sites and picturesque landscapes. The NHK's program "The Silk Road," for example, had glued many Japanese viewers to their televisions. At the same time, sports, concerts, arts, and other cultural exchanges had been sharply increased. The Japanese were particularly impressed by the glamorous archeological exhibits from China, which gave them a new sense of pride for their cultural heritage from this ancient kingdom.

Many Japanese were impressed and flattered by the expressed Chinese eagerness to learn from their successful modernization experience. Hua Guofeng remarked during his visit to Tokyo in May 1980 that the Chinese people admired the vigorous and realistic approach of the Japanese and that China could do well to learn from and study Japan's achievements in industry, agriculture, science, technology, and other areas.[7] China again looks up to Japan, as it did at the turn of the last century, for training a new generation of scientists and technicians. Hundreds of Chinese students have been sent to study at various universities and institutes in Japan. The Japanese government has cooperated by providing special language-training programs for prospective students. Japanese has rapidly replaced Russian and become the second most popular second language (after English) in China.

Numerous Chinese delegations representing people from all walks of life including trading officials, economists, educators, scientists, and engineers have also come to Japan to seek guidance; the number of Chinese visitors to Japan has increased tenfold since the normalization of relations and surpassed ten thousand in 1979. They were very humble and quick to admit the backwardness of China's economy and technology and were extremely flexible in dealing with the Japanese. The Chinese behavior was in marked contrast to the arrogant and dogmatic attitudes of the Russians. This reminded the Japanese of the deep cultural gap between themselves and the Soviet people. Some Japanese were surprised, considering the big gap in ideology and the prolonged separation and lack of communications between the two peoples, to find many striking similarities between the Chinese and themselves, which they could not even find in their contacts with the Americans with whom they have maintained close relations for more than three decades. Indeed, Japan's deep consciousness of feelings of closeness toward China may continue to bind Tokyo to Peking in a subtle yet not insignificant way.

The Japanese, however, though sentimental and carried by "mood,"[8] are very practical people. The shrewdness of Japanese politicians, diplomats, and businessmen is well known to foreigners who have dealt with them. When the

Peking government canceled unilaterally in early 1980 several giant plant contracts with Japanese firms involving more than $1.5 billion it caused an uproar in Japan's political and business circles. Some demanded immediate compensations and warned the Chinese of the serious consequences that might have on the overall Sino-Japanese economic relations if Peking failed to respond to Japanese business interests. The Japanese government was reluctant and refused to extend additional low-interest loans to China before the Chinese demonstrated their ability to resolve the current economic problems. The Japanese press joined some high-ranking officials in urging a businesslike manner, based on cool and careful cost-benefit calculations, in settling contract disputes and other economic transactions with the Chinese. The press was particularly harsh in criticizing the mishandling of economic policies by the Peking government.

Clearly, emotional linkage cannot shield the bilateral relationship between China and Japan from conflicts. National interests always come first in bilateral relations. Sino-Japanese relations have been and will continue to be determined by political and economic developments in both China and Japan, the overall foreign policy strategies of the two countries, and, above all, the changing international environments.

THE TREATY OF PEACE AND FRIENDSHIP

The connection between China's bilateral relations with Japan and its global strategy was dramatized by the prolonged (almost four years) and arduous negotiations that eventually led to the signing of a peace and friendship treaty between Tokyo and Peking on August 12, 1978. Ever since the beginning of the negotiations in spring 1975 the prospect of agreement by the two sides on the terms of the proposed peace treaty was clouded by the thorny "antihegemony" clause. As it became a well-known fact that "hegemony" was a Chinese code word for Soviet expansionism, Tokyo resisted the inclusion of such a clause in the peace treaty. Proposals and counterproposals were exchanged yet there was no breakthrough three years after the initial negotiations.[9]

There were signs, however, of changing mood in the Japanese society favoring an early conclusion of a peace treaty with the PRC by fall 1977. The Japanese business community, facing increasing difficulty in trading with the United States and Western European countries, demanded for expanding trade with China. Domestic pressure for the resumption of treaty negotiations with Peking increased as the leaders of big business were convinced that the peace treaty was a prerequisite for signing lucrative trade agreements between China and Japan. This protreaty mood was boosted, ironically, by Soviet attempts to block Japan's move toward concluding a peace treaty with China. The heavy-handed Soviet diplomacy that warned the Fukuda government of "retaliatory measures" from Moscow had apparently backfired. The unyielding Soviet stand on its territorial dispute with Japan and its refusal even to discuss the issue during Foreign Minister Sunao Sonoda's visit to Moscow in January 1978 also infuriated the Japanese. Furthermore, Tokyo was indignant at the Kremlin's unilateral publication of the Soviet draft proposal to Japan of the "Treaty of Good Neighborliness and Cooperation" on February 23 in *Izvestia*, and rejected the proposal as humiliating and unacceptable. Seeing no improvement of Soviet-Japanese relations, the Fukuda Cabinet decided to tilt toward China and reopen the treaty talks with Peking in March 1978.

Fukuda, however, was undecided as to the specific date of resuming the treaty talks because of strong opposition from conservative and pro-Taiwan Diet members of the ruling Liberal Democratic Party (LDP), who cautioned Fukuda of concluding a hasty peace treaty with the PRC at the expense of Japan's national interest and relations with the Soviet Union. Some LDP members also demanded the Chinese acknowledgment of the Japanese territorial rights over the disputed Senkaku (Tiao Yu Tai) Islands, which are claimed by Tokyo, Peking, and Taipei, as a precondition for a peace treaty between the two countries.

The stalemate in the peace treaty negotiations hindered the development of closer relationships with Japan and annoyed the Peking leaders who were eager to import high-technology products and obtain financial support from the Asian industrial giant. The urgency of concluding a peace treaty with Japan was heightened by the intensifying dispute with Hanoi over Indo-China and the latter's drifting away toward the Soviet Union that aroused Peking's concerns about Soviet encirclement from the south. The signing of a peace treaty with Japan would serve as a counterweight, from Peking's perspective, to the Soviet-Vietnamese alliance and forestall a similar, though very unlikely, Soviet-Japanese cooperation. In an apparent attempt to break the logjam of negotiations, Deng Xiaoping indicated in March 1978 that the inclusion of the antihegemony clause in the peace treaty would not imply joint Sino-Japanese action against a hegemony-seeking third power. He agreed that Japan and China each had its own foreign policy and should make its own independent decision in such matters.[10] Deng's statement was clearly aimed at alleviating the Japanese fear of provoking repercussions from the Russians.

Despite (or because of) China's flexible position on the antihegemony clause, opposition by the pro-Taiwan Diet members of the LDP remained strong. There were no clear signs of diplomatic breakthrough. It was at this point on April 12 that the Senkaku incident occurred. Armed Chinese fishing boats intruded into the disputed territorial waters of the Senkaku Islands. The effect of the Senkaku Island incident was inconclusive. In any event, the Fukuda government proposed the reopening of the treaty negotiations by the end of May and agreed to the separation of the Senkaku issue from the treaty. One can easily argue, however, that with or without the incident, because of the favorable American attitudes and rising domestic pressure for an early conclusion of the treaty, the Japanese government would renew treaty negotiations at about the same time or even earlier and would not object to the shelving of the territorial issue.

The Sino-Japanese Treaty of Peace and Friendship was concluded and signed in Peking less than three weeks after the renewal of treaty negotiations. The antihegemony clause declares that neither of the contracting parties should seek hegemony in the Asia-Pacific region or in any other region, and that "each is opposed to efforts by any country or group of countries to establish such hegemony." Article IV accommodates the Japanese wish not to offend the Soviets by specifying that "the present treaty shall not affect the position of either contracting party regarding its relations with third countries." However, both Moscow and Washington chose to ignore Article IV and interpreted the treaty as anti-Soviet.

TRADE AND ECONOMIC RELATIONS

The signing of the peace treaty had had profound impact on the development of bilateral relations between the two countries and the momentum triggered by this historical event is likely to remain strong in the 1980s and beyond. The immediate effect of the treaty was the rapid increase of the two-way trade between the PRC and Japan. The initial long-term trade agreement that was signed in February 1978 was renegotiated in March 1979 and the two sides agreed to extend the effective period from eight years (1978-85) to thirteen years (1978-90). The agreed amount of trade was expanded from the original $20 billion to $40 billion or $60 billion for the period covered by the agreement. The Chinese promised the Japanese a steady supply of oil and coal in the coming years while importing high-technology products and complete industrial plants and equipment from Japan. The two-way trade between the two countries soared to over $9 billion in 1980, a $2 billion increase over the previous year and more than double the trade value of 1977. More importantly, perhaps, the value of Sino-Japanese trade has since 1977 consistently surpassed the value of Soviet-Japanese trade and the gap appears to be widening. In 1980, the two-way Soviet-Japanese trade amounted to only $4.1 billion, less than half the value of Sino-Japanese trade of the same year.

Furthermore, the Chinese were seeking loans from the Japanese government and commercial loans from Japanese banks. Commercial loan agreements of more than $10 billion were signed in 1979 and 1980 between the Bank of China and the Bank of Tokyo and other Japanese banks. In addition, the Ohira government offered to lend the Chinese $1.5 billion low-interest loans for China's ambitious infrastructure projects and to help the Chinese to explore the supposedly oil-rich Bohai Bay. Prime Minister Masayoshi Ohira pledged that Japan would try every feasible way to help China modernize. As a symbol of friendship between the two countries, Ohira promised to assist in building a memorial hospital in Peking, to be equipped with advanced technology and facilities. In return, the Chinese government promised the Japanese business leaders that China would implement the contracts, which were suspended in

February 1979 and unilaterally canceled a year later by the Chinese partly because of the lack of funds, as soon as satisfactory arrangements for deferred payments could be worked out. A Chinese delegation headed by Vice Premier Gu Mu in September 1979 even went so far as to invite Japanese industrial leaders and bankers to invest in joint venture projects with the Chinese, including the exploitation of oil in the area near the disputed Senkaku Islands.[11]

The Chinese, of course, were fully aware of the pivotal position of Japan in China's global foreign policy strategy. Indeed, Peking's careful cultivation of its bilateral relations with Tokyo had been closely paralleling China's strategic calculations. The signing of the Treaty of Peace and Friendship and the inclusion of the antihegemony clause in the treaty were clearly calculated Chinese moves in winning the Japanese to China's side in the Peking-Tokyo-Moscow strategic triangle. A strong tie with Japan may not break the Soviet encirclement from the north. Japan, after all, is still a very weak military power. It would nevertheless increase the stakes of any Soviet move that intends to intimidate Tokyo or Peking. It would be a nightmare to the Kremlin leaders to see the formation of a formal military alliance between the highly industrialized and technologically advanced Japan and the populous and modernizing China. The Soviets were eager to seek financial and technological assistance from the Japanese to develop the Eastern Siberian frontier. Therefore, the Russians did not adopt any overt retaliations against Tokyo for its obvious tilt toward Peking.

STRATEGIC CALCULATIONS

Japan is also a crucial factor, from the Chinese viewpoint, in the Peking-Tokyo-Washington triangular relations. There was no coincidence that four months after the conclusion of the Sino-Japanese peace treaty a breakthrough was reached in negotiations between Washington and Peking concerning the establishment of diplomatic relations between the two countries. An antihegemony clause similar to that included in the Sino-Japanese treaty was also inserted in the Washington-Peking joint communique of December 15, 1978, which announced the establishment of formal diplomatic relations between the PRC and the United States. Unlike the Peking-Tokyo-Moscow triangle, however, in which Tokyo is regarded by the Chinese as a counterweight to the Soviet threat, Japan is considered by Peking as the indispensable coordinator in the Peking-Tokyo-Washington triangle and in its united front strategy. The Chinese government has publicly acknowledged that the U.S.-Japanese security treaty plays an important role in stabilizing Asian security. Deng Xiaoping himself commented on that point to a group of visiting Japanese editorial writers on September 6, 1978, saying that Japan's relationship with the United States was more important than its relationship with China.[12] Peking was convinced that only a strong American-Japanese military alliance could serve as a counterveiling force to the expanding Soviet navy in the Pacific. Furthermore, Peking made no secret that it would like to see Japan strengthen its Self Defense Force. China may not wish to see a nuclear-armed or a militarized Japan; a viable Self Defense Force that could impose unacceptable cost to Soviet military incursion would certainly be welcomed by Peking. As long as China remains highly sensitive to Soviet military threat, a Peking-Tokyo-Washington entente is probably a best policy option for the Chinese.

There is little doubt that the PRC's relations with Japan have been and will continue to be determined to a large extent by the development of Sino-Soviet relations. The deteriorating relations between Moscow and Peking are likely to push the latter ever closer to Tokyo and Washington. The Russians may have a short-term strategic advantage over the Peking-Tokyo-Washington triangle because of their vastly superior military posture over the Chinese in the Asian continent and their formidable navy in the Pacific. In the long run, however, the Soviet Union is no match to the combined industrial and military power of the United States, Japan, and China. The Kremlin leaders may have only two policy options: either to launch a preemptive military strike, by a nuclear or a large-scale conventional attack to destroy China's military and industrial capabilities, or to accept the new configuration of world politics and to accommodate the Chinese. There is strong evidence to suggest that most Soviet leaders have considered that the cost of risking a full-scale war with the Chinese is simply too high and unacceptable. The successful launching of China's first intercontinental ballistic missile (ICBM) in May 1980, which could reach the entire Soviet Union, would certainly strengthen the position of the soft-liners in Moscow. That does not mean, of course, that confrontations between the two Communist countries are going to decline in the immediate future. It does suggest, however, that the Kremlin leaders may incline to reopen the dialogue with their counterparts in Peking and to negotiate the unsettled issues concerning relations between the two countries.

There were also indications to suggest that the Chinese may be in the process of reconsidering their policy toward the Soviets. Peking agreed to the resumption of ministerial level negotiations between the two countries in September 1979. Although the first round of negotiations held in Moscow failed without producing any conclusive results and further negotiations were halted by the Chinese after the Soviet invasion of Afghanistan, the very fact that a new dialogue had begun was itself highly significant. It may take years for the two sides to reconcile their deeply rooted apprehension and mistrust, yet one should not rule out the possibility of a Sino-Soviet rapprochement in the 1980s.

It is short-sighted, however, as some observers have suggested, to regard any Sino-Soviet rapprochement as detrimental to the Peking-Tokyo-Washington entente.[13] The return to a Soviet-Chinese alliance of the early 1950s is simply beyond the realm of possibilities. The termination of the 30-year Sino-Soviet alliance in 1980 signaled a watershed in the two countries' bilateral relations — it had put Peking and Moscow on an equal and realistic footing in future negotiations. A new phase of Sino-Soviet relations has begun. Future detente or entente between Moscow and Peking, if it is going to happen in the 1980s, is likely to be a result of common desire from the two sides to accommodate each other in an increasingly interdependent world. After all, the two sides would have nothing to lose by cooperating or coexisting with each other and stand only to lose, even for the eventual winner, by direct confrontation. Seeing in this light, indeed, a genuine rapprochement between China and the Soviet Union in the 1980s and beyond would contribute to China's national security as well as to the stability of Asia and would be welcomed by Tokyo and Washington.

THE PROSPECTS

Because of Japan's unique position as a common base in the Peking-Tokyo-Washington strategic triangle and the Peking-Tokyo-Moscow triangle,[14] Japan occupies a pivotal position in China's calculations. Japan's pivotal role in the Peking-Tokyo-Washington triangle was demonstrated at the first summit between President Ronald Reagan and Prime Minister Zenko Suzuki in May 1981. Suzuki reportedly urged Reagan to expand "cooperative relations" with the PRC and argued that a strong China was crucial to the peace and stability of Asia. In the communique issued after the summit, concern of relations with the PRC was given the priority for the first time in similar documents between the two countries over the stability of the Korean Peninsula.[15]

Likewise, Tokyo could easily tip the balance of the Peking-Tokyo-Moscow strategic triangle by changing its policy toward the Soviets. After the conclusion of the Treaty of Peace and Friendship between China and Japan, the Soviet Union had increased its military presence in the northern islands claimed by the Japanese, in an apparent attempt to deter the Japanese government from moving too close to Peking. The Soviets, however, underestimated the sensitivity of the Japanese and their determination to resist any intimidation by coercion.[16] Ironically, it was precisely this Soviet "gunboat diplomacy" that had pushed Tokyo ever closer to Peking.

This does not suggest that Japan would seek a military alliance with the PRC. In fact, the Japanese government has been very cautious to prevent sending any signals that might imply Sino-Japanese military cooperation. The Japanese government has also reiterated that the ban on arms sales to Communist countries including the PRC will be strictly imposed. Clearly, Japan does not want to provoke any Soviet repercussions. Peking, probably more than the two superpowers, is well aware of this Japanese sentiment and aspiration for an independent role in global politics. In a skillful diplomatic move, Deng Xiaoping denied flatly that China would seek any military cooperation from Japan.[17] Deng thus alleviated the fear of some Japanese who were worrying that moving too close to China may one day lead to some form of military cooperation between the two countries. Japanese-Chinese relations, therefore, would continue to flourish despite, or because of, the absence of military alliance.

Future Sino-Japanese relations also hinge to a large degree on the prospects of China's modernization programs. Post-Mao leadership has concentrated its efforts in modernizing China's backward economy. The 1980s may well be proven the crucial decade in China's new Long March toward modernization. As Deng Xiaoping himself has put it, China is going either to make or break it in the 1980s. Judging from China's economic performance of the past three decades particularly the recent post-Mao years, despite some serious drawbacks such as inflation, budget deficits and stagnant energy supplies, the PRC stands a better than average chance to attain a sustained 5 to 7 percent economic growth well into the 1980s and beyond.

As China's drive toward modernization picks up momentum, its quest for international influence and prestige is likely to become increasingly an important factor in Peking's policy calculations. In its dealings with Moscow, Tokyo, and Washington, Peking would be more assertive. China's position in the quadrilateral relationship would be strengthened and its views would be taken more seriously by other powers. Because of the common interest in Asia, the frequency of political consultations between Peking and Tokyo regarding regional and global affairs is likely to increase. The first ministerial level meeting between the two countries was held in Peking in December 1980. The two governments, however, realizing the difference in national interests, agreed to disagree. The Chinese government, for example, refrained from criticizing Tokyo's Indo-China policy, despite the latter's intent to continue aid and other assistance to Vietnam.

The complementary nature of the two economies suggests that Sino-Japanese trade may continue to grow, albeit less dramatically than in recent years, into the 1980s. The Chinese obviously have problems in increasing the amount of crude oil supplies to Japan; China's crude oil to Japan for both 1981 and 1982 was reduced by the Chinese government to 8.3 million tons from the initially agreed 9.5 million tons and 15 million tons respectively. The prospects of increasing supplies of Chinese steam and coking coal look much brighter. Peking reassured Tokyo that total Chinese coal export to Japan may reach or surpass 10 million tons by 1985, a big jump from the 1 million level of the 1970s. With the world's third largest proven coal reserve and Chinese priority in developing their coal mines, China should have little difficulty in meeting the target of coal exports to Japan. It is short-sighted, however, to assess future trading relations between the two countries from the prospects of China's energy and other raw material supplies to Japan alone. As China's economy continues to expand and the current consumer-oriented economic policy remains unchanged, China will become an increasingly important market for Japanese products. Likewise, when Japan's industry becomes more technology/knowledge-intensive, the domestic Japanese market will become more open to China's manufactured goods.

The *Nitchu yuko mudo* (Japan-China friendship mood) that has developed in Japan since the establishment of diplomatic relations with the PRC in 1972 may have already served its purpose of promoting friendly contacts between the two peoples and has begun receding and fading away.[18] Taking its place, however, a stable and permanent government-to-government relationship has been firmly established. After decades of confrontation and mistrust, the two countries have finally begun to approach each other with better understanding and on a more realistic basis.

NOTES

1. Japan Communist Party's *Akahada* [Red Flag], December 12, 1979.

2. The *Asahi Shimbun*, for example, well known for its strong pro-Cultural Revolution stand in the 1960s, made a dramatic turnabout in recent years by dispatching neutral and sometimes negative reports from China.

3. Yoshikazu Sakamoto, "Sino-Japanese Relations in the Nuclear Age," *Journal of Social and Political Ideas in Japan* 4, no. 3 (December 1966): 64.

4. For example, Saburo Okita, the former foreign minister and Tokyo's special envoy to Peking in February 1981, lectured the Chinese leaders on the inflationary nature of their economic policies and the mismanagement of plant projects that led to cancellations and postponements. See John Lewis and David Bonavia, "The Honeymoon Is Over." *Far Eastern Economic Review* (February 20, 1981): 46-47.

5. The survey was conducted nationwide with an 80 percent returning rate. The findings were reported in the *Asahi Shimbun*, September 29, 1980.

6. *Peking Review*, November 3, 1978, p. 14.

7. *Beijing Review*, June 9, 1980, p. 11.

8. Minoru Takeuchi, "Japan-China Friendship-Myth and Reality," *Japan Quarterly* 28, no. 1 (January-March 1981): 23-29.

9. For the developments of Sino-Japanese relations since 1972 until the start of initial negotiations on the peace treaty see A. M. Halpern, "China and Japan Since Normalization," in *Dimensions of China's Foreign Relations*, ed. Chün-tu Hsüeh (New York: Praeger, 1977), chap. 5. For a detailed account of the negotiations between Japan and China that led to the conclusion of the peace treaty see Hong N. Kim, "Sino-Japanese Relations in the Post-Mao Era," *Asian Affairs: An American Review* 7, no. 3 (January-February 1980): 161-81; and Chae-Jin Lee, "The Making of the Sino-Japanese Peace and Friendship Treaty," *Pacific Affairs* (Summer 1979): 420-45.

10. *Asahi Shimbun*, March 15, 1978.

11. *Beijing Review*, September 14, 1979, p. 5.

12. As quoted in Shinkichi Eto, "Recent Developments in Sino-Japanese Relations," *Asian Survey* 20, no. 7 (July 1980): 736.

13. One student of Chinese foreign policy, however, suggested that Sino-Soviet rapprochement may give the Americans additional leeway in dealing with the two Communist countries and hence should be welcomed by Washington. See Gerald Segal, "China and the Great Power Triangle," *China Quarterly*, no. 83 (September 1980), pp. 490-509.

14. For an excellent discussion on the pivotal position of Japan on the two strategic triangles see Tang Tsou, Tetsuo Majita, and Hideo Otake, "Sino-Japanese Relations in the 1970s," in *China and Japan: Search for Balance Since World War I*, ed. Alvin D. Coox and Hilary Conroy (Santa Barbara: ABC-Clio, 1978).

15. For the English text of the communique see the *Japan Times*, May 10, 1981.

16. For an interesting account of persistent Soviet underestimation of Japan and heavy-handed Soviet diplomacy toward Tokyo see Joseph M. Ha, "Moscow's Policy Toward Japan," *Problems of Communism* 26 (September-October 1977): 61-72.

17. Shinkichi Eto, "Recent Developments," p. 736.

18. Minoru Takeuchi, "Japan-China Friendship," p. 24.

4

KOREA IN CHINA'S FOREIGN POLICY

Chün-tu Hsüeh

China's foreign policy toward Korea is influenced by the following basic factors: historic relations between the two countries, the principles of proletarian internationalism, China's concern with its security because of geographic proximity, the common problems of the unification of a divided country, and the maintenance of the balance of power in East Asia, that is, China's relations with Japan, the United States, and the Soviet Union. Apart from national security, these factors do not always carry the same weight in the formation of China's policy toward Korea. One consideration may exercise stronger influence at one time, while the interplay of other factors may be decisive at other times. A change in one of these variables or the interaction of China's relations with other powers may result in policy changes by all the actors concerned with the Korean Peninsula. Needless to say, Korea's own decisions cannot be completely ignored. This chapter first will analyze China's policy toward Korea within the above framework and then discuss Korea's response to the Sino-American rapprochement.

TRADITIONAL RELATIONS

It is well known that the traditional relations between China and the states surrounding it — Korea, Burma, Annam (Vietnam), and others — constituted an international system based on concepts distinctively different from the Western system of international law. China was a "superior state," while Korea and Vietnam were "dependent" or "subordinate states." The concept of dependent states can be understood only in the context of the traditional Confucian cultural relations, rather than by the Western legalistic concepts. Traditional Sino-Korean relations were different from the suzerain-protectorate and suzerain-vassal relationship, which involve legal implications, including certain obligations on the part of the suzerain state to manage the foreign and military affairs of the vassal state.

Several official statements and incidents may be cited to illustrate this point. In 1591, the king of Korea replied to Hideyoshi, the Japanese warrior who had aspired to rule East Asia from Peking, in these words:

> You stated in your letter that you were planning to invade the supreme nation [China] and requested that our Kingdom join in your military undertaking. . . . We cannot even understand how you have dared to plan such an undertaking and make such a request of us. . . . For thousands of years, from the time . . . the founder of the Kingdom of Korea received the investiture from the Chou dynasty, up to our own time. . . . Our two nations have acted as a single family, maintaining the relationship of father and son as well as that of ruler and subject. . . . We shall certainly not desert "our lord and father" nation. . . .[1]

The famous and favorite statement often repeated by China's Foreign Office in the 1870s also puzzled the Western international lawyers: "Korea, though a dependence of China, is completely autonomous in her policies, religion, prohibition, and orders. China has never interfered [with] it."[2] Indeed, in the old international order of East Asia, China exercised power with restraint. As U.S. Minister George F. Seward wrote in 1879:

> It is not too much to say that it has been within the power of China for a very long period to overrun and subdue these petty states. . . . A great people fillling all their territory to the limit of its sustaining power, but remaining for centuries self-contained, regardful of their own dignity and place, but regardful also of the rights of the petty powers about them, is a spectacle not very common in the history of the world. It is one upon which we may pause to raise the question whether a state capable of such conduct has not, for some reason, a poise and balance of judgment and temper greater than we have been in the habit of attributing to her, and which entitles her to a large measure of respect and esteem.[3]

For two centuries prior to the 1870s China had seldom interfered with Korea's internal or foreign affairs, in spite of their nominal tributary relations. The change of policy was partly due to a response to foreign design in Korea. A direct interference in Korea's domestic politics occurred in 1882, when China sent troops to Korea to restore order. China took hostage of the regent, who was the father of the king and leader of the conservative faction. Three years later, when China decided to permit the regent to return to Korea, the Peking imperial edict (September 20, 1885) declared:

> The Court is aware that filial piety is the most important virtue and that in the dependent state that virtue is regarded highly. . . . The Board of Rites should inform the said [Korean] King that [the release of his father] is our extraordinary benevolent act. . . . The said King should carefully take lesson from the past mistakes and . . . devote [his] whole heart in the administration.[4]

It is probably impossible to find any similar statements defining the relations of two countries in Western international law.

It should be stressed, however, that Western scholars have often tended to overemphasize the concept of the Middle Kingdom and of the inequality of nations of the tributary system as if it were the only international system that China recognized and practiced. As a result, Chinese international posture has often been distorted. In the 1950s, some leading scholars in Chinese studies went so far as to say that it was one of the reasons why the West could not get along with the People's Republic of China. The fact of the matter is that for more than a century since 1842, China had not been accepted as an equal in the "family of nations," and that one of the main objectives of China in modern time has been to achieve equality. Furthermore, Russia was not included among the list of tributaries in an official Chinese document published in 1820, and it is doubtful that missions from the West at the end of the eighteenth century and throughout the nineteenth century were so considered by the Manchu government.[5]

PROLETARIAN INTERNATIONALISM

Since the inauguration of the Democratic People's Republic of Korea (DPRK) in 1948 and the establishment of the People's Republic of China (PRC) in 1949, Korea, or at least its northern part, has remained culturally and politically orientated toward China after the interval of half a century. Of course, the common ideology shared by the two countries now is communism rather than Confucianism. Nevertheless, since the 1950s, the regional international system of East Asia, as far as China, North Korea, and, before 1975, part of Indochina are concerned, is in some respects reminiscent of the historic Confucian system of the family of nations. While the description of relations between China and Korea in terms of "father and son" or "elder brother and younger brother" reflects the traditional Confucian concept of the family of nations in the old traditional order of East Asia, the DPRK and PRC are now on equal terms as "class brothers." It may not be too farfetched to suggest that "brotherhood" is akin to the concept of fraternal national socialist solidarity, and by and large China has served as a model for the development of Korea (DPRK), particularly before the Great Leap Forward and the Cultural Revolution, as it did in the imperial past. However, although these and other aspects of the traditional Chinese-Korean relationship continue, there is a qualitative difference between the traditional government and social structures of China and Korea and their contemporary socialist systems.

On the whole, relations between China and the DPRK have conformed to the principle of proletarian internationalism. It may be mentioned that the Chinese support of North Korea during the Korean War and the Chinese aid to North Vietnam in the latter's struggle against the French and the United States were partly based on security and ideological reasons. The fact that the socialist camp no longer exists as a result of the Sino-Soviet conflicts in the 1960s and the Chinese punitive action against Vietnam in 1979 does not necessarily mean that proletarian internationalism is no longer an operational code and ideology, although it has become much less important than nationalism and the balance of power in the makeup of China's foreign policy in the 1980s.

CHINA'S SECURITY AND THE BUFFER STATE

Korea is located on the border of northeast China. The two countries are separated by the Yalu River. Relations between them, as between the Chinese and Vietnamese before 1975, often have been described as close as "lips and teeth." The analogy is indicative of the Chinese view of Korea as a buffer state, vital to China's national security.

Within 60 years (1894-1953), three major wars were fought in East Asia because of Korea, two of which involved China directly. China was forced to fight the Japanese in 1894-95, when Japan attempted to dominate Korea. In 1950, China, pressed by Stalin, sent "volunteers" to fight against the United States in order to save North Korea and to counter America's threat. At that time, North Korea was actually the responsibility of the Soviet Union.[6] Perceiving Korea as the "lips" to China's "teeth," Peking found it necessary to intervene. The intervention fully demonstrated not only "proletarian internationalism" but also China's perception of Korea's importance to China's security. Although China had reestablished itself as a major power in East Asia after World War II, it was the Korean War that most enhanced its international status prior to its acquisition of nuclear weapons.

Korea is a classic example of a buffer state in East Asian politics.[7] Many aspects of the Korean War have remained obscure, but one thing that appears quite clear is that China was unjustly condemned as an aggressor by the United Nations, and that the Chinese intervention was actually motivated by fear of America's threat to Chinese security.[8] When the United States ignored the repeated private and public warnings that China would "not sit idly by" if U.S. forces crossed the thirty-eighth parallel, it became imperative for China to move in to preserve North Korea's position as a buffer state. The intervention served both China's national interests and the ideological demand for international socialist solidarity.

PEKING, PYONGYANG, AND THE TAIWAN QUESTION

Although China's influence in Korea was naturally enhanced as a result of the Korean War, China seemed not to have made any special effort to increase its influence at the Soviet's expense. Indeed, China had intended to withdraw all its troops from Korea earlier than 1958. By October 1954, China had already withdrawn 87,900 men, and an additional 52,200 were pulled out between April and October 1955. The final withdrawal was delayed until October 1958 because of an urgent request by the Pyongyang government.[9]

As Sino-Soviet relations began to deteriorate after 1959, Peking began to pay special attention to Pyongyang as China sought ideological and political allies in the dispute. At first, the North Koreans scrupulously avoided taking sides in the Sino-Soviet dispute; then Pyongyang slowly gravitated toward the Chinese position. During the Cultural Revolution, China was too preoccupied with internal struggle to have an effective foreign policy, and relations between the two countries were at an all-time low.

China's moves to improve relations with North Korea after 1969 were consistent with its general pattern of behavior toward many foreign countries. The warming trend was signaled by Chou En-lai's visit to Pyongyang in April 1970. The Chinese-Korean joint communique subsequently stressed the revival of Japanese militarism, calling it a "dangerous force of aggression in Asia." The communique called for further consolidation of friendship and unity between the two peoples based on their common struggle against American imperialism in Korea, Vietnam, and Taiwan.[10] This statement was a direct response to the Nixon-Sato communique of November 1969, in which the Japanese prime minister stated that "the Republic of Korea was essential to Japan's own security" and that "the maintenance of peace and security in the Taiwan area was also a most important factor for the security of Japan."[11] Peking was also aware of the Soviet attempt to contain China through a "system of collective security in Asia," which was formally proposed by CPSU Central Committee General Secretary L. I. Brezhnev in June 1969 at the international Communist Party meeting in Moscow.

As the world entered the 1970s, all the major powers concerned with Korea favored detente in the peninsula. Shortly before the announcement in July 1971 that President Richard Nixon was to visit China in 1972, the Chinese delegate to the Korean Armistice Commission attended a meeting for the first time since August 1966. In an interview with James Reston in August 1971, Chou En-lai repeated that "a way should be found to bring about a rapprochement between the two sides in Korea and to move toward a peaceful unification of Korea." Furthermore, the "Korean question is also linked up with the problem of Japanese militarism."[12]

In the Shanghai communique issued at the end of President Nixon's visit to China in February 1972, Peking declared its firm support of the DPRK's "eight-point program for the peaceful unification of Korea" and its stand for the abolition of the U.N. Commission for the Unification and Rehabilitation of Korea, while the United States pledged that it would "support efforts of the Republic of Korea to seek a relaxation of tension and increase communications in the Korean peninsula."[13] And a *People's Daily* editorial promptly endorsed the July 4, 1972 joint statement of the North and South.[14]

Although not in the same sense as Korea, Vietnam (before unification in 1976), or Germany, China is a divided country. Therefore, Peking must take Taiwan into account in the formulation of its policy toward Korea. As early as 1950, as a result of President Harry Truman's decision to send the Seventh Fleet to the Taiwan Straits after the outbreak of the Korean War, the Peking government had considered the "U.S. armed intervention of Korea and aggression on Taiwan of China" to be two "serious and closely related" problems.[15] Indeed, the dialogues and negotiations in the Korean Peninsula may establish the direction and reveal the thinking of the Peking leaders on the unification of Taiwan. Both Taiwan and South Korea are supported by the United States. As a corollary of the Sino-American rapprochement, Peking naturally favors relaxation of tension in the Korean Peninsula. As the tension in Asia diminishes, the United States will have to live up to its commitments in the Shanghai communique.

In the communique, the United States "reaffirms its interest in a peaceful settlement of the Taiwan question by the Chinese themselves . . . [and] the ultimate objective of the withdrawal of all U.S. forces and military installations from Taiwan. In the meantime, it will progressively reduce its forces and military installations on Taiwan as the tension in the area diminishes." The relaxation of tension in the Korean Peninsula (as well as in Indochina), therefore, has direct bearing on the withdrawal of America's military presence in Taiwan. The Korean dialogues should create a favorable atmosphere for discussion of the reunification of the divided countries.[16]

Subsequently, Peking's peaceful overtures to Taiwan have been intensified. The publicity given to Chang Shih-chao's trip to Hong Kong in May 1973 was the most dramatic move by Peking,[17] followed by the release of large number of "war criminals" and KMT agents in 1975. Peking and Pyongyang appeared to have acted in concert concerning their respective unification problems. When Kim Il Sung put forward a new policy line embodied in five propositions in June 1973, it was promptly supported by China the next day.[18]

Apparently, there had been close consultation and coordination before the new line was advanced, and China certainly had Taiwan in mind. In fact, on many occasions Taiwan was mentioned when the Korean unification problem was being discussed.[19] Of course, there are significant differences between South Korea and Taiwan with respect to their adversaries. South and North Korea may be considered almost equals, but Taiwan is merely a province of China. In terms of population, territory, and military strength, Taiwan can hardly be compared with the mainland. Hence, the unification of China can only mean the "absorption" or "liberation" of the province by Peking. This was one of the reasons why Taiwan did not follow South Korea's flexible policy in response to the Sino-American rapprochement. In fact, Taiwan has continued to adhere to a "no contact" policy even though since 1979 Peking has offered generous terms and talked only in the context of "unification," not "liberation."[20]

Both Koreas have tolerated "dual recognition"[21]; however, Pyongyang has opposed Seoul's "two Koreas" representation in the United Nations. It suggested instead to join the United Nations under the single name of the "Confederal Republic of Koryo." Peking, on the other hand, has always insisted that it would not establish diplomatic relations with any country that recognizes the government in Taiwan.

BALANCE OF POWER

Chinese foreign policy toward Korea may also be viewed in the context of China's relations with Japan, the United States, and the Soviet Union, as well as their bilateral relations with each other and Korea. As mentioned earlier, Peking made no special effort to increase its influence in North Korea at the expense of Moscow during the period of Sino-Soviet "solidarity" in the 1950s. It was only after the deterioration of the relationship that China began to woo North Korea in order to win an ideological and political ally in the dispute with the Soviet Union.

It has been mentioned that China favored relaxation of tension in the Korean Peninsula as a result of the Sino-American rapprochement. Japan's role in Korea always has been of great concern to China. After the establishment of diplomatic relations between Japan and South Korea in 1965, there has been an increasing economic dominance of South Korea by Japan. The Nixon Doctrine (July 1969) expected Japan to play a leading role in Asia. The Nixon-Sato communique (November 1969) stated that the Republic of Korea was "essential" to Japan's own security and that Taiwan was "a most important factor for" the security of Japan. China has toned down its attack on the revival of Japanese militarism since the establishment of diplomatic relations between the two countries in September 1972. However, Peking cannot support a united Korea that would be primarily responsive to Japan and serve once again as a springboard for Japan's aggressive continental policy; nor can China support a policy that Korea would come under Soviet rule, as in the case of Outer Mongolia. It would also be unacceptable for China to support the unification of Korea, which would constitute the triumph of South Korea. Any one of these developments would upset the existing balance of power in the area and threaten China's security. Although the Korean Peninsula is barely larger than Minnesota, the combined population of South (38 million) and North (18 million) would make Korea the sixteenth most populous nation in the world, only a little behind Italy, the United Kingdom, and France. Furthermore, the combined armed forces of North and South, totaling more than 1 million, would place Korea's as the fifth largest in the world's standing armies.[22]

While China's intervention in the Korean War was motivated by concern for national security, America's response to the outbreak of the Korean War also can be explained partially by its concern for the security of Japan, which was recognized as a vital U.S. interest.

KOREA'S RESPONSE TO THE SINO-AMERICAN RAPPROCHEMENT

"The Korean people," declared an editorial of the *People's Daily*, "are the masters of Korea."[23] Nevertheless, Korea is inevitably affected by the decisions of great powers. As one observer remarked: "The future of Korea as well as her past is inextricably tied to her geographical position."[24] Historically, Korea has always had to contend with the power rivalries of its neighbors – Russia, China, and Japan. Japanese aggression toward Korea led to the Sino-Japanese War of 1894-95. It was followed by a decade of Russo-Japanese rivalry that culminated in the Russo-Japanese War of 1904-5. After years of championing Korea's independence, Japan finally annexed the country in 1910. After World War II, the United States and the USSR replaced Japan as the dominant powers in the peninsula.

Korea has good reasons to be suspicious of great powers. After all, until after the surrender of Japan, "Koreans played no part whatsoever in planning or decision making regarding Korea's future."[25] Furthermore, the country was divided by the United States and the Soviet Union in 1945. The leaders of the South and the North owed their existence to their respective mentors, and the DPRK was saved from almost certain annihilation only by the timely intervention of China in 1950. As a result of the resumption of diplomatic relations between Japan and South Korea in 1965, Japan once again plays an increasingly important role in the Korean Peninsula.

Although Kim Il Sung declared in September 1971 that the change in Sino-American relations would have "no direct relation to us,"[26] it is obvious that the Sino-American rapprochement has had a profound effect on Korea. In fact, by the time Chairman Mao had decided to welcome President Nixon to visit China,[27] North Korea was also beginning to change its militant posture to a more moderate stance toward South Korea.

Initially, South Korea was apprehensive about the Sino-American rapprochement, as illustrated by the comment made by the Korean ambassador to the United States concerning Nixon's announcement of his forthcoming trip to China: "While we welcome this dialogue between these two world giants, at the same time we are understandably in a quandary as to the future of our peninsular vis-a-vis the policies of the United States, China, the Soviet Union and Japan."[28] In May 1972, Lee Hu Rak, director of the South Korean Central Intelligency Agency, secretly visited North Korea, where he met Premier Kim Il Sung and Kim's younger brother to discuss a broad range of political issues. Then the Second Vice Premier Pak Song-chol traveled to Seoul to meet President Park Chung Hee. From these meetings came the July 4, 1972 communique.* There is no doubt that Sino-American rapprochement was the underlying factor in the initiation of the dialogue between the North and South Koreas. However, after the breakthrough, the dialogues soon deteriorated. By the spring of 1974, harsh words again were exchanged and tensions were renewed. Both Pyongyang and Seoul want unification — but on different terms. Pyongyang wants the complete withdrawal of American forces from the peninsula, while Seoul favors the conclusion of a nonaggression pact for peaceful coexistence between the South and the North. The death of Park Chung Hee in October 1979 did not seem to have any effect on the North-South relations. Kim Il Sung's reiteration of a unification proposal in October 1980 and South Korean President Chun Doo Hwan's proposal (January 12, 1981) that the two parts of Korea exchange visits by their top leaders have had no significant effect on the North-South relations.

The Sino-American rapprochement was a gain by Peking and, by extension, for Pyongyang. Before December 1970, only 58 countries had diplomatic relations with the PRC; by July 1981, 124 countries had recognized Peking. The DPRK also has broken out of its previous international isolation. Between 1948 and 1970, only 31 countries had established diplomatic relations with North Korea. Since then it has been recognized by an additional 21 states. In June 1973 it was granted permanent observer status at the United Nations.

Geographically and militarily, North Korea is in a somewhat advantageous position. The country is supported by China and the Soviet Union, the two continental powers that border North Korea. The treaties between the DPRK and its two allies (July 1961) call for immediate military and other assistance in case of military attack from any nation. South Korea, on the other hand, is supported by two maritime powers — the United States and Japan — separated from the peninsula by sea. The Korean-American mutual defense treaty of 1953 provides that in the event of an armed attack, each party "would act to meet the common danger in accordance with its constitutional processes."[29] The Japan-ROK treaty of 1965 contains an ambiguous article that provides the basis

---

*On June 1, 1972, I arrived at Seoul, where I talked to some of the officials on the National Unification Board. I gained the impression that they were extremely suspicious of North Korea. They asked me a number of questions concerning the mission of George C. Marshall, who was sent to China by President Truman to mediate negotiations between the Kuomintang and the Chinese Communists in December 1945. I did not know then that the South and the North were engaged in the secret negotiation that resulted in the July 4 joint communique.

for the speculation that the Japanese government "self-defense" force might come to the aid of the ROK within the framework of the U.N. forces.[30]

The two Koreas reacted differently to the establishment of diplomatic relations between China and Japan in 1972. Seoul was concerned about whether or not Tokyo would honor the 1965 ROK-Japan treaty, while Pyongyang enthusiastically pursued the new development in Sino-Japanese relations. As a corollary to this development, the DPRK is prepared to promote friendship with the ruling Liberal Democratic Party of Japan, and to develop trade, travel, and cultural exchange with Japan before diplomatic ties are established — a Peking-Washington model. Since September 1971, the Japanese press and politicians have been invited to visit Pyongyang. A close examination of policies and statements emanating from Pyongyang and Peking "suggests that North Korea intends to follow a set of policies complementary to those of the Chinese People's Republic, with some of the same basic tactics being pursued."[31]

It is interesting to note that there has not yet been any significant improvement in relations between Peking and Seoul or between North Korea and the United States. Peking is opposed to a two Koreas policy, and it will be unlikely to establish any official contacts with Seoul. North Korea has repeatedly proposed replacing the existing military armistice agreement with a peace agreement with the United States;[32] the State Department has always reacted coolly to the suggestion. In the fall of 1979, North Korea, in an apparent bid to open a dialogue with the United States, secretly invited several U.S. congressmen to visit that country. But none has made the trip except one (July 1980). Washington's basic policy is to support the dual entry of both South and North Korea into the United Nations without prejudice to their eventual reunification. If North Korea and its allies would improve their relations with South Korea, the United States would be prepared to take similar reciprocal actions. Furthermore, the United States would not discuss security arrangements on the Korean Peninsula without South Korea's participation; nor would the United States agree to terminate the UN command without new arrangements that would preserve or replace the armistice on a new, permanent legal basis. Washington repeatedly proposed that the United States, PRC, North Korea, and South Korea hold a conference to find a solution acceptable to all parties.[33] After Jimmy Carter was elected to the presidency in 1976, he wanted to live up to his campaign promise by withdrawing American ground forces in South Korea together with nuclear weapons within four or five years. Later, for a number of reasons, he changed his mind. In July 1979, he extended his trip from Tokyo to Seoul. The U.S.-South Korea joint communique proposed holding a "three-way talk" by the two Korean governments and the United States on the Korean problem. The Reagan administration, however, disavowed the tripartite conference's solution. Instead, it endorsed South Korean President Chun Doo Hwan's proposal of personal meetings between South and North Korea. Pyongyang's position, however, has always been in favor of negotiations without the participation of South Korea.

The strain between South Korea and the United States because of the human rights issue has been greatly lessened since President Chun's visit to Washington shortly after President Ronald Reagan's inauguration in 1981. The Reagan administration is opposed to further withdrawal of U.S. forces from Korea, and it has given more consideration to security for the making of foreign policy.

CONCLUSIONS

The future of Korea is closely related to the future interaction among the major powers concerned with the Korean Peninsula. Given the same trend of the international situation, neither China, the United States, nor the Soviet Union desires a war in Korea or increased tension in the area.[34] When Kim Il Sung visited Peking in the wake of the Vietnam debacle in April 1975, there was a serious concern in Washington and Seoul for the Korean situation, but it turned out to be a false alarm.[35] China and the Soviet Union no longer take concerted policy on Korea, but they share some common goals, such as peaceful unification of Korea. Although the Russians have also supported a series of moves taken by North Korea since 1971, the Soviet policy today is also in favor of maintaining the status quo. The Koreans, of course, are capable of taking independent action, but it is unlikely that either North Korea or South Korea can wage a civil war on a sustained basis without assistance and support from their respective allies. It appears that two Koreas will continue to exist on a semipermanent basis while working out a formula of unification. Both sides will continue to stress the need for the common goal, while accusing each other of the violation of their agreement or bad faith.

It goes without saying that a unified Korea oriented to one side would be unacceptable by the other. But it is doubtful that Korea could be neutralized and excluded from power bloc struggles.[36] The DPRK's confederation proposal seems to present a realistic formula that would permit the temporary continuation and coexistence of two separate systems and two different ways of life, while, at the same time, fulfilling the desire of the Korean people for the ultimate unification of their country. Furthermore, it would maintain the existing balance of power in the area.

Prior to Sino-American rapprochement and normalization, the objective of China's policy toward Korea both ideologically and in terms of security consideration was to establish a united Communist Korea friendly to Peking or, alternatively, as a modus vivendi, a divided Korea in which the South need not be Communist but should be free from American military presence. While South Korea and the United States might be prepared to formalize Korea's division on the German model, Pyongyang and Peking were opposed to the two Koreas policy. They maintained that U.S. forces should be withdrawn from South Korea and that the Korean question should be resolved by the Korean people themselves, free from any foreign interference.[37]

China's foreign policy has dramatically been shifted since the 1970s, but officially its Korea policy seems to have remained the same.[38] On many occasions, Peking has reaffirmed its support for the Korean reunification by peaceful means, and endorsed Kim Il Sung's effort to remove U.S. troops from South Korea. One may argue that the withdrawal of American military forces from Korea is inconsistent with China's policy to support the U.S. military power to counter the Soviets in various parts of the world, and that North Korea, as in the case of North Vietnam in the past, has never joined Peking's international united front against the Soviet Union. What will happen after the conquest of South Korea by the North is unpredictable in view of China's bitter experience in the aftermath of the Vietnamese unification.

The PRC and the DPRK share the same ideology, but their national interests are not entirely identical. North Korea might be willing to take a greater risk in war, but it is absolutely necessary for China to have peace in order to carry out the modernization programs. South Korea is supported by the United States. Taiwan continues to maintain close economic and cultural relations with the United States and Japan, nonrecognition of Taiwan by both notwithstanding. In the early 1970s both Peking and Pyongyang hoped that Sino-American rapprochement would encourage Washington to withdraw from the area. They believed that once this was accomplished, the Chinese and the Korean peoples would be able to resolve their respective problem of unification. China is still greatly concerned with the Soviet influence in North Korea, but its anxiety over South Korea's being supported by the United States has been greatly reduced after the normalization and the subsequent significant improvement of U.S.-Chinese relations. China's foreign policy toward Korea has been determined to a larger extent by the interactions of these considerations and variables.

NOTES

1. Quoted in M. Frederick Nelson, *Korea and the Old Orders in Eastern Asia* (1945; reprint ed., New York: Russell & Russell, 1967), p. 76.

2. Quoted in Frederick Foo Chien, *The Opening of Korea* (Hamden, Conn.: Shoe String Press, 1967), p. 16. According to Chien, the origin of this statement by China's Foreign Office (Tsung-li Yamen) is probably to be found in answers the Foreign Office gave to Minister Williams of the United States and Minister Rutherford Alcock of England regarding their requests for the Foreign Office to ask Korea why the nationals of their two countries had been mistreated. See the correspondence between the Yamen and the two ministers in March 1869, *Ch'ing-tai ch'ou-pan i-wu shih-mo: T'ung-ch'ih ch'ao* [History of the Management of Barbarian Affairs during the T'ung-chih Reign], vol. 57 (Peiping: National Palace Museum, 1929-30), pp. 23-28 (hereafter cited as IWSM). Earlier, in May 1867, the Yamen, in conversation with the French minister, had made the same statement when France asked for permission to preach in Korea, ibid., vol. 42, p. 54; Chien, *The Opening of Korea*, pp. 214-15.

3. Seward to Evarts, December 11, 1879, in *Papers Relating to the Foreign Relations of the United States, 1861-1928* (Washington, 1862-1943), 1880, p. 179, quoted in Nelson, *Korea and the Old Orders*, p. 106.

4. National Palace Museum, ed., *Ch'ing Kuang-hsü ch'ao Chung-Jih chiao-she shih-liao* [Documents on Sino-Japanese Relations, Kuang-hsü Reign], vol. 8 (Peiping, 1932), p. 41, quoted in Chien, *The Opening of Korea*, p. 189.

5. G. Jamieson, "The Tributary Nations of China," *China Review* 12 (1883): 96. For an inquiry of legal equality among the feudal states, see Shih-tsai Chen, "The Equality of States in Ancient China," *American Journal of International Law* 35 (1941): 641-50. See also Richard L. Walker, *The Multi-State System of Ancient China* (Hamden, Conn.: Shoe String Press, 1953). It may be mentioned that, although the equality of states has been regarded as a basic principle of modern international law, it is also a question much disputed in academic circles ever since the last quarter of the nineteenth century. Chen, "The Equality of States," pp. 641-42.

6. The Soviet advisers, who were with the North Korean army, were recalled shortly before the outbreak of the war in order to avoid their capture, which might have precipitated a Soviet-American confrontation. See *Khrushchev Remembers* (New York: Bantam, 1971), p. 403.

7. For a brief and unsatisfactory discussion of Korea from the standpoint of the buffer state concept and the balance of power, see Hans J. Morgenthau, *Politics Among Nations*, 5th ed. (New York: Knopf, 1973), pp. 176-77; see also Ku Kwhan Sul, "Some Bases for Negotiation of Buffer States: The Korean Case," mimeographed (Cambridge, Mass.: Center for International Affairs, Harvard University, 1965).

8. In an article written several days after the outbreak of the Korean War, and published in the New York *Sheng-huo tsa-chih* [Life Magazine] 1, no. 4 (July 16, 1950), I concluded that should the U.S. forces march north of the thirty-eighth parallel, "the war would be enlarged." The article is included in Chün-tu Hsüeh, *Shih-nien tsa-lu* [Selected Writings of a Decade] (Hong Kong: Universal Book Company, 1964), pp. 143-47. For the origin and other aspects of the Korean War, see *Khrushchev Remembers*, pp. 400-7; I. F. Stone, *The Hidden History of the Korean War* (New York: Monthly Review, 1952); and Allen S. Whiting, *China Crosses the Yalu* (New York: Macmillan, 1960).

9. Broadcast of the Pyongyang Domestic Service in Korean, October 8, 1969, cited by Rinn-sup Shinn, "Changing Perspectives in North Korea: Foreign and Reunification Policies," *Problems of Communism*, January-February 1973, p. 58.

10. See *Peking Review*, April 10, 1970, pp. 3-5, 6-24, for other related reports and documents. In the joint communique issued at the end of the visit of the Rumanian delegation headed by Chief of State Nicolae Ceausescu on June 15, 1971, Kim Il Sung again opposed the revival of Japanese militarism. For the text of the communique, see *Rodong Shinmun*, June 15, 1971.

11. *United States Foreign Policy, 1969-1970: A Report of the Secretary of State* (Washington, D.C.: U.S. Government Printing Office, 1971), p. 503.

12. Frank Ching, ed., *The New York Times Report from China* (New York: Avon, 1971), p. 105. The editorial of January 29, 1972 appealed for the peaceful unification of Korea.

13. For the text of the Shanghai communique, see *Peking Review*, March 3, 1972.

14. Editorial, "A Good Beginning," *Renmin Ribao* [People's Daily], July 9, 1972.

15. Chou En-lai, telegram to UN Secretary-General Lie, November 11, 1950. The Information Department of the Chinese People's Anti-America and Aid-Korea Headquarters, ed., *Wei-ta ti k'ang-Mei yuan-Chao yun-tung* [The Great Anti-American and Aid-Korea Movement] (Peking: People's Publishing House, 1954), pp. 42-43.

16. Chün-tu Hsüeh, "The Shanghai Communique: Its Significance and Interpretation," *Asia Quarterly* (Brussels), no. 4 (1973), pp. 279-85. See also Chün-tu Hsüeh, "Nixon's Visit to China and Asian Politics," *Joongang Ilbo* [Central Daily News], Seoul, February 29, 1972 (in Korean).

17. *Peking Review*, June 1, 1973, p. 4. Subsequently, numerous articles speculating on Chang's mission have been published abroad. He was a follower and close friend of

Huang Hsing in the Republican revolutionary movement that overthrew the Manchu dynasty. I saw him again in Peking on November 3, 1971. One of his daughters is married to former Foreign Minister Ch'iao kuan-hua. For a biographical sketch of Chang Shih-chao (1881-1973), see Howard L. Boorman, *Biographical Dictionary of Republican China*, vol. 1 (New York: Columbia University Press, 1967-71), pp. 105-9.

18. The support was expressed by Premier Chou En-lai at a banquet given by Colonel Moussa Traore, head of state and president of the government of Mali, June 24, 1973; *Peking Review*, June 29, 1973, p. 5.

19. For example, see editorials, *Renmin Ribao*, June 25, 1973 and June 25, 1975; *Peking Review*, June 29, 1973, p. 7; and *Peking Review*, June 27, 1975, p. 5; see also Joint Communique of the Government of the People's Republic of China and the Government of the Democratic People's Republic of Korea, *Peking Review*, April 10, 1970, pp. 4-5; May 2, 1975, p. 10.

20. In a letter addressed to Taiwan by the Standing Committee of the National People's Congress, dated January 1, 1979, the Peking government made it clear that it would "respect the status quo of Taiwan" after unification and suggested that there should be direct trade, direct postal exchange, and travel between both sides. On September 30, 1981, NPC Standing Committee Chairman Ye Jianying elaborated the unification policy by saying that after unification, Taiwan, as a special administrative region, could retain its armed forces and maintain its current socioeconomic system as well as its way of life. For Ye's nine-point policy, see *Beijing Review*, October 5, 1981, pp. 10-11.

21. Fifty-two countries have diplomatic relations with both Koreas. In addition, South Korea maintains consulates general while North Korea has embassies in three countries. In Burma, both Koreas have only consulates general but not embassies. For details, see *1979 Handbook of the Countries in the World: Official Guide Nos. 79-130* (Seoul: ROK Ministry of Foreign Affairs, 1979).

22. It is interesting to note that Korea had no military tradition and that Korea's armed forces had been exceedingly feeble for more than 200 years before the Japanese occupation. It is the United States, however, that is partly responsible for the militarized policy in South Korea since the 1960s. See Gregory Henderson, "Korea in United States Policy" (Paper presented at the sixty-ninth Annual Meeting of the American Political Science Association, New Orleans, September 1973), pp. 7-8.

23. *Peking Review*, April 20, 1973, pp. 12-13, in English.

24. David I. Steinberg, *Korea: Nexus of East Asia* (New York: American-Asian Education Exchange, 1968), p. 39.

25. Gregory Henderson, "Korea," in *Divided Nations in a Divided World*, ed. Gregory Henderson, Richard Ned Lebow, and John G. Stoessinger (New York: David McKay, 1974), p. 49.

26. Kim Il Sung, interview with managing editor, *Ashai Shimbun*, September 25, 1971. For the text of the interview, see *Journal of Korean Affairs*, October 1971, pp. 49-52.

27. Edgar Snow, *The Long Revolution* (New York: Random House, 1972), pp. 171-72.

28. Dong Jo Kim, address at the National War College, March 8, 1972; *Korean Report*, Spring 1972, p. 11. Kim "applauded President Nixon's efforts to ease world tensions." Ibid., p. 13.

29. U.S. Department of State Bulletin, October 12, 1953, p. 484.

30. The government of Japan denied having made such a commitment. According to Article III of the treaty, the signatories confirm that the government of the Republic of Korea is the only legal government in Korea as specified in Resolution 195 (III) of the UN General Assembly. This ambiguous formula was designed to meet the ROK government's claim that it was the legitimate government of all Korea while at the same time avoid the implication that Japan recognized the ROK jurisdiction over North Korea. For a discussion

of the security aspect of the ROK-Japan treaty, see Kwan Ha Yim, "Korea in Japanese Foreign Policy" (Paper presented at the annual meeting of the American Political Science Association, New Orleans, September 1973). See also, Shigeru Oda, "The Normalization of Relations with the Republic of Korea," *American Journal of International Law* 61 (1967): 41. For an analysis of the Korean alliances, see Astri Suhrke, "Gratuity or Tyranny," *World Politics* 25, no. 4 (July 1973): 508-32.

31. Robert A. Scalapino, "Changing Relations Between the United States and the Chinese People's Republic and the Impact Upon the Republic of Korea," statement before the Subcommittee on Asian and Pacific Affairs, U.S. House of Representatives, Committee on Foreign Affairs, May 4, 1972; *Korean Affairs*, April 1972, p. 26.

32. Pyongyang *Times*, March 30, 1974; also Kim Il Sung's remark to a Japanese delegation on September 14, 1980.

33. For example, Secretary of State Henry Kissinger, statement to the UN General Assembly, September 22, 1975. Also his speech before the Downtown Rotary Club and the Chamber of Commerce, Seattle, Washington, July 22, 1976; see U.S. Department of State, Bureau of Public Affairs, Office of Media Service, PR 351, pp. 5-6.

34. George Ginsburgs, "The U.S.S.R. and the Issue of Korean Reunification," *International Conference on the Problems of Korean Unification, August 1970: Report* (Seoul: Asiatic Research Center, 1971).

35. It has been suggested that Kim's visit was not necessarily initiated by the DPRK leader: if the North Koreans wanted to use the Indochina situation to further their revolutionary strategy toward South Korea, Kim would have also visited Moscow. Young Hoon Kang, "Kim Il Sung's Trip to Peking," *Journal of Korean Affairs* 5, no. 1 (April 1975): 47-51. In May 1976, British Foreign Secretary Anthony Crosland was reportedly told in Peking that all talk of a new war in Korea was "out of the question." Washington *Post*, May 12, 1976, p. A19. According to Fuji Kamiya, "The Prospects for Peace in Korea," in *U.S.-Japan Relations and the Security of East Asia*, ed. Franklin B. Weinstein (Boulder: Westview, 1978), p. 182, Kim attempted to go to Moscow after Peking. He was unable to do so because of Brezhnev's illness – a convenient excuse for the Soviet leader to avoid meeting Kim under those circumstances.

36. Cf. Steinberg, *Korea*, p. 8; and Henderson, "Korea," p. 15.

37. Joint Communique of the PRC and the DPRK, April 26, 1975, in *Peking Review*, May 2, 1975, p. 9.

38. See, for example, an analysis of the reopening of the Korean dialogue, *Beijing Review*, March 17, 1980, pp. 12-13; also a report on the Third World Conference for the Independent and Peaceful Reunification of Korea, *Beijing Review*, April 6, 1981, pp. 9-10.

5

CHINA AND THE ASEAN STATES: FROM HOSTILITY TO RAPPROCHMENT

Shee Poon Kim

China's relations with the Association of Southeast Asian Nations (ASEAN), formed by Indonesia, Malaysia, the Philippines, Singapore, and Thailand on August 8, 1967,[1] have shifted from hostility in the 1960s to rapprochement since the mid-1970s. Some of the questions to be asked are: Why was China hostile to the ASEAN states and vice versa? Why did Malaysia, the Philippines, and Thailand decide to establish diplomatic relations with China in 1974-75, but Indonesia and Singapore did not? What are the contemporary problems in Chinese-ASEAN relations, and why? Finally, what are the prospects for Sino-ASEAN ties?

This chapter deals first with China's attitudes toward ASEAN, and then looks at the ASEAN states' policies toward China. The final section analyzes the contemporary problems and assesses the prospects for Sino-ASEAN ties.

It is pertinent to mention that security, ideology, ethnicity, and trade are relevant variables in the Sino-ASEAN relationship. Any meaningful assessment of the patterns of Sino-ASEAN interaction must take into consideration the milieu in which the decision makers operate, since foreign-policy outputs may be due to internal or external determinants, or to a combination of the two.

CHANGE OF CHINESE POLICY

China's immediate response to the formation of ASEAN was one of apprehension. Chinese leaders perceived ASEAN to be a regional organization somewhat like SEATO (1954) manipulated by the United States to implement its anti-China policies. Indeed, two of the ASEAN member states, the Philippines and Thailand, were also members of SEATO. Thus from the very beginning China's attitude was uncompromisingly hostile, condemning the association as "a new anti-communist alliance."[2] Furthermore, the formation of ASEAN coincided with China's Cultural Revolution and U.S. escalation of the Vietnam War. Even prior to the formation of the association, China had reacted strongly when Thai personnel, for example, were involved in the Laotian conflict in the early 1960s. In 1965, China began to give more support to the Communist Party of Thailand (CPT) and warned the Thai government that a people's war was underway. It can be argued that China's behavior during this period (as will be seen below) evolved in response to the security threat posed by the Thai-U.S. alliance, rather than as an attempt to promote revolutionary war in the kingdom. Thus China's support of the three Indochinese states and the CPT was defensive rather than offensive. In the same way, China's criticism of ASEAN as an organization "propped up by U.S. imperialism to serve its war efforts" stemmed from security considerations rather than from any ideological rejection of the association.[3] China's hostility toward ASEAN can best be understood from an analysis of its attitudes toward Thailand. The kingdom has long been important to China's security, partly because of its proximity to the Chinese border and partly because of Thailand's close alliance with the United States.

China's policies toward Thailand can be divided into three periods. During the first period (1949-58), China preferred to adopt a moderate policy, which culminated in the Bandung Conference in 1955. When Marshall Sarit Thanarat came to power in a coup in 1959, the situation was altered. China's futile efforts to neutralize the U.S.-Thai alliance after Thailand became a member of SEATO gave way to a period of hostility (1959-70) that was a response to the security threat posed by this close alliance with the United States.[4] A lessening of Sino-Thai tensions has since 1971 turned China's main objective to ensuring that the security threat can be minimized and, eventually, removed.

China's hostility toward Thailand after 1959 was due to a number of factors. First and most important was the Thai leaders' decision to get directly involved in the Indochinese war. Second, Thailand continuously rejected China's overtures to promote people-to-people or state-to-state relations. Third, Thailand continued to oppose the admission of China to the United Nations. Fourth, the close ties between Thailand and Taiwan and Thailand's insistence on a "two China" policy proved to be a stumbling block. The phasing out of the first two irritants ushered in the period of detente that developed slowly after May 1971 and led to the establishment of diplomatic relations in July 1975.

It can be seen from this brief account that China's attitude toward Thailand depended on its perception of whether and to what extent its security was being threatened. If the risks increased, China became hostile; if the risks decreased, the reverse behavior could be expected. The evidence collected in my study of Sino-Thai relations from 1949 to 1975, as well as other American scholars' findings on China's policies toward the Southeast Asian states, confirms this.[5]

The fact that China is more preoccupied with its security than with spreading revolution can also be seen from its policies toward fraternal Communist Parties in the region. The evidence so far derived from the ties of the Chinese Communist Party (CCP) with the CPT indicates that when U.S.-Thai relations were close, the CCP vigorously supported the CPT. Conversely, when Thailand became more self-reliant, less dependent on the United States, and, most importantly, less strongly anti-China, the CCP allowed its bonds with the CPT to lessen. China's relations with the Communist Party of Malaya (CPM) and the Communist Party of Burma (CPB) also confirm Peter Van Ness's hypothesis that "the likelihood of the country being endorsed as a TR [target for revolution] varies according to important aspects of its government's relative official friendliness or hostility toward Peking."[6] Hence, one can conclude that China's support of the CPT in the 1960s and its call for a people's war were not motivated primarily by ideological considerations, as security rather than the spread of communism has thus far been the most important determinant in China's policy toward Thailand and the other non-Communist Southeast Asian states. One can further argue, based on concrete evidence, that China at times tried to use the CPT to exert pressure upon Sarit Thanarat and the Thanom-Prapass administration to adopt a policy in line with China's objectives. For example, in 1979 China advised the CPT to cooperate with the Thai government against the Socialist Republic of Vietnam (SRV).[7]

Similarly, China's main concern in its relations with the "overseas Chinese" in the region is to protect or to promote its own national interests rather than the interests of the "overseas Chinese" in Southeast Asia. For example, China was very vocal when the SRV adopted an anti-ethnic Chinese policy after implementation of the new economic zones in March 1978, but it preserved a complete silence when the "overseas Chinese" were ill-treated by the Pol Pot regime. China's behavior in the field of trade also indicates that this behavior may at times be motivated by consideration of China's national interests, especially in a state of nonrecognition. China's trade policy toward Thailand prior to the establishment of diplomatic relations had been very much guided by political considerations rather than sheer business motivations.[8]

By the end of the 1960s, Mao was convinced that the United States would soon disengage from Indochina, thus lessening the danger to China's security from the United States and, by implication, also lessening the threat from ASEAN. The consequence was an observable toning down of Peking's previously sharp criticism of the United States and a corresponding decrease in its hostile attitude toward ASEAN. Simultaneously, Radio Peking increased its criticism of the Soviet Union both in volume and substance and now singled out "social imperialism" as its number-one enemy in the world.

After China's admission to the United Nations in 1971, its foreign policy entered a new stage. Since 1972, China has repeatedly expressed its interest and at times has proven keener than its ASEAN counterparts in promoting bilateral state-to-state relations with the individual ASEAN states on the principles laid down at the Bandung Conference. China used a number of tactics in its search for the establishment of diplomatic relations with the ASEAN states. For example, it had cultivated people-to-people diplomacy by inviting various sports teams from the ASEAN capitals to Peking, followed up by semiofficial delegations and then official visits by the two teams. It tried to use intermediary and international organizations such as the United Nations to solicit the political friendship of the ASEAN states. And Peking attempted to improve its international image by adopting a more pragmatic attitude toward third world countries.[9]

The presence of U.S. bases in the Philippines is no longer perceived as a threat to its security. On the contrary, the U.S. presence is regarded as an important bulwark against the Soviet Union's growing inroads in the region. For this reason, China has privately expressed its wish to Thai leaders that they refrain from asking the United States to close down its bases in the kingdom. China even reportedly advised Prime Minister Kukrit Pramoj on how to minimize the threat from the CPT.[10] Finally, China's decision to seek closer relations with the ASEAN states can be traced to the Maoist ideological parlance, i.e., both ASEAN and China belong to the third world, both have struggled against Western colonialism and imperialism. Moreover, there is a unique element in China's national character, i.e., to help the poorer, weaker, and smaller states against the richer, stronger, and more "wicked" powers — and ASEAN fits the description of a state in need of aid.

But beneath China's new, flexible diplomacy, which culminated in Deng Xiaoping's visit to the three ASEAN capitals in November 1978, was a deeper concern. China's principal objective at that time was to counter the growing influence of the Soviet Union in Indochina and its disturbingly close alliance with the SRV.

THE ASEAN STATES' PERSPECTIVES

Malaysia

In May 1974, Malaysia established diplomatic relations with China. This shift was partly due to a change in leadership. Tun Abdul Razak, who came to power in September 1970, ended the era of Tunku Abdul Rahman's (1957-September 1970) anti-Communist and anti-China policy. The Tunku advocated a "hands-off" policy of nonrecognition toward China because he was convinced that normalization with China would impede Malaysia's efforts at nation-building. He feared that any official Chinese presence in Kuala Lumpur might enable it to subvert the 4 million Chinese in Malaysia (37.7 percent of a population of 14 million).[11] Furthermore, the Sino-Indian war of 1962 convinced the Tunku that China is an expansionist power, prone to adventurism.[12]

Tun Razak, who came to power in the wake of the May 13, 1969 racial riots, recognized the need to get the support of the Chinese community. Moreover, he assumed — correctly, as it turned out — that normalization with China would enhance his popularity and give him needed legitimacy as the leader of a multiracial nation. Razak also hoped that by getting Mao's support he could diminish the appeal of the CPM, relegating it to the status of a meaningless revolutionary movement.[13] In addition, he saw a source of economic gain in a rapprochement. He felt confident that China would buy a large amount of rubber — Malaysia's chief export — which in turn would raise the international market price of that commodity.[14] And Razak concluded that the only way to bring to the region that peace and stability essential to Malaysia's economic development was to ask the Peking leaders to support his Zone of Peace, Freedom, and Neutrality (ZOPFAN), which has since 1971 been the cornerstone of Malaysia's foreign policy.

The most important factor, however, that prompted Razak's decision to seek detente with China was the declining presence of Western powers in the region. The turning point came in 1968 when the British government announced its intention of withdrawing its forces and closing the bases east of Suez. In Malaysia and Singapore, both traditionally safeguarded by Britain, this proclamation was received with alarm. Another means of defense had to be found. The second important development was Nixon's visit to Peking in February 1972, which inspired a reworking of ASEAN foreign policy. Thus Razak, troubled by the absence of any strong system of national security, saw at least a partial answer in Peking. He moved cautiously, however, for he met some internal opposition, and suspicion of China was still very strong among the other ASEAN leaders. At first Razak only initiated informal contacts with China, either through friends or through international agencies, without making any move to establish formal diplomatic relations.

On the other hand, there were signs that China was also eager for diplomatic relations with the ASEAN states. This change in attitude can be partly explained in the light of its changing internal political development in combination with the changing pattern of forces in international politics at the beginning of the 1970s. The end of the tumultuous Cultural Revolution, the death of Lin Piao in 1971, and the subsequent rise of the moderates to power ushered in a period of new diplomacy, enabling China first, when Malaysian Finance Minister Tunku Razaleigh visited Peking in 1971, to announce its support of ZOPFAN, and, in 1974, to establish diplomatic relations with Malaysia.

Thailand

The downfall of the Thanom-Prapass regime in October 1973, as a result of student demonstrations, ended a decade of anti-Communist, pro-U.S. foreign policy and initiated a new phase in Sino-Thai relations. Thanom-Prapass' nonrecognition policy had had several motivations. First and most important was their conviction that a close military alliance with the United States was the best way to protect the kingdom's security. Second was China's continued support of the CPT. A third, somewhat less weighty factor was the influence of the powerful Taiwanese lobby in Bangkok and the substantial amount of trade between Thailand and Taiwan.[15] Finally, there was the fear that China could pose a potential threat to the kingdom by using the 3 million Chinese in the country as a fifth column.

The downfall of the Thanom-Prapass regime left the caretaker administration of Sanya Dharmasaki (1973-74) with a heavy legacy of internal problems: continuous student demonstrations, peasant protests, labor strikes, increasing minority pressures in both the northern and southern regions against the central authorities, and a sharp increase in violent activities by the CPT not only in the northern, northeastern, and southern regions but now also in the urban areas. Sanya's administration was in no position to attempt a major breakthrough such as the establishment of diplomatic relations with Peking would be.

It was not until Kukrit Pramoj came to power in April 1975 that some headway was made. The most critical stimuli to Kukrit's decision to normalize relations with Peking were the Indochinese debacle and the Communist victory in Indochina in mid-1975. In the light of these dramatic developments, Thailand's old policy became outdated. Kukrit set as his top priority the solidifying of relations with the three Indochinese states, and especially with the SRV, which had emerged as the most important country in the region. This stance permitted Kukrit to normalize Thai relations with China. He was encouraged by the hope that China might be used to exert influence on the SRV, and he was optimistic that Thai recognition of China would induce China to downplay its support of the CPT.

The Philippines

In line with the Philippine's traditionally pro-U.S., pro-Taiwan foreign policy, President Marcos had consistently upheld a "two China" policy even though China approached the Philippines, together with the other ASEAN partners, with a view to improving bilateral state-to-state relations. However, in the wake of Nixon's trip to Peking, Marcos began to reassess his foreign-policy options. He developed a strategy to minimize his country's dependence on the United States. By the end of March 1972 he had announced the formation of a Special Cabinet Committee whose twofold task was to look into the feasibility of abandoning the "two China" policy and to explore the possibility of Filipinizing the local Chinese schools, newspapers, and Chinese-dominated economy. In addition, Marcos instructed the partially government-controlled National Export Trading Corporation to work on formal trade ties with China.[16] His administration had now established diplomatic relations with six East European socialist states (Yugoslavia, Rumania, Bulgaria, Czechoslovakia, Hungary, and East Germany) as well as with Mongolia, but Marcos continued to move with caution in his dealings with China and the USSR. Sino-Philippine relations improved after Marcos' wife visited Peking in August 1974 and his brother-in-law, Benjamin Romualdez, followed in September. Chou En-Lai then allegedly assured the Philippine leader that the Chinese government would cease its support of the Partido Kommunistang Pilipinas (PKP) insurgent movement in the Philippines.[17] This assurance settled Marcos' decision to formalize diplomatic relations with China in June 1975.

Indonesia

China's enthusiasm in seeking normalization and establishment of relations with the other ASEAN states, Indonesia and Singapore, has so far not been fully reciprocated. Indonesia was the first country among the ASEAN states to establish diplomatic relations with China (on March 28, 1950) and afterward maintained close ties with Peking until the downfall of President Sukarno in 1967. Since then diplomatic relations have been suspended, and normalization has still not taken place. On the contrary, relations between the two countries have deteriorated since Suharto came to power and have indeed reached their nadir as a result of the anti-Chinese riots and violence in 1967 that prompted thousands of Chinese to leave the country. From 1967 to 1971, China was actively hostile to Suharto's government, openly accusing him of being a "Fascist," allowing exiled leaders of the Indonesian Communist Party (Partai Komunis Indonesia or PKI) such as Chairman Jusuf Adjitorop to operate in Peking, and even trying, though without much success, to help PKI leaders revive the defunct organization.[18] Since 1971, China had on a number of occasions expressed its desire to resume normal relations with Indonesia but up to now the latter has not responded with enthusiasm. Indonesia's reaction to Nixon's Peking visit was wary, although the government recognizes that resumption of diplomatic relations with China is inevitable.[19] Indonesia did not oppose Malaysia's recognition of China in May 1974, but it did allude at that time to the necessity for guarding against the ever-present danger that China may subvert the security of the ASEAN states.

Since 1975, there has been growing pressure from some of the more outward-looking generals and liberal civilian politicians to normalize relations with China.[20] These men argue that Indonesia should follow its three ASEAN partners, in recognition of the fact that China's role in the region has been growing stronger. A majority of the military elites (especially the younger army leaders), however, still oppose normalization, out of a fear that China will continue to subvert the security of the country through clandestine support of the PKI and the 3 million Chinese in the country (one-third of whom are still either nationals of China or are stateless).[21] The powerful Islamic groups share this attitude, which in their case is reinforced by their jealousy of the Chinese, who dominate the Indonesian economy and whom they regard at best as stiff competitors and at times as menacing their vested economic interests.[22]

Although during the earlier period of 1977 pressure had been growing within the administration to resume diplomatic relations, a number of developments that took place during the latter part of 1978 made it difficult for Indonesia to normalize relations with China. Deng Xiaoping's visit to Thailand, Malaysia, and Singapore was watched very closely by the Indonesian leaders. After Deng's adamant refusal to forego Chinese support of the PKI, Indonesia decided to postpone normalization of relations.[23] The second and equally important event was China's decision to attack Vietnam in February 1979. This move heightened Indonesia's apprehension that China still may have designs on the country's independence, since the Indonesian leaders perceive that Maoist China can be as imperialistic as feudalistic China was. In fact, one school of thought within the elites in the Ministry of Defense and Security claims that Vietnam and Indonesia share a "China problem" and that a political alignment with Vietnam (which has also tried to play this line) may thus be a reasonable protection against the much stronger and more powerful enemy to the north. In short, the prospects for Indonesia's resumption of diplomatic relations with China depend on many factors, including the changing situation in the international arena, the amount of support given by the opposition parties (especially by the Muslim-dominated PPP), the extent of economic development in Indonesia, and assimilation of the ethnic Chinese. On balance, internal rather than external considerations will determine Indonesia's policy toward China.[24]

At present President Suharto's administration does not see any major advantage in thawing the frozen relations. In fact, the visit of premier Sun Yun-suan and other high ranking government officials of Taiwan to Indonesia in December 1981 indicated quite clearly that Jakarta and Peking are unlikely to resume diplomatic relations in the foreseeable future.[25]

Singapore

Although Singapore's trade relations with China date back to the nineteenth century, political relations took second place to economic ties. Singapore became independent in 1965, after a brief, unhappy marriage with Malaysia (1963-65). Since that time, the People's Action Party (PAP) government, under the leadership of Lee Kuan Yew, has consistently maintained that the island republic will be the last ASEAN state to establish relations with China.

The Singapore government wanted an independent Singaporean identity before it established diplomatic relations with China, as otherwise China might have used the Chinese-educated population against the government. This problem has already been overcome, due to the success of the PAP's economic policy and the leadership's continuous efforts at encouraging bilingualism. Singapore Chinese are vastly different from those of China, and the propagation and implementation of a Mandarin-speaking policy together with the adoption of the *pinyin* system can be interpreted as signs of growing confidence among the PAP leaders that Peking's influence has greatly diminished.

As Singapore's population is about 75 percent Chinese, any hasty attempt by the PAP government to seek closer alignment with China is bound to trigger a negative reaction from the neighboring states. At times this situation has been conveniently and/or intentionally distorted, as by the SRV's accusations that Singapore was a "third China," "an outpost of Peking in Southeast Asia," and "a Trojan horse for China" in the region.[26] Singapore has therefore been very sensitive to regional reactions and since the formation of ASEAN has linked its identity and future to that of the region. Thus despite political contacts and diplomatic visits between Chinese and the Singaporean leaders, the two countries have tacitly agreed to maintain the status quo. Thus far this position has ideally suited Lee Kuan Yew, who is therefore welcome both in Peking and in Taipei.

PROBLEMS AND PROSPECTS

The SRV's blitzkrieg against Kampuchea in December 1978 and the Soviet Union's invasion of Afghanistan on December 27, 1979 have substantially altered diplomatic relations between China and ASEAN. China was deeply disturbed by Hanoi's decision to join COMECON in June 1978. Even worse, from China's perspective, was the signing of the so-called "Treaty of Peace, Friendship, and Cooperation" with the Soviet Union in November 1978, which China perceived as a move by the SRV to assist in reviving Brezhnev's Asian Collective Security System (1969) aimed at encircling China. One of the main motives for China's post-Cultural Revolution termination of its isolationist foreign policy was to acquire outside counterweight against the Soviet Union. Indeed, Peking perceived the Soviet Union's invasion of Afghanistan aggression in that country and the SRV's attacks on Kampuchea as being together part of the Soviet Union's world hegemonism. China's punitive war against the SRV was in this light at least partly a desperate attempt at restoring Kampuchea's independence, and also at teaching the SRV that maintaining its alliance with the Soviet Union would be costly, not to mention border incursions by the Vietnamese.[27]

As part of China's diplomatic offensives and propaganda endeavors aimed at containing and countering the Soviet/SRV's influence and threats, China's Vice Premier Li Xiannian visited the Philippines on March 12, 1978, and in November of the same year Deng Xiaoping himself visited Thailand, Malaysia, and Singapore. China's implied decision to seek a political alignment with ASEAN and to lure the association into a union with the United States, the

EEC, Japan, and the third world against the Soviet Union's "worldwide hegemonism" and the SRV's "regional hegemonism" was made evident from remarks made by Deng Xiaoping during his trip to the United States in January 1979 when he called for the United States and the third world countries to form a united front against the Soviet Union.[28]

China has now reversed its position, seeing a strong and cohesive ASEAN as beneficial to China and as an organization able to halt the Soviet Union's inroads in non-Communist states in the region. This posture can be seen from Deng Xiaoping's statement in Bangkok on November 6, 1978: "ASEAN is farsighted when it adheres to the proposal for establishing a zone of peace, freedom, and neutrality in Southeast Asia. It is our view that in strengthening its own unity and cooperation, ASEAN not only serves the interests of peace, stability, and prosperity in Southeast Asia, but also makes a valuable contribution to world peace and security".[29]

Thailand is the most important country in China's strategic calculations against Vietnam. The kingdom, the frontline ASEAN state, can block any further SRV-USSR inroads into the region, and it is able to resist any further consolidation of power by the SRV over Indochina — for example, by serving as a supply link from China to Pol Pot's forces and as a sanctuary for the Khmer Rouge. Since China established formal diplomatic relations with the kingdom the relationship between the two countries has in general been cordial. During Kriangsak's administration (1977-80) Thailand tilted somewhat toward China, especially after the SRV's invasion of Kampuchea, which destroyed the Kampuchean and Laotian buffer states, the foundation of Thailand's security. This new strategic situation prompted Thailand to seek a multifaceted diplomatic front. Thus China may become important in checking the SRV's potential designs against the kingdom. Also, reversing its move to distance itself from the United States during the democratic period (1973-76), Thailand now wished to form closer ties with the United States.

Thailand's immediate concerns were: first, to ensure that the fighting in Kampuchea would not spill over to the kingdom; second, to halt the continuous influx of refugees who at one point reached higher than the 400,000 mark; and, finally, to assess the intentions of the SRV toward Thailand after the former's consolidation of power over Kampuchea. Thus Thailand's support of the Pol Pot regime has been very strongly motivated by security and national interests, despite its official claim of a neutral stand in this conflict. The underlying motivation behind Thailand's support was the hope that another five years of Khmer Rouge resistance of the SRV would be sufficient for the kingdom to strengthen its armed forces and put its troubled house in order. (There have been 44 governments since the 1932 coup.)

Thailand's hard-line posture in the Kampuchean conflict was inspired by several considerations. First, its support of China's position in Kampuchea could be used as a quid pro quo, as the administration would then be in a position to bargain with the Chinese on minimizing their support of the CPT.

Second, the military leaders hoped that such an approach would facilitate an appeal to Thai nationalism. Third, an important consideration was the chance of gaining U.S. military aid. Finally, a soft approach would be tantamount to admitting the administration's weakness, which in turn might constitute a factor in any future strategic calculations by the SRV against the kingdom.

Hanoi's invasion of Kampuchea contributed to some extent to ASEAN's tilt toward China. ASEAN has become more hostile toward the SRV partly because of the latter's policies toward the refugees and partly because of its occupation of Kampuchea. This hardening in its attitude could be seen from the results of the ASEAN Foreign Ministers' Ministerial Meeting in June 1979, when for the first time in its history the association pointed a finger at Hanoi and asked the SRV to stop the influx of its citizens immediately.[30] This deluge of refugees has drained the national resources of some of the ASEAN states and in Malaysia even threatens the fragile fabric of its multiracial society, as the refugees are mainly ethnic Chinese in origin or are Vietnamese of Chinese origin.

How successful is China's current strategic tilt toward ASEAN? One can argue that the current Chinese-ASEAN entente is a reaction to a common threat from the Soviet Union and Vietnam. From the Chinese perspective, the "Indochina problem" forms part of a large problem to which the Soviet Union is the key. Hence, China-ASEAN relations are a function of Sino-Soviet rivalries: the greater the conflicts, the more will China tilt toward ASEAN. From the ASEAN states' point of view, the roots of the Kampuchean crisis lie in Sino-Soviet rivalries and in China's antagonism to the SRV because of Vietnam's regional hegemonism. Thus ASEAN's main concern is to implement its ZOPFAN, i.e., to ask all the major powers to stop their involvement in the region so that an equilibrium between ASEAN and the SRV can again be attained. The association's top priority is now to ensure the withdrawal of the SRV forces from Kampuchea and the restoration of peace in that country; second, as was mentioned earlier, to prevent the influx of refugees; and, finally, to ensure that Thailand will not also serve as a target for the SRV. China is pursuing similar policies, although it has an ultimate motive of breaking the SRV-USSR alliance, which is not a paramount factor in the making of the foreign policy of the ASEAN states. However, the SRV alliance with the Soviet Union is likely to continue in its present form, despite the manifestation of some strains.[31]

The most thorny problem in ASEAN-China relations has been China's stubborn refusal to forego its support of Communist insurgent movements in the ASEAN states. This posture, for example, has been one of the main stumbling blocks hindering resumption of Sino-Indonesian diplomatic relations. Despite China's diplomatic offensives and its interest in fostering closer relations with the ASEAN governments, it fails to appreciate the ASEAN leaders' intense suspicions of China's two-pronged approach — i.e., on the one hand China has openly endorsed ASEAN, while on the other hand it continues to support revolutionary movements in the ASEAN states — and their ardent desire that

China recall this support immediately. Malaysia, for example, has long been unhappy with China's continuous support of the CPM. The CCP's congratulatory message to the CPM in connection with its forty-fifth anniversary in 1975 was strongly criticized by the United Malays National Organization (UMNO), the dominant Malay ruling party, for being a blatant act of interference in the internal affairs of Malaysia and a breach of Mao's promise.[32] Malaysia's uneasiness over this matter can be seen from the remarks made by Prime Minister Hussein Onn during a speech in honor of Deng Xiaoping's visit to Malaysia in November 1978: "Malaysia would like to be left alone in peace, free from any form of interference, subversion, or incitement."[33] This strain also came to the fore during Lee Kuan Yew's visit to Peking in November 1980, when Lee cancelled a speech he was to have made at a banquet. This step further testified to ASEAN's weariness with China's party-to-party relations, as Lee had intended to touch on this issue openly. The Chinese leaders, however, asked the Singaporean Prime Minister to discuss the matter only in private.

China is now facing a major dilemma. Lee Kuan Yew proposed to China that as a practical solution to their mutual suspicions China should discontinue its support of the Communist revolutionary movements in the ASEAN states. In reply, the Chinese leaders insisted that such a change in their policy would take time.[34] If, however, the Chinese did in fact forsake their support of Communist revolutionaries, the Soviet Union and the SRV might step in to fill the vacuum, and this would only enhance the Soviet Union's influence in the region – a situation the Chinese (and probably the ASEAN states as well) would very much like to prevent.[35] If, on the other hand, China continues to support Communist insurgents, then ASEAN-China relations will remain strained. On balance, China seems to prefer to keep its options open in its relations with the fraternal Communist Parties in the region,[36] although a gradual diminishing of its support can be expected. In fact, it closed the Voice of the Communist Party of Thailand (VCPT) in July 1979 as a friendly gesture to the Thai government.

The ethnic factor also proved to be a liability in China's relations with ASEAN. China's current emphasis on the importance of the "overseas Chinese" role to support their "motherland's" efforts in the Four Modernization Program, for example, heightened Indonesia's apprehensions concerning China.[37] Lee Kuan Yew's remark in November 1980 to Deng Xiaoping that Singapore's national interests lie in Southeast Asia rather than in China is another clear indication of this effect.

With regard to China's current strategy of united front against the SRV, the ASEAN leaders, particularly those in Malaysia and Indonesia, have resisted any push toward China against Vietnam. This stance was expressed by Malaysian Home Affairs Minister Ghazali Shafie: "ASEAN must not succumb to external power and persuasion to seek security through military alliance against Vietnam whether or not Vietnam is backed by external powers."[38] Some of the Indonesian elites even went so far as to suggest a possible diplomatic entente with the SRV to counter Chinese inroads in the region.[39] Similarly, ever since

General Prem Tinsunalond came to power in 1980, he has tried to reverse Kriangsak's tilt toward China.

What, then, are the prospects for China-ASEAN diplomatic relations in the 1980s? As illustrated above, beneath the surface of China-ASEAN rapprochement are deep cleavages. First, the ASEAN region is essentially a Muslim world; about 53 percent of a total population of 240 million are Muslim. In Indonesia, 90 percent of whose inhabitants are Muslim, communism is generally considered to be anathema. One can therefore argue that a main reason why communism has not been successful in the ASEAN states, especially in Indonesia and Malaysia, is because it has difficulties in appealing to Muslims. It is also important to point out that, despite the presence of approximately 15 million ethnic Chinese in the ASEAN region, Maoist ideology has not been adopted by the majority of the Chinese population and that the CPM, for example, has so far not been able to get the majority support either of the ethnic Chinese or of the indigenous population.

Second, their national and foreign policy objectives are very different. China's main concern since the end of the Cultural Revolution has been to minimize security threats from the Soviet Union and restrain its infiltration of China's southern flanks. Thus China's foreign policy toward Southeast Asia during the last three decades has shown a consistent pattern, i.e., any small power in the Southeast Asian region seeking a military alliance with any superpower against China will come under critical attack. We saw this, for example, in the 1960s in the case of the U.S.-Thai alliance. One can expect the same pattern in China's behavior concerning the SRV-USSR alliance, which has been a source of instability in the region. So long as this alliance exists, there is very little chance that an amicable solution to the Sino-Soviet conflict can be achieved. ASEAN's main priority, on the other hand, is realization of its ZOPFAN; the region has to be freed from all major power involvements so that the smaller states can work toward economic cooperation and peaceful coexistence with the three Indochinese states.

On balance, one can foresee that China-ASEAN relations will in the immediate future take the forms of very limited diplomatic cooperation and a gradual expansion of economic ties through trade, but that there will be strains over China's stubborn support of the Communist Parties in the ASEAN states. An ASEAN-China military alliance is out of the question. It is certainly not on the agenda of either side. From the association's perspective, no sooner will the Kampuchean crisis be resolved than the basis for China's diplomatic entente with ASEAN will be dissolved. What, then, does China expect of ASEAN? Security will remain the top determinant in China's policy toward Southeast Asia. Its tilt toward ASEAN has been primarily a function of the Sino-Vietnamese as well as the Sino-Soviet conflicts. On the whole, China would be quite content to maintain its present relationship with the ASEAN governments, provided that they do not adopt a pro-Soviet policy.

NOTES

1. Regarding the original text of the objectives of ASEAN, see *The ASEAN Declaration*, Bangkok, August 8, 1967.

2. *Renmin Ribao*, August 12, 1967, p. 6. See also *Far Eastern Economic Review* (*FEER*), September 28, 1967, p. 637.

3. Ibid.

4. It is important to note that a country's membership in SEATO is not a factor attracting China's hostility. Pakistan, for example, was also a member of that organization, yet China adopted a lenient policy toward that country from 1954-60. See J. D. Armstrong, *Revolutionary Diplomacy, China's Foreign Policy and the United Front* (Berkeley: University of California Press, 1977), pp. 152-55; and Khaw Guat Hoon, *An Analysis of China's Attitudes towards ASEAN: 1967-1976*, Occasional Paper, no. 48, September 1977 (Institute of Southeast Asian Studies, Singapore), p. 19.

5. See Shee Poon Kim, *Thailand's Relations with the People's Republic of China: 1949-1975* (Singapore: Institute of Humanities and Social Sciences, College of Graduate Studies, Nanyang University, 1979). See also Peter Van Ness, *Revolution and Chinese Foreign Policy, Peking's Support for Wars of National Liberation* (Berkeley: University of California Press, 1971); Melvin Gurtov, *China and Southeast Asia: The Politics of Survival, a Study of Foreign Policy Interaction* (Baltimore: Johns Hopkins University Press, 1975).

6. Peter Van Ness, *Revolution and Chinese Foreign Policy*, p. 169.

7. *Bangkok Post* (*BP*), October 21, 1979.

8. See Shee Poon Kim, "The Politics of Thailand's Trade Relations with the People's Republic of China," *Asian Survey* 21, no. 3 (March 1981). See also Lee Gene T. Hsiao, *The Foreign Trade of China: Policy, Law and Practice* (Australian National University Press, 1977), pp. 8-10. Because Thailand suffered a shortage of oil, it bought a substantial amount of crude oil from China at a "friendship price." But on balance, trade has been most of the time in favor of China. This imbalance, however, had created a political issue in the 1970s. Hence China went all out of its way to redress it by buying more goods from Thailand. See Shee, "The Politics of Thailand's Trade Relations," p. 322.

9. China's desire to promote good relations with the ASEAN states can also partly be explained by its recognition of the growing importance and increasing influence that small and medium-size powers have in the international arena. In this sense, China has began to recognize ASEAN's growing role in the region. See Chün-tu Hsüeh, ed., *Dimensions of China's Foreign Relations* (New York: Praeger Publishers, 1977), p. 66.

10. Washington *Post*, July 3, 1975.

11. It seemed to have been one of the Tunku's practices to blame the Maoist agents for the political disturbances in Malaysia during the racial riots in 1969. See Tun Abdul Rahman, *May 13, Before and After* (Kuala Lumpur: Utusan Melayu Press, 1969).

12. See *Foreign Affairs Malaysia* (*FAM*) 3, no. 3 (n. d.): 48.

13. *New Nation* (Singapore), May 11, 1974.

14. Rubber was the most important commodity in Malaysia's exports to the PRC and accounted for years for more than 90 percent of Malaysia's exports to that country. In 1974, for example, rubber represented 30 percent of Malaysia's total export earnings and 15 percent of her gross domestic product. See John Wong, "Sino-Malaysian Detente: Economic Basis," *Asia Research Bulletin* (*ARB*), August 31, 1974, pp. 2916-17.

15. For trade data see Shee, "The Politics of Thailand's Trade Relations with the People's Republic of China," p. 318.

16. *The Straits Times* (Malaysian edition) (*ST*), August 8, 1972.

17. Interview, November 1975.

18. *Renmin Ribao*, December 3, 1969, p. 6; *SCMP*, no. 4558, December 1969, p. 17; *Peking Review* (*PR*), July 14, 1967, p· 15. According to Taiwanese sources, it was estimated that about 700 PKI members were in the PRC during this time. See *Today Mainland* (Taiwan) 323, March 1, 1969.

19. Adam Malik, the then Indonesian foreign minister, for example, pointed out that unless the overseas Chinese are reeducated, it is unlikely that Indonesia would establish normalization of relations with Peking. See *New Nation*, June 10, 1974. For an Indonesian perception of China see Franklin Weinstein, *Indonesian Foreign Policy and the Dilemma of Dependence from Sukarno to Soeharto* (Ithaca: Cornell University Press, 1976), pp. 88-95. The top army leaders, for example, prefer to wait as long as possible. See p. 123.

20. See Leo Suryadinata, "Problems and Prospects for Sino-Indonesian Ties," *The Asian Wall Street Journal (TAWSJ)*, January 24, 1980. Indonesia's foreign minister, Mochtar Kusumaatmaja, holds this view. See, for example, *Southeast Asian Record* 1, no. 32 (January 18-24, 1980): 1.

21. Leo Suryadinata, ibid.

22. The anti-Chinese riots in Kudus, Java, in 1906, for example, were due to economic competition between the indigenous Indonesian population and the alien Chinese.

23. This refusal prompted Mochtar Kusumaatmaja to make the following remark: "Indonesia was seriously working to normalize relations with China, but now it will be very difficult to realise this soon." See *TAWSJ*, November 24, 1978, p. 13. Indonesian papers also hit at Deng Xiaoping's remarks. See, for example, *ST*, November 15, 1978; and *Survey of World Broadcasts (SWB)*, FE/5969/A3/7, November 15, 1978. The Weinstein study also shows that most of the Indonesian elites perceive China poses the most serious threat to the country's independence. See *Indonesian Foreign Policy*, pp. 92-93; and *ST*, August 29, 1980.

24. *Foreign Broadcasting International Services (FBIS)*, March 11, 1981, N2; *Christian Science Monitor (CSM)*, June 12, 1979.

25. Commentary, Xinhua News Agency, December 12, 1981.

26. *SWB*, FE/6262/A3/12, November 3, 1979; and *SWB*, FE/6223/A3/2, September 19, 1979.

27. For the Chinese position of the punitive action, see *Beijing Review*, March 23, 1979, pp. 19-27.

28. *Nanyang Siang Pau* (Singapore), February 2, 1979.

29. New York *Times*, November 7, 1978, p. 10; *CSM*, September 9, 1977, p. 3.

30. *SWB*, FE/6156/A3/6, July 2, 1979.

31. *FEER*, February 27-March 5, 1981, pp. 32-33; and *FEER*, March 27-April 2, 1981, p. 9; and *FEER*, June 12-18, 1981, p. 27.

32. *Bangkok Post (BP)*, July 1, 1975; and *Survey of China Mainland Press*, no. 5850, May 12, 1975, pp. 42-43. See also *South China Morning Post*, June 23, 1975; and *ST*, June 23, 1975; Washington *Post*, July 1, 1975.

33. New York *Times*, November 13, 1978; and *AWSJ*, November 14, 1978, p. 3.

34. *FBIS*, December 10, 1980, N1; and *Asia Week*, November 21, 1980.

35. This could be the main reason why Deng Xiaoping refused to give a pledge to end the support of the CPT when he was interviewed by Thai journalists in Peking prior to his visit to Bangkok in November 1978. *ST*, October 14, 1978. He also repeated that China would adhere to its dual policy of state-to-state and party-to-party relations. *Asia Week*, November 10, 1978, pp. 33, 34.

36. Prime Minister Zhao Ziyang is, however, reported to have remarked during his visit to Thailand in February 1981 that Peking would seek to avoid that its relations with the Communist Parties in the area harm the country's ties with the ASEAN states. See New York *Times*, February 2, 1981, p. 3.

37. New York *Times*, November 14, 1978.

38. *FEER*, May 18, 1979, p. 15.

39. *Christian Science Monitor*, June 12, 1979, p. 12.

6

SINO-FRENCH RELATIONS:
A FRENCH VIEW

Jean-Luc Domenach

The differences in scale and conditions between China and France are considerable. What, then, could have been the significant effects exerted on an enormous state "more ancient than history"[1] whose efforts toward modernization, if successful, would bring it to the forefront among world powers by its relations with an old Western country, indeed still rich and vigorous, but forced by its dimensions and geographic position to envisage its future within a wider European framework? The paradox of Sino-French relations lies in the fact that, despite the failures and illusions provoked by their short history (and in a certain sense, because of them), they have favored China's modernization to an extent that should neither be overrated nor overlooked.

EXPECTATIONS

There is some truth in the argument that the most important and most significant chapter in Sino-French relations was its initial one. In fact, diplomatic recognition of the Peking government by France under General de Gaulle in 1964 not only enabled bilateral relations between the two countries to develop but was probably also part of a vague yet innovating strategic plan.[2]

To say that there had been no way of predicting this decision is a sheer understatement. In the nineteenth century, France took part in the military-economic assault on China led by the Western powers. By arrogating the protection of the Catholic missions, it assured itself of solid bases on Chinese territory (in particular, a concession at Shanghai and a leasehold area in Yunnan province) and eventually conquered Annam in 1885 after putting its all into a fierce struggle.[3] During the first half of the twentieth century, France's political influence lessened while many nationalist Chinese intellectuals came under its cultural influence during their studies abroad: among the founders of the Chinese Communist Party, we find a large number of "former French residents" — Ch'en Tu-hsiu, Chou En-lai, Deng Xiaoping, Chen Yi.[4] According to the treaty signed on February 28, 1946, France ceded its leasehold areas and concessions back to China, its recent ally. But, starting in 1945, the Indochinese question had begun embittering relations between the two countries, first of all because the nationalist government had sought to reintroduce itself in Vietnam, and, second, because the Chinese Communists were supporting the Vietminh rebellion in that country. Once the Ho Chi Minh government had been recognized by Peking in January 1950, the two countries, already members of opposing camps, became declared enemies. Today we know that Giap's troops had had at their disposal a powerful assistance from the Chinese. The 1954 Geneva Conference, which marked the end of the first Indochinese War, attested to an amelioration in Sino-French relations: it was achieved through the joint efforts of Pierre Mendès-France, president of the French Council of Ministers, and Premier Chou En-lai, who were both, albeit for different reasons, anxious to put an end to this conflict.[5] Limited contacts were subsequently resumed: commercial missions were exchanged semiofficially, while progressive writers such as Jean-Paul Sartre, French Communist Party officials, and liberal politicians like Edgar Faure or Francois Mitterrand paid visits to Peking to express their desire that diplomatic relations be reestablished. However, this evolution was vigorously stemmed by the fear, held by successive French governments, of offending Washington, and especially by Peking's clamorous support of the Algerian rebellion.[6]

In the 1950s the Chinese press scarcely missed an occasion to vent its contempt for French militarism and colonialism. General de Gaulle, who never showed any particular fondness for Asian realities nor any special talent in handling the Indochinese affair, first appeared to have no sympathy for Communist China. However, beginning in 1962-63 both France and China underwent similar evolutions in their diplomacy. While de Gaulle, finally relieved of the colonial bond, gradually began defining line by line a strategic world policy, independent of U.S. tutelage, Peking, left in growing diplomatic isolation through its break with Moscow, was exploring the channels of a revolutionary strategy hostile to both revisionism and imperialism.

Thus in the eyes of many third world governments Peking and Paris might have appeared to be elaborating a median line of strategy — one of independence and development in face of the Soviet-American understanding that has become reality through the nuclear test ban treaty of 1963. No doubt, neither Paris nor Peking hedged any illusions about the future. At all events, there would be two immediate advantages to establishing diplomatic relations: it would open up the possibilities of bilateral economic cooperation, since China was seeking new suppliers outside the Soviet camp; above all, it would quite dramatically underline the new-found independence of each of the two partners with respect to their former protectors. This explains why the announcement of Paris' diplomatic recognition of Peking in January 1964, followed shortly by the rupture between Taipei and Paris, provoked a certain hidden displeasure in Moscow and outright rage in the United States. In the eyes of the Washington officials and commentators, who were increasingly obsessed with the Vietnam War, General de Gaulle's spectacular gesture did not appear to be that "recognition of realities" which received the almost unanimous approval of French public opinion (excepting some moderates and a parliamentary group of the Socialist Party), but rather pure and simple "treason."[7]

Were the French and Chinese leaders as daring and resolute as many commentators then thought them to be? Had their rapprochement in fact been accurately prearranged? This seems unlikely since their relations were to be rapidly marked by signs of mutual disappointment. Once both sides had scored successes in prestige and reaped economic gains from the exchange of ambassadors, the basic political limits to a Sino-French dialogue quickly became evident: while Paris was chiefly interested in strengthening its position vis-a-vis Washington and in improving its relations with Moscow,[8] Peking was again giving a more leftist turn to its revolutionary strategy directed primarily toward young states and third world national liberation movements, and was irritated by France's excessive pretensions of playing an important role in the resolution of the Indochinese conflict and by its rather lukewarm reprobation of American aggression in Vietnam. Therefore, even if we consider that the project of a Sino-French political axis was the deeper reason behind the diplomatic rapprochement between Paris and Peking, we must immediately recognize that it was never executed, not even in the domain of disarmament where the conjunction of French and Chinese interests was most evident.[9] Two internal political events killed these projects in *embryo*: in China the Cultural Revolution caused Chinese diplomacy to slumber for more than three years (1966-69) and led to a number of restricted incidents between France and China;[10] in France, the events of May-June 1968 weakened General de Gaulle's position and obliged him to moderate his ambitions abroad. The conjunction of the Cultural Revolution with the Paris students' rebellion (in whose midst the Maoist groups proved to be particularly active) temporarily modified China's image in France: it was no longer that far-off and highly reputed empire General de Gaulle had spoken of, but now appeared as an advancing revolution whose model threatened to overcome the West itself.

The stabilizing of the political scene, both in France as well as in China, did not give way to any renewal of pre-1966 relations and hopes. In fact, beginning in 1968-69, the general lines of the French and Chinese diplomatic policies changed. While Paris was tempering its relations with Washington, Peking, alerted of the seriousness behind the Soviet threat by a number of major border incidents, gradually abandoned its opposition to the two superpowers and began a process of reconciliation with the United States. Indeed, an atmosphere of friendly relations was progressively reestablished between the two capitals. As stated in the *Far Eastern Economic Review*, France "enjoyed a privileged position in China."[11] It was in fact the only Western country to maintain a large embassy there. France sent a number of ministerial and parliamentary delegations to Peking in 1970 and 1971 where they were heartily received by the Chinese authorities. In autumn of 1971, Paris crowds applauded, successively, Peking's minister for foreign trade and one of the vice-ministers of foreign affairs. The fact that Chou En-lai himself was present at the French embassy on July 14, 1971, the day of the French national commemoration, characterized the excellence of the two countries' relations. Yet, between France and China, the era of great expectations was past, succeeded by that of discrete good services. It appears that General de Gaulle (particularly at the time of President Nixon's visit in March 1969) and his ambassador in Peking, Etienne Manac'h, aided in the establishment and good functioning of the first Sino-American contacts, notably in connection with the Vietnam conflict.

However, as soon as the United States and China began dialoguing directly and discovered their growing political convergence, Sino-French relations began to lose interest for Peking and, to a lesser extent, for Paris as well. France's position in China began to weaken and lose its savor. From 1973 to 1979, despite a number of minor oscillations due in part to France's growing commitment in easing the political strains in Europe, but above all to internal political agitation in China,[12] relations between Paris and Peking were characterized by three phenomena. First, they continued to be particularly cordial: either out of faithfulness or in view of preparing for the future, both governments constantly found new reasons for dealing tactfully and granting special favors to one another. This gave rise to a series of symbolic privileges that could be cleverly presented as political. Thus, Monsieur Pompidou became the first Western head of state to pay an official visit to Peking (September 1973); Paris became the first Western capital to receive the visit of an important Chinese Communist leader (Deng Xiaoping, May 1975); and, again, it was in France that Hua Guofeng began his European trip in the fall of 1979. Second, although the bilateral Sino-French relations have evolved less brilliantly than was first hoped, development has nevertheless been incontestable. Trade has increased sixfold between 1964 and 1979. Cultural relations that started on a small scale with an agreement concluded in October 1965 were practically broken off in 1967, but were seriously resumed in the fall of 1973. The two-year agreement signed in October 1979 has intensified and extended them to include the social sciences. Exchanges have multiplied in highly specialized fields. Thus, as early as March 1976, France organized a large scientific and technical exposition in Peking. Since 1979, one Chinese delegation after another has been received in France, as has been the case, moreover, in most of the Western countries. Finally even though regular advisory procedures have not been formally established, political relations have been very good, as is shown by the number of ministerial delegations exchanged by both parties (a total of eight for the year 1978 alone). After the Soviet invasion of Afghanistan, the fact that, with respect to Moscow, Paris adopted a more moderate attitude than Washington provoked no open difficulties in Sino-French relations.[13] Back from a fact-finding trip to the United States, Chinese Vice-Minister of Foreign Affairs Zhang Wenjin stopped over in Paris in March 1980 to confer with French diplomats. The year also witnessed Deng Yingchao's visit to France, and President Giscard d'Estaing's visit to China. Of course, today, there are still a number of important issues on which Paris and Peking disagree: in the eyes of the Chinese leaders, the French are wrong in putting faith in a European detente and in the usefulness of a friendly dialogue with Moscow since the Soviets interpret such an attitude as a sign of weakness; moreover, for a number of years now, Peking has stopped believing in the virtue of a Europe independent of the United States. But both French and Chinese leaders have decided to insist on the points held in common, points that are in fact important: they concern major principles such as national independence, major world problems, as, for example, disarmament (which must be total and not used as a means of assuring the condominium of the two superpowers), but also certain specific, regional problems, such as peace in the Near East (which should not favor the USSR but must not exclude the Palestinians) and particularly Africa, where their two policies are highly convergent on the primary issue of containing the Soviet advance. However, although relations between the two countries are still emphasized in official speeches, they have lost much of their importance. Despite its interest in Indochina, French diplomacy has become less overbearing; today, it is paying increasing attention to Africa, the Mediterranean basin, and Europe. Without renouncing its great principles of disarmament, it has done its utmost to maintain more confident relations with the United States while keeping up constructive exchanges with the Soviet Union. On the other hand, Chinese diplomacy since 1974 has multiplied its relations with various European governments, in particular those that are the most concerned about the Soviet threat, and has established ties of "quasi alliance" with the United States since 1979. Thus, it has been led to attach less importance to its friendship with France, although the latter still remains an attractive, and moreover hardly avoidable, intermediary for China in Europe. However, France's desires for independence appear to be steadily losing their usefulness, while its attachment to Soviet friendship is an irritating factor, and its efforts in favor of Vietnam seem inappropriate. As for the rest, China is still weak in terms of power but potentially strong because of the future that it claims for itself and that others, often so naively, ascribe to it; China has woven such a dense network of world relations that it can now do without France's good offices. We cannot exclude on principle the possibility that Sino-French relations will again become more intense. But should this happen, France will have to commit itself concretely and firmly to the process of modernization (particularly military) launched by China. And this is a policy that France's general choices presently prohibit it from adopting. Considering the hopes that the surprise decision had raised in 1964, the balance of Sino-French relations is and may well continue to be disappointing in the eyes of many observers.

LIMITATIONS

In point of fact, the relations between Paris and Peking after 1964 were globally marked by a disequilibrium between reality and the spoken word. China and France vie with one another in efforts to call attention to their history, to the greatness of their respective cultures, and to the political importance of their relations. As early as 1957, Chou En-lai declared to Gerard Philippe, the famous progressive actor, that "the love of France exists in the heart of every Chinese."[14] In 1970 Mao Tse-tung confided his admiration for General de Gaulle to Minister Bettencourt — "We are both military men, we can understand one another."[15] Subsequently, the Chinese mass media have hardly stopped praising the similarities, political as well as cultural, that are said to bring the two countries closer together. It adds color to its demonstrations with stereotype references to the French Revolution, Victor Hugo, the Paris Commune, Chou En-lai's stay in France, and the effort of General de Gaulle. These official compliments seem to tally with a sincere attachment to France on the part of many Chinese leaders and intellectuals. To a great extent, their attitude can be explained by France's cultural influence on several generations of Chinese students and by their general admiration for the way of life in that highly industrialized country. While France's technical achievements clearly receive less acclaim than do the American or West German ones, they are by no means overlooked. In contrast to the attitude usually found in other Asian countries, the Chinese do not look down on French individualism and passion for culture but, rather, are envious of them or compare them to specifically Chinese traits of character: some even consider China to be "the France of the Far East." France's great nineteenth-century writers, especially those held in high respect by the Marxist tradition (for example, Stendhal, Balzac, Zola), have always been remarkable best-sellers among the well-educated Chinese. Before being reprinted in the early 1970s, a number of short stories by de Maupassant in Chinese translation circulated as publications of a *samidzdat* in southern China. On the French side, praise has been even more extravagant, but subject to a paradoxical evolution. In the beginning, during the era of the great expectations, de Gaulle entertained no illusions about Chinese communism. He justified establishing diplomatic relations with Peking much more in recognition of a certain reality and the long-term interests of France and the Western world than out of any cultural or political sympathies. Nor did he have any illusions about the causes behind the temporary political convergence of France and China. As for his advisers, they heavily emphasized the economic advantages that France would derive from its new relations with China.[16] Curiously enough, when Sino-French relations began losing political momentum during the Cultural Revolution, the French became more and more extravagant in their praise. The progressive Parisian intelligentsia, liberated from the influence of the French Communist Party by the May 1968 movement, gave vent to boundless Maoism that reached its peak with the work by M. A. Maccchiochi, *De la Chine*.[17] This Parisian Maoism has, in face of the facts, proved to be as excessive as it was inconsistent.[18] Under the influence of a small number of lucid Sinologists,[19] and impressed as they were by Maoism's posthumous destiny in China after 1976, the most ardent flatterers of the Peking regime changed camps after 1977.[20] The spontaneous pro-Maoism of a great number of French writers and politicians close to the government will have proved more constant, more influential, and, in the long run, more interesting for the history of ideas. The most perfect prototype of this kind of writing, which is on the borderline between literature, travel narrative, and political thought, will certainly have been the work of Alain Peyrefitte, a Gaullist minister and accomplished writer. Almost 1 million copies of his book *Quand la Chine s'éveillera* have been sold to date.[21] The political sympathy of such authors is derived from their national appeal for China: it is the emergence of a source of power that appears most admirable in the Chinese experience, perhaps because it reminds the French and the Europeans of their own political obligations. As Alain Peyrefitte stated, "We are inclined to be Maoist for China just as we are Gaullist for France."[22] In spite of the rise to power of Valéry Giscard d'Estaing, a president who owes considerably more to liberal traditions than to the Gaullist heritage, this pro-Maoism has hardly regressed, for it proves to be less vulnerable to internal Chinese evolution than was the appeal of the progressive intelligentsia abroad. Although it has ceased to exert any substantial influence on French diplomatic practice as a whole, it still continues to impregnate both the language of some French diplomats and the conduct of certain specialized affairs.

In point of fact, Sino-French relations have, in the eyes of many observers, failed to produce results proportional to the stress placed on them in official speeches or to the vast ambitions attached to them.[23] In the political sphere, the Sino-French axis has never gotten beyond the initial stage. France's good offices (along with those of Rumania) as an intermediary between China and the West were never spectacular enough to bring it any great advantages. Since 1973, France is no longer a power with a world calling nor even really a politically privileged Western partner for China, but simply the European country that China is inclined to treat with circumspection because of its past, the originality of its position, and the influence it exerts over certain governments in the third world — and this, by the way, is becoming less and less evident. Whereas in 1975, Deng Xiaoping had visited France alone, in 1979 Hua Guofeng also traveled to West Germany, Great Britain, and Italy. Barring a rather improbable change in the orientation of French and Chinese diplomacy, the French privileges, even the symbolic ones, should continue to dwindle. Actually, the militant anti-Sovietism manifested by Prime Minister Margaret Thatcher's government has made possible a noticeable rekindling of Anglo-Chinese relations. The German

Federal Republic is one of China's top trade partners. During an official visit to Bonn in October 1979, Hua Guofeng conveyed to Chancellor Schmidt China's comprehension for West Germany's present line of foreign policy. Even Italy, where the Communist Party holds major positions in local government authorities, no longer fills Peking with apprehension: in April 1980 the Chinese leaders extended an invitation to the head of a party whose "revisionism" had once been so loudly denounced in the mid-1960s.

But not only has the political dialogue lost much of its significance, bilateral Sino-French relations also remain basically limited. Cultural exchanges have been intensified and diversified. To the 25 scholarship holders that France sends each year to study in China have been added a large number of scientific missions. As for the Chinese, since the winter of 1978-79, they have accepted the financing of scientific training in France for more than 150 Chinese students and researchers. The presence in France in April 1980 of a dance troupe from the Peking Opera and the subsequent visit to China of the *Comédie française* are indicative of a substantial boost in artistic exchanges (basically limited, however, by the problem of distances and by their official nature). What is more, France is furthering the instruction of its tongue in China by financing a dozen foreign language assistants there. An interesting joint project together with the University of Wuhan involves the instruction in French of several scientific courses. However, the development of Sino-French cultural exchanges has met with two specific obstacles: the insufficiency of the funds that France is willing to devote to this sector, due to her overall choices, and the Chinese leaders' strong preference for the English language. In fact, French is unable to hold out against the advance of rival languages except in a number of specialized fields and in a few universities. It may also be justified to ask just how far the Chinese authorities will be prepared to go in expanding joint cultural projects in fields where French thought has shown its greatest originality in the past 35 years: in philosophy, sociology, ethnology, and psychoanalysis.

The economic aspect is the weak link in Sino-French relations. Although it has grown in importance, bilateral trade is still highly irregular. In fact, neither Chinese exports to France nor French exports to China (particularly the key-in-hand factories of recent years) correspond to permanent needs. In reality, their evolution depends on the cycle of Sino-French relations: each high point results in an advancement of trade (for example, in 1965-66, after diplomatic recognition, and after President Pompidou's trip to China, 1974-76) and is rapidly succeeded by a drop (in 1977, France was only thirteenth on the list of China's trade partners). Sino-French trade is relatively independent of Chinese political and economic cycles: it was hardly touched by the Cultural Revolution, but we might also add that French exporters derived less profit from the opening of the Chinese market in 1977-78 than did their Western and Japanese competitors. In 1979 France was only China's seventh commercial partner, and Sino-French trade accounted for no more than 0.3 percent of foreign exchanges and 2 percent of China's international trade. Indeed, some slight progress has been achieved in the past two years: commercial missions have multiplied and each of the two partners has a better idea of what he may expect from the other. The leading role played by large-scale projects has been fading to make room for a tide of less irregular deals. Limits to possible progress are set by France's excessive price conditions, by the stiff competition of the Japanese and the West-Germans, both technically and financially, as well as by the disappearance of any political preference for French products.

THE FRENCH ROLE

If the concept of "modernization" is used in the strict sense, i.e., to mean economy and technology, France can be said to have played only a minor role in the modernizing of China. A primary cause of this is that France, after its political rapprochement with China, proved in many cases technically and financially not competitive enough. Furthermore, whatever other promises China may have made to take the two countries' political relations into consideration, it has kept a most exact account of price conditions, and some of its leaders have finally come to the conclusion that, in all but very special sectors (e.g., Berliet lorries), French exports are technically and financially behind their Western competitors. We must acknowledge that, on the whole, and since both 1949 and 1977, the USSR, Japan, and the United States as well have played a more influential and at the same time more problematic role in the modernization of China and France.

However, "modernization" can also be understood in another manner, in a wider and more profound sense: not only as the technical and economic development process by which China is striving to rejoin the world's most advanced nations, but more generally as the economic, political, diplomatic, and even cultural process by which China, in renewing its ties with the real world (and not just the world vision of the Marxist-Leninist vulgate), is preparing its entrance in the ranks of the most developed nations and its peaceful contribution to world order. From this viewpoint, the role played by Sino-French relations may well have been greater than is commonly imagined.

First of all, the exchange of information has been facilitated by the establishment of diplomatic relations and the exchange of first-rate ambassadors on both sides.[24] What is more, this has opened a window for China to a world where it once had practically no access, i.e., to French-speaking Africa, Europe, and the West in general. For the first time, China entered into direct contact with a Western regime for reasons other than the settling of a dispute, without being limited by the cold war or trade negotiations. For the first time, in dealing with the de Gaulle regime, Mao Tse-tung, who had been a party to all kinds of highly realistic alliances and compromises during the epic times of his struggle for power, gave a try to diplomatic cooperation with a capitalist government. A lesson was drawn from the 1964 experience: cooperation proved difficult but not impossible. There was less reason to forget this lesson after the Cultural Revolution when the Soviet threat revealed the necessity of a rapprochement with the United States since France was still present, offering its good services. It must be noted that the Gaullist leaders had envisaged the possibility of this intermediary role for France as early as 1964. In 1971 Alain Peyrefitte stated that "France is one of the best channels that China can possibly use, at least occasionally, in view of normalizing its relations with the exterior."[25] It has subsequently become a fixed doctrine in French diplomacy that France's China policy is not oriented simply toward short-term profitability but, in a longer term, toward favoring China's reinsertion in the international concert of powers. This reinsertion could lead Peking to temper its diplomatic behavior and perhaps its domestic policy. As early as May 1964, Edgar Faure, one of the French diplomats who did the most for the establishment of diplomatic relations between Paris and Peking, stated: "As far as China is concerned, the chief problem is to help this country in passing the same turning point as Mr. K. after the death of Stalin."[26] Specialized and comparative studies on Franco-Chinese relations in the years 1968-72 will still have to be accomplished before we can define with any exactitude France's real influence on the evolution of Chinese diplomacy. In the meantime, we can only say that this French warrant may have advantaged elaboration of China's Africa policy, hastened its admission to the United Nations and, above all, aided in organizing the Sino-American dialogue. Since 1973, its relations with France have also helped China – to an extent that would be interesting to discover as well – to take root in Europe. Perhaps it would be better to speak of the "experience of relations with France" rather than of France's role as "intermediary." Paris helped Peking replace Taiwan in dealing with the European Economic Community authorities, and there is little doubt that the example of Sino-French relations has served as a model for other European governments. It is even more important to consider if this experience, although disappointing on the whole, has not prepared the way for Peking's present concept of European policy. Although in content China's European policy has evolved toward clear pro-Atlantism, the Chinese conception of a European entity that would counterbalance the Soviet power is probably derived from embryonic collaboration once envisaged between China and France.

CONCLUSIONS

It may be concluded that Franco-Chinese relations after normalization have helped China more than France. As friendship with France grew less and less useful, the French position in China declined correspondingly. But, from another point of view, and paradoxically, this decline may be considered as a mark of success. If China no longer feels the need to have a European or a Western patron, this simply indicates that its integration into the world order has already been accomplished and that within this framework it is now acting with vigor and, on the whole, moderation,[27] and that, finally, its ties with the United States and with the other European countries have become sufficiently strong and solid. Briefly, in acting so as to give priority to Western interests over its own, French policy in the Gaullist and post-Gaullist era has favored not only the economic but also the diplomatic modernization of the People's Republic of China. To what extent the election of Socialist Francois Mitterrand to the French presidency in May 1981 will affect the Sino-French relations remains to be seen. To all probability, there will be no significant change.

NOTES

1. This was the expression used by General de Gaulle when announcing the establishment of diplomatic relations between Paris and Peking, January 31, 1964.

2. This interesting phase of Sino-French relations has not yet been studied in depth. However, we may refer to Stephen Erasmus' short article, "General De Gaulle's Recognition of Peking," *China Quarterly*, no. 18 (April-June 1964), pp. 195-200.

3. A rather general historic account of Franco-Chinese relations may be found in *Le Monde*, January 28-29, 1964.

4. Up until 1949 the French Jesuits of the University of Aurora in Shanghai also exercised much influence on their numerous students who today have attained responsible positions not only in Taiwan and Hong Kong but in the People's Republic of China as well.

5. See the remarkable thesis by Francois Joyaux that capitalizes on material from French diplomatic archives: *La Chine et le règlement du premier conflit d'Indochine, Genève 1954*, Publications de la Sorbonne, 1979.

6. When welcoming an Algerian delegation in December 1958, the Chinese leader Burhan Sahidi declared that General de Gaulle had "killed democracy in France with the same bayonet that he used to massacre the Algerian people" (*Combat*, December 6, 1958).

7. See, for example, *L'Aurore*, January 11-12, 1964; New York *Hearld Tribune*, January 23; *Le Monde*, January 24, 25, 26; *L'Aurore*, January 28, 1964.

8. On Gaullist foreign policy, see, among others, Edward A. Kolodziedj, *French International Policy under de Gaulle and Pompidou* (Ithaca: Cornell University Press, 1974).

9. *Le Monde*, November 1-2, 1964.

10. In particular, in January 1967, the incidents between Chinese students in Paris and the French policy, and, in Peking, the "Richard incident" (*Le Monde*, February 3, 1967) and, in the spring of 1968, the enormous Chinese manifestations of support to the French strikers of May 1968 (*Le Monde*, May 22, 25, 29, June 11; *La Croix*, July 24, 1968).

11. *Far Eastern Economic Review*, August 21, 1971.

12. Thus, while there was a stiffening of China's internal policy in the 1975-76 period, little was felt in the sphere of Franco-Chinese diplomatic relations, notably during the Peking visit of French Minister of Foreign Affairs Monsieur Sauvagnargues in November 1975 (*Le Monde*, November 21, 23-24, 25, 1975). On several occasions, up until 1978, the Chinese press published a number of analyses of the French economic situation that Paris considered offensive (see, for example, the *People's Daily* of January 29, 1977, and January 6, 1978).

13. The Communist press in Hong Kong showed a certain irritation over the French moderate attitude. See, for instance, a *Xinwanbao* [New Evening Post] editorial in February 1980.

14. *Le Monde*, March 28, 1957.

15. *L'Express*, August 3, 1970.

16. Prior to the mission led by the former President of the Council of Ministers, a mission led by the French National Employers' Association prepared the diplomatic recognition of China by de Gaulle in the fall of 1963.

17. Editions du Seuil, 1971.

18. The most significant itinerary is that of the revue *Tel Quel* under the direction of the writer Philippe Sollers, who first professed to be rigorously apolitical, then tried a rapprochement with the French Communist Party (PCF), and finally became Maoist before recently advocating the American model.

19. The work that probably had the greatest and profoundest impact was Simon Leys' *Ombres Chinoises* (UGE, 1974).

20. See, for example, C. Broyelle, J. Broyelle, and E. Tsichhart, *Deuxieme retour de Chine* (Editions du Seuil, 1977).

21. Fayard, 1973.

22. *Le Figaro*, August 20, 1971.

23. See, for example, *La Croix*, September 11, 1973; and *Le Monde*, January 18, 1978.

24. France's ambassadors were, in order of succession, Lucien Paye (1964-69), Etienne Manac'h (1969-75), and Claude Arnaud (1975-79). The Chinese ambassadors were Huang Zhen (1964-67, 1969-73), Zeng Tao (1973-77), Han Kehua (1977-79), and Yao Guange (1980-present). All were very high officials; Huang Zhen and Lucien Paye later became Cabinet ministers.

25. *La Croix*, August 27, 1971.

26. *Le Monde*, May 8, 1964.

27. This is the conclusion, concerning China's activity in the UN, drawn by Samuel Kim in *China, the United Nations, and World Order* (Princeton: Princeton University Press, 1979).

7

CHINESE POLICY TOWARD
WESTERN EUROPE:
A NEW RELATIONSHIP
IN THE 1980S

Raymond F. Wylie

EVOLUTION OF A NEW RELATIONSHIP

In recent years, growing relations between the People's Republic of China (PRC) and the nations of Western Europe have become a notable feature of international politics. In a world still dominated largely by the United States and the Soviet Union, Chinese and European leaders have recognized the leverage to be that medium powers can strengthen their positions by developing cooperative foreign policies in the pursuit of common interests. The two sides have not yet developed their relationship to the point of formal alliance, nor are they likely to, in view of the substantial differences between them. Nonetheless, there has been a dramatic increase in their mutual ties, and a continuation of this trend is possible in the immediate future. A new relationship, based on a growing convergence of interests, is gradually taking shape between China and the major states of Western Europe, both on a bilateral basis and within the broader framework of the European Community (EC). This relationship, should it prove durable, will contribute significantly to the emergence of China and Western Europe as major actors in the multipolar global system of the 1980s.[1]

On the Chinese side the possibilities for gain are substantial, and this has stimulated Peking's desire to court the Europeans. The PRC has three distinct foreign policy interests in Western Europe, namely, strategic security, economic modernization, and regional and global influence, in that order of importance. The Chinese hope that closer relations with Europe will give them greater opportunities to pursue a balance of power strategy toward the Soviet Union, and, to a lesser extent, the United States. Better ties will also help provide

Peking with the advanced weapons and technology required to bring China's military forces up to modern world standards. In addition, the PRC has in recent years embarked upon an ambitious program of economic development, involving the acquisition of high-level industrial technology in Western Europe. This will necessitate a greater Chinese export drive in the EC countries to pay for these costly purchases, and avoid excessive trade deficits and overreliance on external financing. Finally, the Chinese believe that stronger links with Europe will help augment their influence in the Asian region and in the global system as a whole. In this light closer Sino-European relations are highly attractive to Peking.

The West Europeans also hope to benefit from better relations with China, but the relationship is asymmetrical, with the Europeans likely to gain rather less than the Chinese. The Europeans hope to use the PRC as a counterbalance to the Soviet Union, although they have no need for Chinese arms or weapons technology in their present underdeveloped state. Likewise, while the Europeans are eager to find new markets in the PRC for their advanced industrial technology, they have only a limited need for the products of China's growing light industry, which Peking is vigorously promoting in the EC market. Still, China's rise to quasi-superpower status will augment the international influence of its partners, and in the long run Europe has much to gain. The Chinese and the West Europeans have in effect become "objective allies" in their search for a new and expanded role in a rapidly changing international environment.

The strengthening of Sino-European ties poses a difficulty for both the United States and the Soviet Union. Hitherto, the superpowers have dealt with the Chinese and the West Europeans as discrete entities often at odds with each other, and not as independent actors pursuing joint foreign policy interests within a loose framework of cooperation. With the emergence of China and the EC bloc as major centers of influence, the evolution of a global balance of power system will become possible. Greater scope will be given to the medium powers as important actors in their own right, and not simply as clients of the superpowers. Such a balance of power system will not necessarily be more stable or conflict-free than the earlier bipolar structure; indeed, precisely the opposite might prove to be the case as more nation-states compete for positions of advantage in an increasingly flexible (and perhaps formless) international order.[2] Nevertheless, medium powers like China and Western Europe (assuming, in the latter case, a modicum of agreement on foreign policy) will have greater opportunities for coordinated action in the pursuit of common goals.

The Chinese were quick to realize this and, following their break with the Soviet Union in the early 1960s, they urged the West Europeans to follow suit and loosen their ties to the United States. Many European leaders were slow to grasp the significance of China's rupture with the Soviets, but French president Charles de Gaulle clarified the issue with his unilateral recognition of Peking in 1964. The other European governments moved slowly, but by 1971 most of them had decided, against weakening American opposition, to recognize the PRC and seat it in the United Nations. The West Germans remained hesitant, however, and it took the Sino-American rapprochement of 1971-72 to convince Bonn of the wisdom of recognizing Peking, which it did late in 1972. The Chinese were quick to respond to these developments, and in the 1970s they played the "European card" with considerable dexterity and success. Indeed, so keen were the Chinese to argue their case for an independent European foreign policy that they sometimes went too far. To many bemused observers, the Chinese, in their fervent exhortations for greater vigilance against the superpowers, seemed to be "plus Européens que les Européens."[3]

BACKGROUND TO CHINESE POLICY

Thus, as we enter the 1980s China's ties with Western Europe have taken on a significance that was not apparent in the cold war years. Relations then were spotty, and often characterized by mutual suspicion, although in some cases trade ties developed at the unofficial level. This situation continued until the early 1970s, when Sino-American relations improved dramatically following Richard Nixon's election as U.S. president. China's relations with the nations of Western Europe were then free to develop normally, subject to the usual dictates of interest and convenience.[4] The 1980s promise to be a period of considerable importance as the two sides strive to define their foreign policy goals free from the constraints of the cold war era.

Since coming to power in 1949, the Chinese Communists have consistently attempted to fit Europe into a well-defined theoretical framework. In the 1950s, for example, Peking adhered to the Soviet "two camp" concept of international relations, in which Western Europe was considered to be a subordinate part of the American-dominated imperialist camp. This rigid view, which denied the possibility of an independent European foreign policy, remained largely intact until the open rift between Peking and Moscow in the early 1960s. Then, in 1964, responding to what they perceived to be a fundamental shift in world forces, the Chinese put forward a new "three zone" interpretation of the international system. In this view, Western Europe was depicted as part of a "second intermediate zone" made up of smaller developed capitalist states allegedly striving for freedom from American control. (It was in this theoretical context that Mao and de Gaulle agreed to the normalization of relations between their two countries.) This theory was modified in 1974, when Peking advanced the thesis that the international system now comprised "three worlds," the second of which included Western Europe, allegedly seeking an independent role in world affairs. The EC states, it was claimed, were still somewhat oppressive at home and exploitative abroad, but they were struggling for independence from both American and Soviet interference and control. To this extent, it was argued, their role in world politics was progressive and hence worthy of support.[5]

From the early 1960s, then, the Chinese have emphasized the growing role of the West European states as middle powers seeking emancipation from superpower domination. Despite a significant modification regarding the United States, which shall be noted later, this characterization continues to inform the PRC's foreign policies toward individual European nations and the European Community as a whole.

Over the years, Peking has built up an effective institutional structure for dealing with policy toward Western Europe. There is a West European department within the Ministry of Foreign Affairs, and its staff includes both area and functional specialists with personal foreign experience.[6] Chinese embassies throughout Europe were expanded and upgraded in the course of the 1970s, and in 1975 the ambassador to Belgium was accredited concurrently to represent Peking's interests at the EC in Brussels. These embassies keep Peking well informed about current developments in their host countries, as does the New China News Agency, which has offices in all the major West European capitals. "People's diplomacy," once so important in times of nonexistent or strained relations at the official level, now plays a less significant role in keeping Peking in touch with European affairs. Yet, it is not to be discounted, for recent years have witnessed a substantial increase in Chinese visitors whose occupations take them to EC countries of potential importance to China's domestic and foreign policy goals.

SECURITY ISSUES

What are these goals in China's present situation, and how do they relate to policy toward Western Europe? The record to date suggests that the Chinese place security issues at the top of their long-range policy agenda. The PRC remains much weaker militarily than either the United States or the Soviet Union, and this is of primary concern to political and military leaders alike. To improve on this situation, two courses of action have been pursued simultaneously: an adroit manipulation of the shifting balance of power and a steady buildup of the weapons industry and the military forces. Western Europe fits admirably into this scheme of things, for the major EC states provide a useful counterbalance in the West to growing Soviet power, while their advanced weapons industries hold out to Peking the prospect of strengthening China's arsenal against the military might of the Red Army. Western Europe also provides the PRC with a potential counterbalance to American power, or, in the present era of rapprochement, to possible overreliance on the United States in the security area. Western Europe is thus a valuable resource for the Chinese defense effort vis-á-vis both Moscow and Washington, although current Peking leaders have continued the Maoist policy of aligning with the United States against the Soviet Union.

Western Europe is gradually modifying its dependent relationship with the United States, and the trend toward a new, distinctive European voice in world affairs is reinforced by the continuing growth of the EC. Despite their earlier opposition, the Chinese are now ardent supporters of European unification, even in its political dimensions, although they are aware of the many obstacles that lie in the way.[7] Still, Peking does not wish to encourage a complete break between Europe and the United States for the simple reason that American military might in Europe is more impressive to the Russians than anything Europe, united or not, is likely to put in its place. So, while supporting the EC and the distant goal of European unification, the Chinese are also careful to voice their approval of a continuing American military presence in Europe. In particular, they are enthusiastic backers of NATO, which is headed by the United States, and even express fears that the alliance might not be strong enough to cope with burgeoning Soviet power.[8] This tolerance of U.S. influence in Europe represents a significant modification of Peking's formal theory that the EC nations are struggling to free themselves from American domination. It is, of course, based on two propositions, namely, that the Soviet Union is more of a threat than the United States to China and Europe alike, and the security interests of both are best served by using American power to counterbalance that of the USSR.

Although Peking has recently improved its relationship with several of the major West European Communist Parties, there has been little agreement on a common policy toward the USSR. Whereas the European Communists stress the importance of constructive dialogue with Moscow, the Chinese party continues to advocate open confrontation with the Soviets in Europe and elsewhere.[9] In their quest for greater security, the Peking leadership has in recent years developed a keen interest in the weapons systems of the major West European states. The PRC's armed forces are large, but poorly equipped, and this is a long-standing issue to which the impatient chiefs of staff have now turned their attention. Even so, they are operating under severe constraints, for, in the context of the Sino-American rapprochement, the political leaders wish to give immediate priority to economic modernization as the basis for all-round growth. Within this limitation, though, the military has been given the go-ahead to upgrade the level of China's defense preparedness, especially in the conventional sector.

There are two separate problems here: the construction of a modern, integrated weapons industry and the provision of ready-made weapons to divisions in the field. Although lagging behind the capabilities of the superpowers, the arms industries of Western Europe can provide both the technological know-how and the weapons systems desired by Peking. Until recently, there has been more talk than action, for the question of arms sales to China falls under the purview of COCOM, a coordinating committee within NATO responsible for monitoring sales of military-related equipment and expertise to Communist states. The Americans, who have the most influential voice in COCOM, have hitherto been reluctant to approve arms sales to the PRC, although there was some softening of their position in the mid-1970s. Lately, however, there has been a dramatic shift in Washington's attitude, prompted in large part by the normalization of U.S.-Chinese ties and the rapid deterioration of U.S.-Soviet relations following

Soviet occupation of Afghanistan in 1979. In fact, recent developments in Washington suggest that the Europeans will face stiff American competition in the sales of defense-related technologies and products to China. During an official visit in June 1981, Secretary of State Alexander Haig assured Peking that the United States is now prepared to sell the PRC a wide range of both defensive and offensive weapons on a case-by-case basis.[10]

There have already been some West European sales in the defense-related market, although negotiations have been more protracted than originally anticipated. The British, for example, have provided Peking with sophisticated artillery control systems, and, more significantly, with facilities for the production under license of a jet propulsion engine with military capabilities. In addition, the supply of ground attack "jump-jets" has been approved by London, and the sale of heavy tanks is under discussion, although no contracts have yet been signed. On their part, the French have concluded sales of general purpose helicopters and heavy duty helicopters with ground surveillance radars. Negotiations are underway on other deals involving antiaircraft equipment, various kinds of missiles, and computers with military applications. The Italians are eager to join in the marketing campaign, and they have been negotiating on a wide range of hardware of interest to Peking, including helicopters, missile guidance systems, and naval ships.[11]

The West Germans have hitherto been reluctant to discuss weapons sales with the Chinese, in light of Washington's previously cool attitude and Moscow's strong opposition to Bonn's participation in the arms trade. Nevertheless, West Germany is the PRC's largest trading partner in Europe and in light of the change in mood on the part of the Americans, it was not surprising that the Germans eventually cast their hat into the ring. Sales have been completed of light utility helicopters and antitank missiles developed jointly with the French. (One of these helicopters armed with six missiles becomes a formidable antitank weapon, something the Chinese military were eager to acquire.) Preliminary talks have been held on a number of other items, including electronic systems, heavy tanks, and various types of armored vehicles. The scale of West German military sales to Peking will likely be influenced by the political relationship between Bonn and Washington, and, equally, Bonn and Moscow. In this delicate area, the West Germans are conscious of the need to tread gently in light of their historical record, and their potentially difficult relations with the two superpowers.

As could be expected, the Soviet Union and its Warsaw Treaty allies have reacted with alarm at the prospect of growing arms transfers between Western Europe and China. Moscow has argued that the European powers are in effect treating Peking as the "Eastern member" of NATO, and the British in particular were castigated for approving the sale of ground attack aircraft, as they are most likely to be put into service on the troubled Sino-Soviet border. The European capitals will have to gauge the desirability of arms sales to Peking in light of Moscow's opposition, and to weigh the merits of Peking's claims against their own relations with the Soviet Union. A massive buildup of Chinese military capability, especially with the active participation of the EC states, is certain to feed Soviet suspicions of the West's ultimate intentions, and to provoke a greater defense effort on Moscow's part as well. Neither outcome would be in the best interests of Western Europe, and arms sales to China will have to be seen in this light. This does not argue against all arms sales to China, but care will have to be taken not to allow anti-Soviet sentiments or hopes of commercial gain to jeopardize the success of detente and arms control negotiations in Europe.[12]

On the other hand, more practical considerations might impede the growth of arms transfers from Western Europe to the PRC. The Chinese connection is not critical to many EC countries, and on occasion they are prepared to sacrifice a potential Chinese market for a real one elsewhere. In November 1980, for example, the Dutch government approved the sale of two submarines to Taiwan as part of a larger trade package. Despite Peking's violent opposition, The Hague permitted the deal to go through, even at the cost of political and trade setbacks with the PRC. With Peking's decision to downgrade diplomatic relations to the chargé d'affaires level, the immediate prospects for increased Dutch sales to China, especially in the military sector, appear bleak.[13] Even if the major EC countries are prepared to give priority to the PRC over Taiwan, Peking's limited resources for military modernization might prove to be a severe obstacle to greater sales. On their frequent "browses" through the European arms markets, Chinese military delegations have expressed dismay at the high costs of the most desired items, and Peking in consequence has shown great reluctance to sign firm contracts of sale. It might well be that Peking simply does not have the financial resources required to underwrite a large-scale program of arms purchases abroad, either in Europe or elsewhere.

ECONOMIC MODERNIZATION

This raises the issue of Peking's ambitious program for economic development, upon which the PRC's military power and much else depends. In the wake of Mao Tse-tung's death and the purge of the "Gang of Four" radical leaders in 1976, a new campaign was launched to achieve what was termed the "four modernizations." It is hoped that a concerted effort for the remainder of the century will bring about major advances in agriculture, industry, defense, and science and technology, at which time China will join the ranks of the world's developed societies. The outcome of this campaign is uncertain, but Peking has stated explicitly that "China needs the European Communities' advanced technology and equipment in its drive for realizing the four modernizations" in the shortest possible time.[14]

The import of these remarks is evident with regard to the modernization of industry and agriculture, which involves the provision of equipment and the enhancement of skills in key technological sectors. Western Europe is especially valuable to the Chinese in both these areas: the British, for example, have sold Peking modern commercial jet aircraft and related aviation equipment, and the French have negotiated substantial deals in computer systems and power-generating equipment (including a recent agreement on a nuclear installation). Likewise, the West Germans have closed sales of large-scale steel mills and chemical plants, and the Italians have signed contracts for smaller deals involving construction and transportation equipment. Recently, a shortage of funds and other problems have forced Peking to initiate an economic readjustment in the EC market and elsewhere, involving a reduction in purchases. Even so this is likely only to be a temporary adjustment to a level appropriate to the country's ability to pay.[15] In addition, major efforts have gone into providing the Chinese with sufficient training to back up their program of importing technology. Chinese technicians spend considerable amounts of time at European industrial sites in order to familiarize themselves with new equipment and techniques, and Europeans involved in installations and start-up programs can stay up to two years or so working on-site in China. This exchange of personnel is gradually building up a reservoir of expertise on both sides, and this will help lay the foundations of a long-term, mutually profitable relationship.

In light of the continuing improvement in U.S.-Chinese relations, Western Europe will certainly be faced with growing American competition in the Chinese technological market. In certain areas of high technology such as aerospace equipment, advanced computer systems, and electronic communications, the Europeans will be at a relative disadvantage. But in much industrial and agricultural technology the situation might be just the reverse: the West Germans, for example, are more up to date in basic steel production than the Americans, and the British are ahead of the United States in rail transportation, an important area of growth in China. These are only two examples of the EC's strength in key technological sectors, and European market managers are certain to capitalize on these areas of superiority.[16] The Chinese are aware of these differences between West European and American offerings, and they are eager to keep the European option alive in the interests of economic efficiency and political freedom of action.

As the current Chinese leaders have discovered, however, the importation of technological systems and skills is extremely expensive in today's market. Peking still leans toward paying for imports directly from export earnings, in order to minimize balance of payments deficits and the need for external financing. There is a new willingness to take on some foreign finance debt, but the principle of maximum self-reliance consistent with rapid economic growth still holds. Therefore, some way must be found to pay for an ever-increasing volume of imports, and this leads back to the balance of trade and the problem of import financing. Until recently, the Europeans have shown more interest in providing Peking with substantial lines of credit (on favorable terms) than in opening up the EC to imports from the PRC. This presents serious problems, for growth in two-way trade can only occur if the Chinese have the wherewithal to pay for (not finance) their huge expenditures — actual and potential — in Europe.

In an effort to diversify its foreign markets, Peking intends to develop roughly equal levels of trade with Western Europe, Japan, and the United States. These are to be its major trading partners, although their ranking will fluctuate according to changing circumstances. (Western Europe has usually been second to Japan, but it will probably be surpassed by the United States in 1981.) The rest of the PRC's trade is to be distributed among the COMECON countries (including the Soviet Union) and the third world. Trade surpluses with these areas can in part offset deficits with the OECD (Organization of Economic Cooperation and Development) nations, but not completely, and this has become an issue of growing concern. In six of the seven years between 1973 and 1979, for example, China has run a substantial trade deficit with the EC countries, most notably West Germany.[17] Despite reducing the imbalance in 1980, Peking remains unsatisfied, for it is running deficits with Japan and the United States as well. Thus, while the Chinese are eager to expand their imports from Western Europe, they are equally desirous of reducing the recurring deficit in two-way trade.

In 1975, when Peking became the first Communist country (Belgrade excepted) to recognize the EC, the Chinese expressed strong interest in working out a formal trade agreement that would put China on a most favored nation basis along with other Western, non-Communist nations. This was successfully negotiated in April 1978, and it calls for the expansion of trade between the two sides on a nonpreferential, most favored nation basis over the five-year term of the agreement.[18] Peking's position was enhanced further in 1980 by an extra provision allowing China to enjoy certain trade advantages currently held by third-world nations trading with the EC. The Chinese, in this regard, accepted the Lomé Convention of 1975 between the EC and the developing nations of Africa as basically sound, and were happy to negotiate a similar status with Brussels. These agreements, it is hoped, will provide an effective framework for the gradual expansion of Chinese exports to Western Europe.

Yet, the problem remains essentially a practical one. While there is a growing Chinese appetite for the technological products of the EC, the same cannot be said of the European desire for Chinese exports. Many Chinese sales to EC countries are in peripheral product lines, including textiles, pig bristles, clothespins, and peanuts. On the other hand, the Chinese do sell substantial amounts of metals to Europe, antimony and tungsten, for example, and there is room for expansion in exports of these and other raw materials as well. As Chinese production comes on-stream, petroleum and its by-products might improve China's position in EC markets, although growth will be limited by China's own expanding needs for energy resources. In the meantime, Peking has indicated a desire to increase exports of light manufactured goods, cloth and finished textiles, and specialty foodstuffs. But opposition from protectionist interests in Europe and from other third world countries (which are competing for the same markets) will probably make the Chinese export drive rough going. Even so, pressure from certain EC members and high-technology industries interested in the Chinese market might weaken this opposition, thus affording China an opportunity for new avenues of growth.[19]

It is in the encouragement of more Chinese imports into Europe, and not in the elaboration of favorable finance arrangements, that the potential for increased Sino-European trade will be tapped. This is now recognized by the EC, which organized an ambitious EEC-China Business Week in Brussels in the spring of 1981. This event, which involved extensive participation from both sides, focused on the need to develop Chinese manufacturing capabilities and marketing strategies in the EC's highly competitive sales environment.[20] Without a steady growth in exports to Europe and other key markets, Peking's current modernization drive will be starved of the foreign reserves critical to its success.

REGIONAL AND GLOBAL INFLUENCE

China's leaders are determined, on the basis of the realization of its enormous economic and military potential, to achieve for their country a greater role in world affairs. They are seeking an international position fully commensurate with their present strength. Beyond the Asian region, the Chinese aspire to a genuine global role, not in the sense that they will be able to dictate policy in remote corners of the world, but only that their opinions will count in determining outcomes of importance to them.

For the moment, however, Peking is content to strengthen its position gradually, and in this undertaking Western Europe plays a significant role. In East Asia and the Western Pacific, for example, an informal agreement on China's preeminence has become the cornerstone of the new international order in the region. Continuing goodwill and even cooperation on the part of the West, Europe, and the United States alike, now serve as legitimizing devices for growing Chinese influence. Peking's harmonious relationship with the British in Hong Kong is highly suggestive in this regard. London has in effect conceded Chinese sovereignty over the colony, and on this basis Peking has adopted a very positive attitude toward British interests. (Likewise, Washington has acknowledged Peking's claim to sovereignty over Taiwan, thus paving the way for closer U.S.-Chinese relations in the Pacific.) Seen in this light, a cooperative policy toward Western Europe reinforces Peking's position as the leading capital of Asia, radiating Chinese influence and, on rare occasions (as in Vietnam in 1979), Chinese power to all corners of the region. Only the Russians are seriously challenging this arrangement, as is evidenced in their steady growth in power in Asia, their proposal in 1969 for a new Asian collective security system, and their persistent attacks on what they perceive (and with some justification) to be an emerging Chinese-Western condominium in the area.[21]

In their quest for a global role for China, Europe fits admirably into the Peking leadership's views on the main currents in contemporary world politics. The Chinese do not regard the countries of Western Europe, either singly or together in the EC, as constituting a "world power." Rather, Europe is described as a "center of world politics," i.e., the major contradiction in world politics today, namely, the struggle between Soviet imperialism and the forces of anti-hegemonism (anti-Soviet forces), takes on its most acute form in Europe. Accordingly, the West European states are urged to look to their defenses in face of the alleged Soviet threat, the main strategy behind which is seen as "a feint to the East in order to attack in the West." The Chinese argue that Moscow's major preoccupation is its power relationship with the United States and its major allies in Europe, and not with China and the East. Participation in the affairs of Europe at the expense of the Soviet Union thus provides Peking with an opportunity to play a critical role at the epicenter of the contemporary international system. Peking's leaders are conscious of the critical role they played during the upheavals in Poland and Hungary in 1956, and they are desirous once again of exercising their influence in Europe. Although at present their resources are limited, they have obviously decided that Europe should be a major zone of concentration in their projection of a global role.

Western Europe fits neatly into Peking's evolving world view, but there are, in addition, certain intangible factors that make this region especially interesting to the Chinese. As the birthplace of the modern international system, Europe has an influence (or at least a prestige) that often goes beyond the actual power of the major states involved. Likewise, European diplomacy remains a factor of considerable importance among the developed nations, and London and Paris can still play significant roles in the third world. For example, Peking is aware that Britain still has great influence in Southeast Asia, and this could be used to China's advantage in combating Soviet powers in the area.[22] Peking thus seeks to establish new points of leverage in Europe itself and, through these, in parts of the developing world still amenable to European influence.

Finally, it should be noted that the Chinese see significant historical parallels between Western Europe and their own country. They regard China as the prototype of all Asian culture, and likewise acknowledge Europe as the font of modern Western civilization. Indeed, a major theme in recent Chinese history is the clash between these two traditions and the need for a reconciliation, and even synthesis, between them. In this view, the cultures of both the Soviet Union and the United States are regarded merely as offshoots from the main European stem, just as Japan and Korea represent variations of the Chinese tradition. Yet, the Chinese are aware that, despite their historical preeminence, both China and Europe were humbled during the twentieth century, and are striving for positions of influence in the new world order of the future. From this perspective, Chinese interest in Western Europe is not surprising, and, other things being equal, this will make the region of special importance to Peking's foreign-policy makers.[23]

CONCLUSIONS

It is now apparent that the hiatus in Chinese-West European relations after 1949 should be regarded as a temporary aberration due to the pressures of the cold war. Neither side had the will or the means to resist the exclusionist policies of the superpowers, and their own diplomatic relations were allowed to wither. In the early 1960s this situation began to change, and since then Chinese policy toward Western Europe has become increasingly positive, as has the European response. Today, both sides are more able to develop policies based on their own national interests without the need to seek approval in Washington or Moscow.[24]

As we enter the 1980s, the Chinese appear determined to achieve a position of world level power, wealth, and influence by the early part of the twenty-first century. It is likely that Peking's policy toward Western Europe will play an important role in the furtherance of this ambitious goal. Indeed, China has, at least in the short run, more to gain than do the EC nations, and to this extent the relationship is somewhat asymmetrical. Still, in the long term, good relations with China will prove increasingly valuable to the Europeans in their search for a voice in world affairs distinct from, and possibly at odds with that of the superpowers.

Despite current trends, various unpredictable factors could possibly weaken the growing links between China and Western Europe. Peking's interest in Europe would, of course, diminish considerably if there were a recurrence of an isolationist mood reminiscent of the Cultural Revolution in the late 1960s. Likewise, a resurgence of leftism in Chinese foreign policy, with an attendant hostility toward the capitalist (or even democratic socialist) states of the EC, would also lead to a rapid decline in Sino-European ties. Either possibility seems remote, so attention must focus on other avenues of change. A substantial improvement in relations with Moscow, leading to Peking's recognition of Soviet hegemony in Europe, and its abandoning of an independent policy there, does not appear to be in the cards. Also unlikely are the chances of a deepening rapprochement between the EC states and the Soviet Union, to the extent that Peking is in effect frozen out and denied the opportunity for an active policy in the region.[25]

Deterioration in Sino-American relations over an outside issue (in Southeast Asia, for instance) might produce a situation where Chinese influence in Western Europe is excluded by Washington, its NATO allies, or, perhaps, both of them acting in concert. Nonetheless, in many important regions and issues, for example, the Middle East and world oil supplies, Chinese policies might be closer to the EC's position than that of the United States. In such a situation, European leaders would probably resist any attempt by Washington to drag them into a serious dispute with Peking. As the international system becomes more pluralistic and open-ended, the traditional alliances of the past cannot be taken for granted. Responses to Chinese foreign policies will be based increasingly on calculated self-interest, which might preclude the possibility of American-European harmony on certain issues.

As Hua Guofeng's visit to various key EC countries in the fall of 1979 suggests, the Chinese are investing heavily in the European connection,[26] and relations are likely to remain strong, to the mutual benefit of both sides. Peking is hopeful that Europe can be persuaded to judge Chinese foreign policy initiatives on their own merits, free from superpower dictates or pressures. On their part, the Europeans are happy to accommodate the Chinese in this goal, for it largely coincides with their own perspectives. In this respect Peking's recent policies have fallen on highly fertile ground, and the Chinese-West European connection has been restored with considerable vigor. Barring the unforeseen, it is likely to become an increasingly important dimension of world politics in the 1980s.

NOTES

1. China is also pursuing an active policy in Eastern Europe, especially toward the Balkan states. A useful survey is Stephen J. Morris, "Chinese Policy Toward Eastern Europe Since 1968," *Contemporary China* 2, no. 3 (Fall 1978): 10-29.

2. For an interesting discussion of this issue, broadly conceived, see Daniel Bell, "The Future World Disorder: The Structural Context of Crises," *Foreign Policy* 27 (Summer 1977): 109-35.

3. Chinese exhortations in this regard were originally directed against both the United States and the Soviet Union, but since the Sino-American rapprochement of 1971-72 Peking has directed its hostility principally toward Moscow. See Dick Wilson, "China and the European Community," *China Quarterly* 56 (October-December 1973): 649-50.

4. For an excellent account of the historical background, see Giovanni Bressi, "China and Western Europe," *Asian Survey* 12, no. 10 (October 1972): 819-45.

5. The "three worlds" theory was first enunciated by Deng Xiaoping on April 10, 1974, in a speech to the UN General Assembly. The text is in *Peking Review*, April 19, 1974, pp. 6-11.

6. For further details, see George P. Jan, "The Ministry of Foreign Affairs in China Since the Cultural Revolution," *Asian Survey* 17, no. 6 (June 1977): 513-29. In the Ministry of Trade there is a West European section within the third bureau that is responsible for overall trade with the West, excluding Japan.

7. For a typical commentary, see *Beijing Review*, January 10, 1980, pp. 14-16.

8. Lately, Peking has argued that Soviet "aggression and expansion" have fostered a greater degree of cohesion and strength within NATO. *Beijing Review*, December 29, 1980, pp. 9-10.

9. On Peking's improving relationships with the Eurocommunist parties, see Richard Breeze, "Comrades Kiss and Make Up," *Far Eastern Economic Review*, March 28, 1980, pp. 33-34.

10. Despite Haig's initiative, U.S. arms sales to China might be impeded by Peking's open hostility to similar sales to Taiwan. *Beijing Review*, June 22, 1981, pp. 11-12.

11. Two preliminary reviews of Chinese-West European arms negotiations are Paul H. B. Godwin, "China and the Second World: The Search for Defence Technology," *Contemporary China* 2, no. 3 (Fall 1978): 3-9; and William T. Tow and Douglas T. Stuart, "China's Military Turns to the West," *International Affairs*, Spring 1981, pp. 286-300.

12. The question of a coordinated West European arms sales policy toward China is discussed briefly in Lawrence Freedman, *The West and the Modernization of China*, Chatham House Papers 1 (London: Royal Institute of International Affairs, 1979), pp. 35-37.

13. For details on the Dutch submarine deal with Taiwan, see "Holland in Asia," *Far Eastern Economic Review*, January 2, 1981, pp. 56-58.

14. Zhou Cipu, "China and the European Communities: Growing Economic and Trade Relations," *Beijing Review*, March 16, 1979, pp. 23-24.

15. Despite Peking's "economic readjustment," the European Commission remains optimistic about the prospects for EC-China trade. See the recent appraisal, "EEC/China: Trade with China Flourishing," *European Report* 704 (July 23, 1980): External Relations, pp. 1-4.

16. For example, see the listing of the chief projects the British have been working on in John Elliott, "British Prospects in China," *Financial Times*, March 9, 1979.

17. Peking's deficit in 1979 amounted to US$1,042 million, out of a total two-way trade of $4,716 million. See the tables in the *Direction of Trade Yearbook 1973-79* (Washington, D.C.: International Monetary Fund, 1980), pp. 60-61.

18. The official text of this agreement is in "The People's Republic of China and the European Community," *Europe Information: External Relations* 17 (Brussels: Commission of the European Communities, 1979).

19. For a cautious appraisal of the scope and future prospects for China's trade with Western Europe, see Freedman, *The West and the Modernization of China*, pp. 23-31.

20. For coverage of this event, see "EEC and China: Still Friends," *The Economist*, April 4-10, 1981, p. 45; and "EEC-China Business Week," *Beijing Review*, April 20, 1981, p. 9.

21. See, for example, "Peking's Foreign Policy: Hegemonism and Alliance with Imperialism," *International Affairs* (Moscow) (March 3, 1980): 45-57.

22. King C. Chen, ed., *China and the Three Worlds* (White Plains, N.Y.: M. E. Sharp, 1979), p. 150.

23. Europeans are also conscious of these historical parallels. As Christopher Soames, the EC Commission vice-president, stated in 1975 when China decided to recognize the EC: "Both of us a people of yesterday, both of us a people of tomorrow." Soames is quoted in Dick Wilson, "China Comes to Brussels," *European Community* 190 (October 1975): 9.

24. To date, however, Peking continues to argue that Western Europe has neither the will nor the means to become "completely independent" of the United States. See Chang Fan, "Western Europe's Independent Role," *Beijing Review*, January 12, 1981, pp. 13-15.

25. Nevertheless, Peking is manifestly hostile to any signs of detente in Europe. See, for example, the stinging attack on Moscow by *Renmin Ribao* Commentator, "Answer to Moscow's 'Detente' Drive," *Beijing Review*, February 25, 1980, pp. 9-10.

26. On Hua's trip, and the future of the new Chinese-West European relationship, see Douglas T. Stuart and William T. Tow, "China's New Diplomacy: The West European Connection," *NATO Review* 28, no. 2 (April 1980): 25-29.

8

CHINA AND EASTERN EUROPE

Karel Kovanda

During the 1960s the erstwhile "socialist camp" disintegrated, ripped right down the middle by the Sino-Soviet split. As the rift between the two Communist giants expanded, most East European countries rallied to the Soviet side. Later in the decade, as China went through the convulsions of the Cultural Revolution, she actually ceased to consider these countries socialist. That attribute she has since reserved for herself — and for a handful of other countries, including, in Europe, Albania and Rumania. Yugoslavia joined this select group in 1977.

The three worlds theory considers these countries, socialist even by Chinese standards, as members of the third world. The Soviet Union's allies — the German Democratic Republic (GDR), Poland, Czechoslovakia, Hungary, and Bulgaria — are classified as second world countries. This is "loyalist Eastern Europe."

This chapter will examine the subtle changes that the Chinese attitude toward these nations has undergone. During the Cultural Revolution, it was one of indifference; but that has since given way to solidarity with mass popular movements against the Soviets, and eventually to an appreciation of difficulties, especially in economic relations, that East European regimes themselves have with Soviet policies. Here lie China's opportunities. I will finally offer some observations on the delicate question of China's contacts with organized opposition in East European countries.

This chapter deals predominantly with *Chinese* attitudes toward the "loyalist countries," and touches only parenthetically and tangentially on the opposite side of the relationship. Much more research effort would be required to deal with that dimension, a project that perhaps remains to be accomplished in the future.

BACKGROUND

The first decade of the People's Republic's existence saw China's relationship with Soviet allies in Eastern Europe dovetail that with the Soviet Union itself. During this period of close cooperation, China became a leading trading partner of Eastern European countries, especially of those that were in a position to help build her industrial base, and close political ties developed as well.

For the Chinese, Eastern Europe was truly terra incognita. It was only during the 1950s, for example, that the study of East European languages was first introduced in Peking, in the First Foreign Language Institute. Unfamiliar with the area and its problems, the Chinese as a rule deferred to Soviet judgment. One consequence was that the Yugoslavs, who after their split with the Cominform in 1948 had hoped for some support from China, instead had their hopes dashed, although there would have existed good reasons for the two "home-grown" parties to explore possibilities of cooperation.[1]

China offered advice when difficulties developed, e.g., urging the Soviet Union to keep out of Poland in 1956 and, conversely, to intervene in Hungary. But she generally recognized this part of the world as being in the Soviet Union's backyard.

The Sino-Soviet split saw Eastern European socialist countries, except for Albania, fall in behind the Soviet lead and break off most relations with China. Eastern European technicians were withdrawn from China in 1960, together with Soviet ones. After the polemics broke out into the open in the early 1960s, the Soviet argumentation was faithfully reproduced in East European media. Rumania was alone in publicizing both sides of the argument, e.g., in the celebrated exchange of letters between the Central Committees of the two large adversary parties, in a determined and remarkably successful effort to preserve some neutrality in the conflict.[2] But apart from Albania the outcast and Rumania the maverick, all other countries loyally continued to follow the Soviet lead.

China still recognized them as socialist, though as not much more than Soviet appendages. Some of them, notably Czechoslovakia, appeared to be more anti-Chinese than others. Thus big play was given in China to the expulsion of Xinhua correspondents from Prague in 1963;[3] and when the *People's Daily* in 1965 published a selection of anti-Chinese pronouncements from the Soviet and allied press, Czechoslovakia led the pack with 22 items, compared with 13 for the Soviet Union and a meager 2 for Poland.[4]

However, not always did the "loyalist countries" interlock with the Soviet Union precisely. Thus in 1964, the GDR felt threatened by Soviet attempts to improve relations with the Federal Republic of Germany. In a manner that a decade later would become a pattern, China was quick to stick her finger into the crack in East German-Soviet relations, purporting to defend East German national interests.[5]

It has been reported that in another instance, Czechoslovakia's Antonín Novotný felt rattled by the abrupt ouster of his old friend Khrushchev in 1964, and signaled his displeasure to Moscow by, inter alia, temporarily halting the anti-Chinese polemics in the Prague press.[6]

These subtleties do not amount to anything substantial; they left no lasting mark on the generally poor relations between China and the "loyalist countries." They do, however, suggest that even for the closest of Soviet allies there existed some latitude for independent action, short of Rumania's studied neutrality. The extent of that latitude was never fathomed, though, let alone utilized.

The polemic between the two giants was also aimed at public opinion. In this "battle of the minds," the Soviet Union won hands down. In no "loyalist country" did the public find the Chinese argumentation attractive. True, there was a mysterious Polish Communist Party founded in Albania in 1965; and in Prague, there was a tiny group of people around the philosopher Zbyněk Fišer, who in 1968 formed the Association of Marxist Left, with pro-Chinese inclinations.[7] But generally speaking, the public was exceptionally, for once, in agreement with their own leaders, and willing to back the Soviet position.

The reasons for this virtually complete and thus unparalleled support for a Soviet position would deserve a separate study, but insights gained from living in Eastern Europe suggest several. The average East European was interested in the minimum of creature comforts that in the 1960s finally appeared to be attainable. The Soviet position allowed for that, the Chinese did not. The Chinese argument of the inevitability of war was scary, and rejection of peaceful coexistence seemed foolhardy. Most particularly, the continued Chinese praise for Stalin was universally considered abhorrent or, at best, incomprehensible.

And finally, there was the simple matter of rhetoric. In public relations, the Chinese were their own worst enemies, talking only to the converted but hardly even trying to influence the hypothetical waverer. All told, criticizing the Soviet Union from the Left was the last thing Eastern Europeans were ready for. While the Soviets were bad, the Chinese were, or appeared to be, even worse.

With the outbreak of the Cultural Revolution, China wrote off the "loyalist countries" altogether, rejecting them for being as revisionist as the Soviet Union, and occasionally even more so, e.g., when they experimented with forms of economic reform that would decentralize controls over the economy and reintroduce elements of the market mechanism. China no longer considered them socialist. Even internal Chinese translations of documents from party congresses and the like consistently referred to them as "revisionist parties." Thus while the first half of the 1960s saw the loyalists at a distance from China, during the Cultural Revolution they were on the other side of the fence.

SOCIAL-IMPERIALISM

In 1968, China was paying great attention to the upheavals in Western democracies. The French May events were supported by manifestations of millions, and student demonstrations in other countries, including Yugoslavia, received great publicity as well. Developments in "loyalist countries," however, were ignored; conspicuously absent was any coverage of the Polish student demonstrations in the spring of 1968.

However, the Soviet invasion of Czechoslovakia in August 1968 led to a major change in China's position, marked by an effort to gradually improve relations with Eastern Europe. At first, China's support was offered to the Czechoslovak people, embattled against Soviet forces.

The support was selective. The Chinese were wary of anything different from their particular brand of Marxism. Consequently, the Prague Spring itself, the period of democratization that preceded and provoked the invasion, was seen as just another brand of revisionism — inasmuch as any thought was given it at all. China was still intensely preoccupied with her own domestic affairs, and foreign relations in general, let alone foreign relations with unfriendly countries, were not high on the list of priorities. According to information gathered in Peking, detailed accounts of Czechoslovak developments of 1968 were absent even in Chinese internal publications.

China did, however, take note of increasing tension developing between Czechoslovakia and the "Warsaw Five," i.e., the Soviet-led group that in July 1968 invited the Czechoslovak leadership for a dressing-down to Warsaw (the invitation was not accepted) and a month later participated in the actual invasion. Whether China drew any conclusions from this is, however, unclear.

From the Czechoslovak point of view, no matter how far-reaching were the domestic changes implemented at this time, foreign policy remained substantially unaffected, and China was virtually ignored.[8] It has been asserted that some elements of the Prague leadership did suggest seeking contacts with the Peking leadership, possibly with Rumanian mediation; but such ideas were summarily rejected for fears of further antagonizing the Soviets.[9] Both Czechoslovakia and China were too preoccupied with their own domestic problems: the Prague Spring and the Cultural Revolution. These processes were so dissimilar in content, methods, language, and ideology that their participants ignored each other almost totally, although better communications, if practicable, might have been beneficial — certainly to Czechoslovakia.

But if the Prague Spring was just another brand of revisionism, the invasion was a different matter altogether. The Chinese immediately evaluated this brutal instance of interference in the internal matters of another country as a far greater offense than mere revisionism. It was the first major military exercise that the USSR had undertaken beyond its borders since becoming, from the Chinese perspective, completely revisionist, and boded ill for the future. China coined a new term to describe this behavior: social-imperialism.[10]

The invasion provided a major impetus for rethinking the entire framework of China's foreign policy, a rethinking that eventually led to the evolution of the three worlds theory. The Brezhnev doctrine of "limited sovereignty," first invoked in the case of Czechoslovakia, and the Soviet interpretation of "fraternal internationalist aid" portended a menace to China as well as to her European friends. China responded, among other things, by intensifying relations with Rumania; in fact, the Rumanians sought — in vain — Chinese assurances of tangible support in case of another invasion directed against their own country, an eventuality that for some months seemed a definite possibility. Albania demonstratively left the Warsaw Pact, of which it had been only a nominal member for several years, anyway.

China reordered her foreign policy priorities. Now, struggle against the newly recognized menace of "social-imperialism" took precedence over the struggle against mere revisionism. One consequence was a painful reexamination of relations with Yugoslavia, China's long ideological whipping boy. The logic was inescapable: revisionist though Yugoslavia might be, the country had successfully fended off every Soviet effort at domination. The ideological polemic was abated and eventually ceased completely.[11]

Meanwhile, China reserved some very harsh words for the Dubček leadership; not surprisingly, perhaps. These leaders had failed to rouse the nation into armed resistance — and had indeed asked it to stay calm while the tanks were rolling in: the ultimate perfidy of revisionism. Once kidnapped to Moscow, they gave in completely. After they signed the so-called Moscow Communique of August 27, 1968, and the accompanying secret Moscow Protocol, Chou En-lai described them as a "clique of traitors" that had "fallen on their knees and capitulated."[12] The eventual substitution of Gustáv Husák for Alexander Dubček, in April 1969, was passed over in Peking as no more than a "change of horses";[13] only Husák was even more a Soviet "quisling" and "puppet" than Dubček had been.

China's support for the *people* of Czechoslovakia was another matter. The Chinese press was exuberant about their resistance against the occupation: the actual mass rejection of the Soviet troops in August 1968 and every one of the demonstrations that continued intermittently until August 1969. Prominent coverage was given to the aftermath of Jan Palach's self-immolation in January 1969.[14] China hailed all of this activity — providing it was spontaneous, for even her new perception of contradictions between East European people and the Soviet government that had now burst into the open did not allow her to recognize, much less endorse, any opposition that was *organized*, be it by the National Students' Union or the country's trade unions — no matter how antiinvasion and anti-Soviet their activities were. Similarly, the prominent role of the Dubček wing of the party in organizing the secret Vysočany Party Congress in the invasion days and the guiding and mobilizing role of the clandestine broadcasting stations were entirely ignored. China would support the people, but any kind of their representation of necessity had to be revisionist. Recognizing any such representation would have conferred a degree of legitimacy that was more than the Chinese were ready to give to anybody except strict Marxist-Leninists. These, of course, were as scarce as ever.

Other instances of this policy concerned Poland. In December 1970 riots in several Polish cities toppled the regime of Wladyslaw Gomulka. The Chinese considered these events a manifestation of the "contradictions between the Polish people and the Polish revisionist ruling clique," and expressed their solidarity with the struggling Polish workers.[15] In a repeat performance in 1976, a new wave of strikes swept the country. Again it was described in the Chinese press as an "outcome of sharpening contradictions between the Polish people and the ruling clique."[16] But, as in Czechoslovakia of 1968, no mention of organizations was ever made in a Polish context. The only exception was the inconsequential Polish Communist Party of Kazimierz Mijal, whose Central Committee's "Appeal" was excerpted in the Chinese press.[17]

The task of dissecting the concrete, allegedly revisionist, features of Polish reality in 1970 was left to the Albanians.[18] Whether the Chinese were deferring to the local expertise of their European allies or whether they positively did not want to criticize domestic Polish policies, is open to specualtion. It is worth noting though, that during the Prague Spring, the one major article in the Chinese press that attempted to analyze and criticize Czechoslovak developments was also a translation from the Albanian.[19]

These indications suggest a reluctance to speak out on East European domestic issues. Even if one can only speculate about the motivation, the fact remains that there was a second aspect to the Polish struggles; one which for the Chinese was of even greater importance than the country's "revisionism" that so ruffled the Albanians.

COMMON LANGUAGE

While predominantly an internal affairs, the 1970 events in Poland were considered by the Chinese also as a manifestation of the crisis of the "colonial rule of Soviet revisionist social-imperialism in Eastern Europe."[20] In 1976, again the "arch-criminals" behind the Polish crisis were "the revisionist masters of the Kremlin."[21]

There was more. While people in Poland were struggling with higher prices of daily necessities, governments in all "loyalist countries" were struggling with higher prices of energy, imposed by the USSR.

By the mid-1970s, China was in quite a different mood and the targets of her diplomatic efforts were changing. Instead of exclusively courting revolutionary regimes and movements, Peking was opening up to all countries opposing the Soviet Union. Now, the USSR's economic policies were meeting with discontent even among officials of its allies and realizing this, China considerably broadened her interest in Eastern Europe.

In many ways, responding to the issues of Soviet economic pressures was not new. Independent and comprehensive economic development was one of the original issues that in the early 1960s propelled Rumania into its autonomous position within the Soviet bloc — with respect to the Council of Mutual Economic Aid (CMEA), in the Sino-Soviet rift, and even in the Warsaw Pact.

Nevertheless, before adopting her new outlook China had not been very sensitive to troubles that the "loyalist countries" were having with Soviet economic policies.

China now embarked on mining this newly discovered lode of discontent. She noted instances of unequal trade practices between the USSR and its East European partners: buying cheap (e.g., agricultural products from Bulgaria or ships from the GDR) and selling dear; she pointed out that some countries were forced to tailor their production to Soviet needs, and to discontinue production when these needs were satiated, and that some industries were under direct and extremely tight Soviet control, such as the Czechoslovak uranium industry, and so forth.[22]

The major grievance that China reacted to was the steep hike of oil prices. In 1975 the Soviet Union doubled the price for its oil exported to Eastern Europe — and further increases followed. China pointed out that the Soviets were reneging on their contractual obligations, and that their unwillingness and/or inability to supply all the fuel East European countries needed for their planned economic development was wreaking havoc with their planning processes.[23] They even argued that the USSR had first enforced its monopoly of gas and oil supplies onto its CMEA partners, causing some coal-rich nations such as the GDR and Czechoslovakia to neglect their coal industry, and then manipulated oil prices to ensure their subservience.[24]

An important target of Chinese criticism was the CMEA itself, which allegedly serves the interests of Soviet neocolonialism (or social-colonialism, as it has also been dubbed).[25] In 1971, a comprehensive program of economic integration started being implemented within the CMEA, including production, science and technology, foreign trade, currency, and finances. China argues that East European countries have consequently found themselves economically more dependent than ever on the Soviet Union, and that various mechanisms of integration — such as long-term planning, international division of labor, and the loyalists' cooperation and financing of large-scale projects for extracting raw materials in the Soviet Union — deprive CMEA members of resources needed to develop their own national economies, and restrict their sovereignty. "Plunder" is just about the mildest expression the Chinese use to describe these practices.[26]

Conversely, while pointing the finger at the Soviet Union, China pats the loyalist backs for efforts to seek other ways of meeting their requirements and to extricate themselves from their overwhelming economic dependence on the Soviet Union. These especially include efforts to diversify energy sources, to raise the degree of self-sufficiency in grain and in fuels, and to expand ties with countries of the second and the third worlds.[27] Self-sufficiency (or "self-reliance") is of course a favorite Chinese concept, and cooperation of the countries in the second and the third worlds was becoming an ever more important Chinese leitmotif during the 1970s.

In addition to economic issues, China has echoed various East European national aspirations that tend against the Soviet Union. This too is not entirely news. Even in 1964, Mao Tse-tung talked about "the many places occupied by the Soviet Union." The Soviets, he said, "appropriated a part of Rumania. . . . Having cut off a portion of East Germany, they chased local inhabitants into West Germany. They detached a part of Poland, annexed it to the Soviet Union, and gave a part of East Germany to Poland as compensation."[28]

China has since continued to view with understanding occasional Rumanian voices emphasizing the Rumanian character of Bessarabia (now Soviet Moldavia).[29] While she has not directly opposed the postwar European frontiers, except inasmuch as they sanctify the great-power spheres of influence, China has supported German national aspirations for reunification, and no longer (as in 1964) necessarily on East German terms. In 1975, for example, China noted that the new USSR-GDR Treaty of Friendship, Cooperation and Mutual Assistance, signed in October of that year, omitted all references to the aim of reunification of Germany, references that had been contained in the previous 1964 treaty.[30] The aim of the new treaty, according to a Chinese commentary, is to keep Germany "perpetually divided."[31]

One of the most astounding oblique attacks on Soviet postwar East European policy concerned Poland. "It is still within living memory," editorialized the *People's Daily* in 1978, "that after the war, a Soviet Marshal of East European origin was sent by the Soviet Union to an East European country to control the army there, but was finally driven back to Moscow." Thereby, the article argues, the Soviet Union interfered in the internal affairs of another country.[32]

That was an allusion to Marshal K. R. Rokossovsky, who was sent to Poland after the war, only to return to the Soviet Union in the wake of the 1956 unrest in that country. This particular attack suggests that even Stalin's policies are not immune to criticism when China feels it convenient. The Rokossovsky episode was one of scores in which the Soviet Union went against the national interests of Eastern Europe, and China might well bring up others whenever useful in the future.

In another expression of her support for East European nationalism, China reported favorably on a protest movement launched in 1976 in Poland, against proposed constitutional changes that would have linked the country even closer to the Soviet Union.[33] The variety of other areas in which the Soviet Union is trying to get a firmer grip on the "loyalist countries" and which have been brought up by the Chinese includes cooperation in foreign affairs, ideological cooperation, and the military integration of the Warsaw Pact.

The crucial point of China's new attitude toward the "loyalist countries" is this: criticism of their economic and other conditions is aimed, not at the countries themselves, but at the Soviet Union. Their difficulties are seen as being caused not by incorrect domestic policies or by ideological deviations (a line the Albanians would be more likely to adopt) but strictly by the pernicious Soviet influence. Any attempt to scotch it is laudable, no matter what its ideological underpinnings. Prague Spring, if repeated today, would certainly be a most welcome event, even in Chinese eyes, and in private conversations, the Chinese will readily admit as much.

The Chinese position is clear: her original efforts to seek allies among the East European *people*, dating back to the invasion of Czechoslovakia, were broadened during the 1970s to include East European *governments* as well. Furthermore, many of the data and arguments used in Chinese pronouncements are culled directly from East European sources, including high government officials. They are no longer considered "quislings," "puppets," or "revisionist cliques"; now they are potential allies. "Both the *popular struggle* of East European countries against their colonial domination, and the tendency of some *ruling groups* in Eastern Europe to drift apart from the Kremlin" have been recognized.[34]

In highlighting the differences between the "loyalist countries" and the USSR, China is following at least two aims. One is to aggravate the various hairline fractures within the Soviet bloc, thereby seeking to loosen its cohesiveness and gain tactical advantages that can be further exploited. China hopes that these fractures might broaden, and perhaps make some of the "loyalist countries" view China with less animosity (to say the least), while at the same time weakening the Soviet position.

The second aim is connected with China's "special relationship" with Rumania. China's criticism of CMEA, for example, is the same as Rumania's. This is particularly so in economic questions. By highlighting complaints about Soviet economic and integrationist policies, especially when such criticism originates with the loyalists, China helps legitimize Rumania's lack of enthusiasm about these policies, indirectly shielding that country from possible retribution.

China's new accent on differences between not only the people but also the governments of Eastern Europe and the Soviet Union has of course to do with her entire new foreign-political line. This was eventually formulated in the three worlds theory. As elaborated in November 1977,[35] East European countries generally belong to the second world. Rumania, and possibly still Albania, are considered socialist; as such, they belong to the third world, together with underdeveloped nations. Yugoslavia presumably also used to be considered a second world nation, but since the spectacular rapprochement that followed President Tito's 1977 visit to Peking, China acknowledged its socialist character, too, and consequently must have reclassified it as a third world country.

The section of the three worlds theory dealing with the "loyalist countries" deserves to be quoted verbatim:

> The East European countries have never ceased waging struggles against Soviet control. Since the Soviet occupation of Czechoslovakia, the people's resistance has continued to grow. In 1976 the Polish people repeatedly launched widespread movements to protest the inclusion of a provision on the Polish-Soviet alliance in the new Constitution, and there were workers' strikes and demonstrations in which slogans

like "We want freedom," "We want no Russians" were raised. The governments of some East European countries have also shown a more perceptible tendency to oppose Soviet control. There have been open complaints in some articles in their press, for example, "principles of . . . mutual benefit have been violated partially and in varying degrees," there have been statements that the relationship of the East European countries to the Soviet Union "cannot be built on the basis of one socialist country constantly making sacrifices for the benefit of another," and that the attempt to "co-ordinate everything can in practice only lead to 'not coordinating anything' "; and there have been demands as those for "considering the specific interests of each CMEA country" and for maintaining an "independent national economy." As the Soviet Union steps up its contention for world hegemony, Eastern Europe becomes a forward position in Soviet preparations for war against Western Europe and the United States. Soviet control and interference in the East European countries through the Warsaw Treaty Organization has become increasingly intolerable. Thus uneasiness is growing among East European people and the struggle to defend their independence, security and equal rights is gathering momentum.[36]

The strategic line with respect to countries of both the second and the third world is to seek points of common interest and to include these countries, as far as possible, in the united front of the broad antisuperpower, especially anti-Soviet, struggle. There is also a place in this front for the "loyalist countries." China has therefore completely given up criticizing, and thus antagonizing, their governments.

Thus, for example, in 1977 Egypt decided to close down consulates and cultural centers of the USSR and of the "loyalist countries." China hailed the move against the USSR — but did not mention that four other countries were involved as well.[37]

This attitude is obvious also in Chinese propaganda directed exclusively to these countries — the broadcasts of Radio Peking. After several years of preparation, broadcasting in East European languages was initiated in the immediate aftermath of the 1968 invasion of Czechoslovakia. Zhang Xiangshan, director of the Central Broadcasting Administration, explained in a 1979 interview with this writer how the character of the broadcast has changed over the years. During the Cultural Revolution, he said, it was directed exclusively at China's supporters around the world. Since the fall of the Gang of Four, however, it has been gradually changing its orientation so as to appeal to the average listener. In broadcasts to Eastern Europe with which this writer worked for two years, China never criticized leading authorities of the target countries.

Criticism is reserved for the Soviet Union — and for Cuba and Vietnam, considered to be outright Soviet pawns. These countries are attacked openly and mercilessly. But the "loyalist countries," even when they get involved on their side, are spared. East Germany, for example, might be sending military and security advisors to a number of African and Arab countries — but this role has never, to the best of my knowledge, been openly critcized by the Chinese.[38]

This discreetness has yielded some results. Definite shadings were discernible in the positions of the "loyalist countries" vis-á-vis China. Communiques of the most hard-line nations, among them Czechoslovakia and the GDR, would devote an entire paragraph to attacks on China, whereas similar communiques issued by more moderate members, such as Poland and Hungary, would mention China only in one sentence or so.

The measure of success of Chinese efforts is also indirectly suggested by the attacks they are subjected to. Thus Vasil Bil'ak, the international secretary of the Czechoslovak Communist Party and a noted hard-liner, has attacked China precisely for her "differentiated policy" toward East European countries, noting (quite correctly) that it is aimed at "corroding their bonds and isolating them from the Soviet Union."[39]

China's relations with Hungary in particular had warmed up considerably in the mid-1970s. Xinhua News Agency came out with an unusual tribute in 1975, celebrating the thirtieth anniversary of Hungary's liberation from nazism. It spoke highly about Hungary's struggle against nazism and against Czar Nicholas I — and never mentioned the 1956 revolution, suppressed, with Chinese acquiescence, by the Soviet Union.[40] A number of sympathetic reports on Hungary were broadcast by Radio Peking to that country. In fact, since 1978 it seemed very likely that contacts between the two countries would have intensified considerably.[41] Other matters have, however, since thwarted these encouraging developments; I shall return to them in the conclusion.

OPPOSITIONS

Commitment to cooperation with second world countries, even when such cooperation is only a potential matter for the future, leaves the Chinese in a dilemma when it comes to dealing with their internal opposition. Such questions are especially tough in nondemocratic countries where opposition is by definition illegal. How does one acknowledge an opposition without alienating the courted government? The Chinese answer has been to recognize only Marxist-Leninist pro-Chinese organizations (which, however, are nonexistent in the "loyalist countries"). Beyond that, China takes note only of those opposition activities that have a clear anti-Soviet edge, ignoring, at least in public pronouncements, activities directed against the home governments.[42]

As for the "loyalist countries," the Polish petition movement mentioned above serves as one such example, anti-Soviet demonstrations in East Berlin in 1978 are another one.[43] As indicated above, even the mass movements in Poland in 1970 and 1976 were interpreted, at least in part, as anti-Soviet.

The Charter 77 movement in Czechoslovakia is the exception that proves the point. On the eve of the tenth anniversary of the invasion, the Chartists issued a statement declaring the occupation illegal. The statement was duly noted in the Chinese press.[44]

Much more interesting, however, was the Chinese treatment of the charter's original manifesto, issued in January 1977. It met with a worldwide acclaim that even the Chinese could not sensibly ignore. However, the Chinese press hailed it as a manifestation of the people's "resentment against the Soviet occupation and control of the country, and of their determination to fight for political rights." The article in *Peking Review* then went on to point out how the charter was attacked in Soviet media.[45]

The fact is, though, that the Charter 77 was most viciously attacked by Czechoslovak authorities, and that the original manifesto did not even mention the Soviet Union or its occupation of Czechoslovakia. The Chinese had to impute to it certain elements that it did not actually contain. It would seem that if the charter had not been presented as an anti-Soviet document, irrespective of its actual content, it could not have been presented at all.

This indicates exactly how delicate China's East European policy is: trying on the one hand to wean loyalist leaders away from the Soviet Union, while on the other hand, having to recognize the legitimacy of organized struggle against these same leaders, executors of Moscow's will. Strictly speaking, one can interpret the original Charter 77 manifesto the way the Chinese did (i.e., as opposition to the Soviet rule) only if one considers the local Czechoslovak leadership to be an extension of Moscow. This would no doubt be correct to a large extent; but once admitted, there is hardly any point in differentiating the Czech leaders from their Moscow patrons and trying to unite with them against Moscow, as the three worlds theory would dictate.

In the particular case of Czechoslovakia, this is indeed what the Chinese might well have concluded, too. Czechoslovakia, one of the most dogmatic of the loyalist regimes, has waged a particularly vituperative unrelenting verbal war against China. No matter what changes occur in Peking, no matter which people are in the leadership, attacks of Czechoslovak leaders and media never abate. And it just might be that, the three worlds theory notwithstanding, China has written off the Prague leadership as potential allies altogether.

The one indication of this possibility is the particularly cordial relationship that has developed with the Czechoslovak opposition. Contacts have existed at least since 1972. *Listy*, the main journal of the opposition in exile, edited in Rome by Jiří Pelikán, has over the years given substantial, continuous, and on the whole favorable coverage to Chinese affairs. The contacts culminated in the fall of 1979 when Pelikán visited China and held wide-ranging talks with Chinese representatives. (Incidentally, when Pelikán was the president of the International Union of Students in the early 1950s, Hu Yaobang, now chairman of the Chinese Communist Party, was a leading Chinese delegate to this organization.) While no details about the visit are publicly available, its success is apparent from the stridency with which both Czechoslovak and Soviet media attacked it.[46]

Another, more speculative, indication supporting the hypothesis that China might have selected Czechoslovakia for special treatment is the fact that no known contacts exist with the Polish opposition, which is at least as important as that in Czechoslovakia. It is unclear, however, whether the lack of contacts is a result of a conscious political decision based on continuing hopes to improve relations with the Polish leadership, or whether it is a result of incidental factors.

CONCLUSIONS

In addition to the political, anti-Soviet dimension of China's more subtle advances toward the "loyalist countries," China has been demonstrating a greater interest in Eastern European affairs in general. She is exerting a perceptible effort to deal with East European problems on the level of serious scholarship rather than of mere ideological labels. In many respects, contemporary Chinese developments, since the death of Mao Tse-tung and the fall of the Gang of Four, resemble various East European efforts of 15 to 20 years ago to come to grips with their own Soviet-Stalinist heritage, and there is, therefore, ample room for comparing experiences.

One can detect a fresh interest, for example, in problems of the economic reform in Hungary, an interest very relevant to China's own efforts at reforming her system of economic management. The present writer was invited a number of times to lecture on the abortive Czechoslovak economic reform of the mid-1960s and on developments of the Prague Spring in general, invariably meeting with a very sympathetic and interested response. None of the new Chinese research on East European affairs has been made public as yet; but for internal use, the Chinese have translated important reference material such as Z. A. B. Zeman's *Prague Spring*, the "Last Testament" by Josef Smrkovský, one of Dubček's top lieutenants, and probably other writings as well.

In the late 1970s, China might have finally been reaching for the first fruits of her new appreciation of East European realities, possibly in the shape of considerably improved relations with Hungary. Such an improvement would have given some useful balance to the extraordinarily good relations China now enjoys with Yugoslavia and Rumania,[47] relations which the Soviet Union no doubt considers exceedingly egregious. However, so far, China has gone empty-handed, as a result of events far removed from Eastern Europe.

The new variable was Vietnam. The increasing hostilities between China and Vietnam, and China's 1979 military punitive action, pitted all "loyalist countries," without exception, on the Vietnamese side. They all stiffened their stance against China. Even Hungary's János Kádár lashed out against China in unusually harsh terms, forgoing his earlier promising prudence.[48] Czechoslovakia, ever the preeminent hard-liner, attacked not only China but also Yugoslav coverage of the conflict[49] (which, for that matter, certainly did not wholeheartedly endorse the Chinese position). As long as China's conflict with Vietnam is acute, her efforts in Eastern Europe will be hamstrung.

The wave of strikes that started in early July 1980 in Poland seemed for a few weeks to have been of the same nature as the earlier wave in 1976: a protest against higher prices and lack of food. However, the formation six weeks later of an interfactory strike committee in Gdansk transcended in its significance anything that Poland had seen in recent decades. The Solidarity labor union and the process of renewal have become entrenched features of Polish politics, and only a Soviet invasion or internal armies could dislodge them.

The many parallels between the Polish developments and the Prague Spring are obvious. Contrary to the 1968 situation, the Chinese press reports about Poland have been relatively evenhanded. True to form, they usually cover a crisis on the Polish domestic scene only after it is over; but then it can be used as an illustration for the main line of the Chinese argument that "the Polish people are fully capable of solving their own problems."[50]

The Chinese view of the Polish reform movement itself is ambiguous. On the one hand, it parallels some aspects of China's domestic policies. Fair coverage is thus given to aspects such as abuse of official power, the retiring of discredited leaders, and to the progress toward economic reform.[51] On the other hand, the existence and strength of Solidarity is probably not viewed with the same equanimity. That is a phenomenon the Chinese would not care to have emulated in China, and it is presented practically as a result of the Polish workers' need for self-defense,[52] implying perhaps that had the authorities been competent, there would have been no need for such a forceful movement emerging from beyond the officially controlled framework of society. Interestingly, the Catholic church, which is playing an eminent role in the reform movement, is ignored altogether, no doubt a reflection of strained relations between Peking and the Vatican, Polish pope or not.

The ambivalence of the Chinese evaluation of Poland•is reflected in the formulation that people may take "different stands" and hold "different points of view" concerning these events,[53] and let's not argue about who's right. Crucially, however, no matter how one views the situation, it is strictly a Polish affair; that is to say, it is no business of the Soviet Union. As Premier Zhao Ziyang remarked, "Poland's domestic problems must be solved by the Polish people themselves."[54]

Here, the parallels with Czechoslovakia in 1968 are explicit and invoked often — with respect to Soviet threats, fabricated sensationalist news items, maneuvers, party-to-party threatening letters, and so forth. The Chinese people, needless to say, "support the Polish people in their just struggle to safeguard their independence and sovereignty."[55] And yet, such protestations aside, it is entirely unclear what an actual invasion would mean for China.[56]

Poland represents a windfall for China, a sample of centrifugal tendencies of "loyalist countries" coming to fruition much faster than anyone had expected. The fruit is not quite ripe, though. Poland's autonomy in domestic affairs has not yet affected her foreign policy — if indeed it ever will. But if the Soviets tolerate developments in Poland much longer, that country's new brand of national communism will sooner or later open a dialogue with China's brand. China's efforts to develop a new sensitivity toward the peculiarities of Eastern Europe will then have paid off. But the martial law declared by the Polish government in December 1981 has greatly changed the situation.

NOTES

1. See Ross Johnson, "Yugoslavia and the Sino-Soviet Conflict, 1948-1974," *Studies in Comparative Communism* 7, nos. 1-2 (Spring-Summer 1974): 184-203. Cf., e.g., Robin Remington, "China's Emerging Role in Eastern Europe," in *The International Politics of Eastern Europe*, ed. Charles Gati (New York: Praeger, 1976), pp. 82-102; and M. Kamil Dziewanowski, "China and East Europe," *Survey*, no. 77 (Autumn 1970), pp. 59-74.

2. For a history of Sino-Rumanian relations, see Robert R. King, "Rumania and the Sino-Soviet Conflict," *Studies in Comparative Communism* 5, no. 4 (Winter 1972): 373-93. A detailed look at the minute differences perceptible in the approach of European Communist countries toward China in October 1959 can be found in "Eastern Europe Looks at China," *East Europe* 9, no. 10 (October 1960): 4-8.

3. *Peking Review*, July 26, 1963, p. 4; August 2, 1963, p. 5; August 30, 1963, p. 9.

4. Ibid., November 12, 1965.

5. Ibid., September 11, 1964. For a detailed analysis of East German-Chinese relations almost up to the Cultural Revolution, see Carola Stern, "Relations between the DDR and the Chinese People's Republic, 1949-1965," in *Communism in Europe*, vol. 2, ed. W. E. Griffith (Cambridge: MIT Press, 1966), pp. 97-154. See also Hemen Ray, "Peking und Pankow — Chinas Engagement in Osteuropa und das Verhaltnis zur DDR," *Europa Archiv*, no. 16 (1963), pp. 621-28; "Die ideologische Achse Peking-Pankow," *Aussenpolitik*, no. 6 (1962), pp. 820-26; and "Deutschlandpolitik des Kommunistischen China," *Politik und Zeitgeschichte*, April 19, 1969, pp. 3-27.

6. "Moravus," *Listy* (Rome), no. 6 (1971). For a detailed treatment of Sino-Czechoslovak relations, see Karel Kovanda, "Die Tschechoslowakei und China," in *Opposition ohne Hoffnung?* ed. Pelikán and Wilke (Hamburg: Rowohlt, 1979), pp. 115-33.

7. Cf. *Rudé právo*, May 11, 1968.

8. The most authoritative word about this comes from Jiří Hájek, Czechoslovakia's foreign minister of the time. He writes that "the Czechoslovak Communist Party's attitude of reserve vis-á-vis China was based on that country's negative attitude, and on concern not to do anything that the Soviet Union, which was particularly sensitive to the Chinese question, could interpret as a provocation." *Praga: Diez años después* (Barcelona: Laia, 1979), p. 151n. Translated from the French, Paris: Seuil, 1978.

9. "Moravus"; Galia Golan, *Reform Rule in Czechoslovakia, 1968-69* (Cambridge: At the University Press, 1973), p. 204n.

10. The term "social-imperialist" was first employed by Chou En-lai in his address at Rumania's National Day reception in Peking, August 23, 1968. See *Peking Review*, August 23, 1968, Supplement, p. iv.

11. For details of the first stage of Sino-Yugoslav rapprochement, see Johnson, "Yugoslavia and the Sino-Soviet Conflict." For a broader view of the shift in China's position at this time, see Ishwer C. Ojha, "A Comparison of China's Policies Toward Western and Eastern Europe Covering the Period After the Czechoslovakian 'Invasion,' " *Asian Quarterly*, no. 2 (1965), pp. 111-25.

12. *Peking Review*, September 6, 1968, p. 7.

13. Ibid., May 6, 1969, p. 48.

14. Ibid., September 6, 1968, p. 9; October 25, 1968, p. 8; November 8, 1968, p. 29; November 15, 1968, p. 29; February 7, 1969, p. 15; see also, e.g., January 25, 1974, p. 14.

15. Ibid., December 25, 1970, p. 17.

16. Ibid., July 2, 1976, p. 21.

17. Ibid., July 16, 1976, pp. 26-27.

18. Ibid., January 1, 1971, p. 23.

19. *Renmin Ribao*, August 10, 1968.

20. *Peking Review*, December 25, 1970, p. 17.

21. Ibid., July 9, 1976, p. 8.

22. These issues receive constant attention in the Chinese press. For a sampling of articles, cf., e.g., ibid., April 13, 1973, p. 17; January 4, 1974, p. 27; June 14, 1974, p. 18; July 5, 1974, p. 24; August 8, 1975, p. 32; November 12, 1976, p. 24. China was on the other hand hardly in the position to help out. For China's trade with Eastern Europe, see, e.g., Ernst Hageman, "The Foreign Trade of the PRC with East European Countries," *Soviet and East European Foreign Trade* 7, no. 1 (Spring 1972): 56-86 [originally in *Vierteljahrshefte zur Wirtschaftsforschung*, no. 1 (1971)].

23. *Peking Review*, February 21, 1975, p. 20, for the GDR; June 6, 1975, p. 29, for Czechoslovakia.

24. Ibid., February 21, 1975, p. 20; *Beijing Review*, August 24, 1979, pp. 22-23.

25. *Red Flag*, no. 11 (1977).

26. There is an unending stream of articles dealing with the CMEA. Cf., e.g., *Peking Review*, November 29, 1968, p. 24; March 28, 1975, p. 19; June 6, 1975, p. 22; October 10, 1975, p. 17; June 4, 1976, p. 21, February 4, 1977, p. 22; August 19, 1977, p. 41; December 16, 1977, p. 23.

27. Cf. ibid., November 19, 1976, p. 31; and *Beijing Review*, February 9, 1979, p. 29, on increasing ties between the two Germanies; *Peking Review*, September 26, 1975, p. 28, on grain production; ibid., July 25, 2975, p. 12, on lignite production in the GDR; June 17, 1977, p. 29, on CMEA countries' ties with the West.

28. In an interview with Japanese journalists, quoted, e.g., in W. E. Griffith, *Sino-Soviet Relations 1964-1965* (Cambridge: MIT Press, 1967), p. 28.

29. Cf., e.g., *Peking Review*, April 23, 1976, p. 32.

30. Ibid., October 24, 1975, p. 22.

31. Ibid., November 14, 1975, p. 15. For interesting remarks concerning the interplay between Sino-Soviet and Soviet-German relations, see Joytirmoy Banerjee, "The Asian Dimension of East German Foreign Policy," *China Report* 15, no. 4 (July-August 1979): 31-39.

32. *Peking Review*, July 7, 1978, p. 24.

33. Ibid., February 13, 1976, p. 30.

34. Ibid., September 3, 1976, p. 28 (emphasis added). Stephen J. Morris makes a similar argument in "Chinese Policy Toward Eastern Europe Since 1968," *Contemporary China* 2, no. 3 (Fall 1978): 10-29.

35. *Peking Review*, November 4, 1977, pp. 10-41.

36. Ibid., pp. 30-31. References omitted.

37. Ibid., December 16, 1977, p. 28.

38. More recently, however, the Chinese press did mention military treaties that the GDR has signed with South Yemen and Ethiopia. Cf. *Beijing Review*, January 21, 1980, p. 11.

39. *Rudé právo*, March 20, 1978.

40. *Peking Review*, May 2, 1975, p. 26.

41. Note also the report on the remarkable success of the Chinese pavilion at a Budapest industrial exhibition, in ibid., November 11, 1977, p. 29. Bohdan O. Szpurowicz suggests that China's relations with Hungary are "less cordial." This seems to be an

unsubstantiated "hunch" in an otherwise thorough review of "The Sino-COMECON Connection," *Contemporary China* 2, no. 3 (Fall 1978): 30-63.

42. According to Dieter Heinzig, Peking informally approached East European countries in early 1978 with proposals to improve relations. See his "Sowjetisch-Chinesische Beziehungen nach Mao Tse-Tungs Tod," *Bundesinstitut für Ostwissenschaftliche und Internationale Studien*, July 1978.

43. *Peking Review*, October 21, 1977, p. 29.

44. Ibid., September 1, 1978, p. 29.

45. Ibid., February 4, 1977, p. 29.

46. *Rudé právo*, November 27, 1979; *Pravda*, November 30, 1979. It is a matter of public record that in the early 1950s, when Pelikán was the president of the International Union of Students, Hu Yaobang, now secretary-general of the CCP Central Committee and member of the Standing Committee of the Politbureau, was a leading Chinese delegate to this organization. Another expression of affinity between the Czechoslovak opposition and Chinese authorities concerns Frantisek Kriegel. Kriegel was the only member of Dubcek's leadership not to sign the humiliating Moscow Protocol in 1968 and until his death was a guiding spirit of internal opposition in Czechoslovakia. His death in early December 1979 was noted by the Xinhua News Agency. In addition, his picture is exhibited in the Museum of the Chinese Revolution; from 1939 to 1942, Kriegel participated as a physician in the Anti-Japanese War in China.

47. For a review of China's recent relations with these two countries, see David A. Andelman, "China's Balkan Strategy," *International Security*, Winter 1979/80, pp. 60-79.

48. Radio Free Europe, "Hungarian Situation Report," no. 19 (October 5, 1979).

49. Idem., "Czechoslovak Situation Report," no. 8 (February 28, 1979).

50. First in *Beijing Review*, September 15, 1980, and then as a refrain in most articles about Poland.

51. See, e.g., ibid., November 24, 1980.

52. Ibid.

53. Xinhua Commentator, December 6, 1980, as reported in *Beijing Review*, December 15, 1980. Practically the same formulation appears also in *Red Flag*, no. 24 (1980).

54. *Beijing Review*, April 13, 1981, pp. 7-8; also June 22, 1981, p. 10.

55. *Renmin Ribao*, June 16, 1981; see also Guo Ping's analysis in *Beijing Review*, July 13, 1981, pp. 26-27.

56. See the conclusions of Jonathan D. Pollack's "Chinese Global Strategy and Soviet Power," *Problems of Communism*, January-February 1981, pp. 54-69.

9

CHINA AND LATIN AMERICA: A "LAST FRONTIER"

Robert L. Worden

CHINA, THE THIRD WORLD, AND LATIN AMERICA

Evolution in China's View of the Third World

The People's Republic of China has long sought an antisuperpower constituency in the nonindustrialized nations of Asia, Africa, and Latin America, Communist and non-Communist countries alike, and especially among the more revolutionary and newly independent regimes. China's influence-seeking effort expanded geographically, first in Asia, then to Africa, and, last, to Latin America, during the first decade of the People's Republic.

Initially, China cooperated with the Soviet Union in trying to consolidate the socialist camp, followed by a period of seeking peaceful coexistence with non-Communist regimes in a world viewed by Mao Tse-tung as one of "intermediate zones" between the two opposing camps. Still heavily influenced by its own revolutionary struggle, support of the wars of national liberation was a large part of China's emerging third world policy in the late 1950s and throughout the 1960s. As domestic politics became more militant during the Cultural Revolution, so too did China tend to view the entire third world as a great battleground against the superpowers, the Western "imperialists," and the local "reactionary" regimes.

In 1974, China proclaimed an end to the "camp" system and came to view the international scene in terms of "three worlds." China was clearly and consistently self-identified as a third world nation. Deng Xiaoping's 1974 elucidation of Mao's "theory of the three worlds" was a new call for a broad

130

united front against the Soviet Union at a time when China was involved in a rapprochement with the United States. It was an evolution that provided China with a rationale for cooperating with all parts of the second and third worlds that were willing, regardless of the class nature of the regimes. It contributed to the post-Cultural Revolution policy of establishing government-to-government contacts in lieu of attempting to support revolutionary movements. Throughout the 1970s, China generally followed the lead of other third world countries in identifying major issues such as calls for a new economic order, nuclear-weapon-free zones, law of the sea, and regional integration, and gave these issues avid support.

The post-Mao period has been characterized by the Chinese Communist Party's line emphasizing comprehensive modernization, a move that meant developing new ties with the second world while sacrificing influence in the revolutionary countries of the third. China did not alter its self-proclaimed status as a developing country of the third world and, in the 1980s, continued to insist that its "fundamental interests are identical with those of other third world countries." While admitting that Mao committed "some mistakes in his later years," his theory of the differentiation of the three worlds was declared "correct" in 1981 and was to continue as a guiding principle for China's foreign policy.[1]

Latin American Connections

Latin America was long the area of least interest in China's post-1949 foreign policy. During the first 20 years of the People's Republic the region seemed nearly impenetrable to the Chinese because of traditional U.S. influences and the existence there of numerous conservative regimes. It was a region of nations that had fought their revolutions 150 years earlier and that was quite distant from China and any of its then-kindred states. If anything, Latin America was the "backyard" — the *houyuan* — of the United States and its leaders were more in tune with the affairs of the industrialized world in China's viewpoint. Indeed, until 1957, Latin America was not even accorded a place in China's developing world aphorism, "Asia and Africa."

The addition of Latin America to China's third world viewpoint was an indication of its recognition of the area not as a willing partner of the developed world but as an area which, as China discerned, was in need of "national liberation." The Cuban revolution awakened China's interest in the region and led its policy makers to focus on revolutionary movements throughout Latin America. China's primary Latin American policy throughout these two decades (support of the "wars of national liberation") was decidedly based on anti-U.S. premises.

Despite the Cuban connection (which became tenuous and unfriendly by the mid-1960s) and propaganda support of left-wing causes in Latin America,

Chinese contacts in the first 20 years were few and of least importance when compared with the rest of the third world. The ideological dispute between China and the Soviet Union further divided loyalties within the already fragmented revolutionary movements in Latin America and lessened opportunities for influential contacts between the Chinese and Communist and leftist forces in the region. However, this factor eventually came to present a more urgent reason for increased Chinese activity in Latin America — the need to respond to a growing Soviet presence there.

China's ability to develop relations with Latin America has been greatly enhanced during the 1970s and 1980s "normalization" period due to contacts in the United Nations General Assembly and through participation in or observation of Chinese representatives at such Latin American issue oriented conferences as the UN Law of the Sea Conference (one session of which was held in Caracas), meetings of the Agency for the Prohibition of Nuclear Weapons in Latin America (China is a signatory of Protocol II of the Treaty for the Prohibition of Nuclear Weapons in Latin America), and sessions of the UN Industrial Development Organization (a session of which was held in Lima).

Improved relations with the United States led to augmentation of the American and Oceanian Affairs Department of the Ministry of Foreign Affairs and the Third Bureau of the Ministry of Foreign Trade, which also are responsible for Latin American relations. Of the 14 diplomatic missions in Latin America as of 1981, all were staffed at the ambassadorial level. Exchanges of vice ministerial and higher level delegations steadily increased during the 1970s and early 1980s although visits were unbalanced with considerably more Latin American leaders visiting China than vice versa.[2]

CHINA'S STRATEGIC VIEW OF LATIN AMERICA

Superpower Contention

The competition between the United States and the Soviet Union for influence in Latin America is considered by China as fierce and long-range. After years of dominance in the region, the United States is seen as having been put in an increasingly unfavorable situation due to the "mounting demands" of the Latin American countries for political independence and economic self-determination, the increasing influence of Western Europe and Japan in Latin America, and the "infiltration" into the region by the Soviet Union.[3]

Most serious in the Chinese viewpoint is that Latin America, "which has always been considered by the United States as within its 'sphere of influence' and its 'strategic backyard,' has in the 1980's become a target of the Soviet Union's offensive global strategy."[4] China sees a Moscow-Havana axis taking advantage of the U.S. decline in influence and strength in Latin America to "penetrate" the region, especially into Central America and the Caribbean — the new center of U.S.-Soviet contention.

China saw the late 1970s and early 1980s as a period of heightened rivalry between the two superpowers in Latin America. For its part, the United States was seen to have "fought zealously to maintain its interests and influence" while the Soviets "tried to infiltrate into this continent under the banner of 'support for the national liberation movements.' "[5]

China saw a possible crisis developing when, in August 1979, U.S. intelligence sources revealed the long-term presence of a Soviet combat brigade in Cuba. The Chinese media expressed mixed feelings about the results of U.S.-Soviet negotiations over the affair and disappointment over the failure of Washington to take a strong stand as had been done during the 1962 Cuban missile crisis. Washington's efforts to counter the presence of Soviet troops (which did not include a demand for their withdrawal) have been closely watched by China since 1979. Stepped-up military exercises in the Caribbean and other demonstrations of U.S. economic and military strength, the exodus of 100,000 Cuban refugees, the emergence of new pro-U.S., anti-Cuban regimes in Jamaica and seven other English-speaking states and territories in 1980, and declarations by President Reagan that the Soviets were the cause behind the Latin American unrest in 1981, were hailed by China as setbacks for the Moscow-Havana axis. Contention between the two superpowers, however, was seen as continuing to "aggravate and complicate inherent contradictions in Latin America, making the situation there still more unstable."[6]

The "contradictions" the Chinese see in Latin America have been exemplified in the Central American countries of Nicaragua, El Salvador, and Guatemala and are caused by "prolonged imperialist and colonialist domination," wide gaps between the rich and the poor, internal political forces under the influence of "social democracy, anarchism, terrorism and other ideologies," and "external factors which foment the upheaval."[7] The main external factor, in China's view, is superpower intervention, direct or by proxy.

The Soviets have long been seen as carrying out intervention through their proxy — Cuba — which, for example, signed cooperation agreements and sent thousands of teachers, military advisers, and other personnel to Nicaragua after the demise of the rightist Somoza regime. The Xinhua News Agency reported in December 1980 that the Soviet Union had shipped 100 pieces of artillery and 100 tanks from Cuba to Nicaragua and that Cuban military personnel had found their way into El Salvador and Guatemala. China became quite critical of Soviet, Cuban, and Vietnamese military aid to the Salvadoran insurgents and U.S. aid to the ruling junta when violence escalated in El Salvador in 1980 and 1981. Their sensitivities were further aroused when Chinese-made weapons were reported to have been used by the insurgents. The Chinese admitted that they had given small arms to Havana in the early 1960s but declared that Cuba, having ulterior motives, had transshipped them to the insurgents.[8]

China has encouraged U.S. responses to the Soviet-Cuban involvement in Latin America and has written in relatively glowing terms of "democratic" movements it would have condemned earlier as reactionary. On the other hand,

Washington's economic and military aid to established regimes has been criticized as generally benefitting the "ruling clique and foreign monopoly-capital" and having "produced few results."[9] Chinese policy clearly favors "political solutions" instead of any form of foreign peaceful or nonpeaceful intervention in the region.

The Chinese were heartened by the 1980 Caribbean election results that "constituted a sharp contrast with the situation a year earlier when rapid advances of pro-Soviet, pro-Cuban forces were visible." The Chinese were gratified when the new pro-U.S. Jamaican Prime Minister Edward Seaga demanded that Havana recall its ambassador from Kingston, accused Cuba of acting as a proxy for Soviet expansionism in the Caribbean, and charged the Cubans of having "set up Jamaica as their espionage centre of the Caribbean."[10] Caribbean countries' pleas for aid and a change in previous U.S. policy for the region have been favorably reported on in the Chinese media.

The Chinese have given other examples of superpower conflicts in Latin America. During the 1981 Peru-Ecuador border war, *People's Daily* (Renmin Ribao) noted, very unspecifically, that "people will recall that Moscow has made use of border disputes between Latin American countries to create tension in the Western Hemisphere and seek benefits for itself." The United States, previously criticized for ineffective Carter administration policies, was shown in a positive light for having joined Argentina, Brazil, and Chile in successfully proposing a ceasefire.[11]

Other areas of critical interest to the superpowers in Latin America, and thus subject to their interference, in the Chinese viewpoint, are oil-rich Mexico and Venezuela, a nuclear-powered Brazil, and strategic choke-points such as the Panama Canal and the Tierra del Fuego-Antarctic Ocean area, which is also rich in proven oil reserves.

As elsewhere in the world, China has supported regional unity, stable economic cooperation, and vigilance against the common Soviet enemy. In Latin America this requires the active participation of the United States in a viable and mutually beneficial regional cooperation. In a give-and-take strategic environment, Chinese policy makers want the United States to give up less and take a more forceful role in resisting Soviet-Cuban pressure in Latin America. In such a situation, however, China does not want the United States to return to the use of a *houyuan* style of imperialism against its southern neighbors.

Cuba

Cuba has been a bothersome issue for China since the mid-1960s. Havana provided the People's Republic with its first diplomatic entry into Latin America and, initially, a base for gaining further influence throughout the region. Although China and Cuba had their own bilateral dispute (over mentorship of "wars of national liberation" and an unsuccessful rice-for-sugar barter arrangement), relations worsened primarily because of the larger rift between China and the Soviet Union. Despite periodic efforts by both sides to improve relations and the maintenance of a status quo in trade relations, rapprochement is not possible without one of two possible developments: normalization of Chinese-Soviet relations or devolution in Soviet-Cuban relations.

Since the probability for these changes occurring in Chinese-Soviet and Soviet-Cuban relations is remote, China will continue to view Cuba as a regional hegemonist, a Soviet pawn, and an anti-U.S., anti-China irritant on the international scene.

Regionally, Cuba is seen as playing the role of troublemaker as it interferes in the internal affairs of its more unstable neighbors. China has long criticized Cuba for interference throughout the Caribbean area. Since the 1980s began, China has complained about Havana's involvement in the Nicaraguan, Guatemalan, and Salvadoran revolution and its exporting over 100,000 unwanted refugees, criminals, social outcasts, and the elderly to the United States in the hope of shifting its own domestic social problems onto its superpower neighbor. Cuba's embarrassing gaff of sinking a Bahamian patrol boat, killing four crew members, and sending warplanes to harrass nearby islands during a fishing rights dispute in 1980 was a relatively minor incident touted by China as a leading example of Cuban hegemonism. Havana was cast in the role of an intransigent regional bully to which the Nassau and other regional governments responded with indignation. The slight show of force by the United States — sending a Coast Guard helicopter to the vicinity — was noted with satisfaction by the Xinhua News Agency, especially since the Cuban MIGs had the temerity to have "buzzed within 18 miles" of the U.S. aircraft. Chinese propaganda on the incident was used also to demonstrate support for the Bahamas' claim to a 200-mile special economic zone.

Cuba's military, political, and economic actions, both in Latin America and in other third world areas, are recognized by China as aiding Moscow's strategic goals. The dispatching of tens of thousands of Cuban troops to Africa to participate in the Angolan civil war and the Angola-Zaire and Ethiopia-Somalia wars (all against Chinese-supported forces) was seen as blatantly mercenary. Cuba was characterized as a "Trojan horse" for the Soviet Union and an extremely dangerous enemy to third world nations with which China seeks closer ties.

The presence of Cuban military advisers in Vietnam and Kampuchea was particularly irritating to China. Starting with Vietnam's invasion of Kampuchea in 1978 — ostensibly, in China's perspective, at Soviet bidding — Chinese propagandists took to calling the Hanoi government "the Cuba of Southeast Asia." China was also angered at the attempt made by Cuba's foreign minister in the spring of 1980 to rally support in Pakistan and India for the Soviet-installed regime in Afghanistan. "An accomplice . . . trying to act as a peacemaker. It's both detestable and ridiculous," declared a Chinese domestic radio broadcast.[12]

In these and other Cuban activities on the international scene, Havana is viewed as trying to harm the reputation of China as a third world leader, offering itself as an alternative. A favorite theme of criticism of Chinese actions in Latin America is China's continuing relations with the Pinochet dictatorship in Chile. Castro has also chastised China for its alleged support of South African attacks against Angola and for its 1979 invasion of Vietnam. China has returned the favor through its attacks on Cuba's hypocrisy as a leading force in the non-aligned movement while doing Moscow's bidding whenever and wherever called upon. In the post-1972 period of U.S.-China entente, China frequently has connected Cuba's international activities with its concerted anti-U.S. and anti-China policies, both of which are seen as serving Soviet intentions. This observation helped China demonstrate the validity of a broad united front, participated in by both the United States and China, against Moscow and its followers.

China's reportage on Cuba's domestic situation presents a grim picture of a socialist state whose revolution has been misdirected and failed to meet the needs of its people and whose leaders have placed themselves in bondage to a foreign benefactor. It is with no little satisfaction that the Xinhua News Agency reports on the large daily amounts of capital and goods that Moscow is forced to transfuse into the Cuban economic and military sectors. The Chinese media declared that "Cuba is a hundred percent Soviet pawn" and "not only a Soviet protectorate, but . . . a Soviet military base in the Caribbean" when the news broke in 1979 that a Soviet combat brigade was stationed in Cuba.[13] Havana also was accused of "pursuing a neocolonialist slave system" by shipping tens of thousands of Angolan children to Cuba to cut sugar cane.[14]

BILATERAL RELATIONS

Diplomatic Exchanges

At the time of writing, China had exchanged diplomatic relations with 14 of the 30 independent governments in Latin America.[15] Of the remaining countries, 11 had ties with Taiwan (a factor that will have long-range impact on China's diplomatic efforts) and five had relations with neither Peking nor Taipei.[16] Prospects are mixed for additional diplomatic exchanges between Peking and Latin American governments during the rest of the 1980s.

The People's Republic of China's diplomatic entry into Latin America came with the exchange of recognition with Cuba in 1960, an action not repeated until Chile and China recognized each other in 1970. The seating of the People's Republic in the United Nations in October 1971 became the turning point in Peking's diplomacy. Since that time it has achieved numerous diplomatic exchanges worldwide including 12 in Latin America.

Future diplomatic exchanges with Latin America, like at least some in the past, will relate to the China policy of the United States. Fluctuations in Washington's China policy will continue to have an impact in Latin American relations with China. Before the 1972 Nixon rapprochement with China's leaders and the signing of the Shanghai Communique — when one of the basic premises of U.S.-China policy was isolation of the People's Republic — Latin American regimes generally followed Washington's lead in regard to China. The conservative regimes in the region avoided contact with Communist nations while more moderate governments such as Mexico, Chile, and Argentina allowed trade and cultural exchanges in the 1949-71 period. Leftist governments in Guatemala (briefly in 1954), Cuba (after 1959), and Brazil (1961-64) developed closer contacts with the PRC but only Cuba under Fidel Castro parted with tradition and established formal relations with the People's Republic. It was Chile's leftist government under Salvador Allende, a one-time visitor to China, that gave China its second diplomatic entry to Latin America.

Latin American UN delegates voted almost unanimously to prevent the seating of the People's Republic in the United Nations as long as the U.S. position on the issue had been eminently clear. In the final vote in 1971, coming after Nixon's announced intention to visit China and as Washington carried out an obviously hopeless action to save Taipei's seat, Latin American countries voted in favor of the People's Republic or abstained in significant numbers.[17]

Once in the UN, Chinese envoys increased their contacts with Latin American counterparts and were able to help facilitate policies favored by governments in the region. China's support of the 200-nautical-mile territorial sea/exclusive maritime zone and the Latin American nuclear-weapon-free zone enchanced its good standing throughout Latin America and won it new ties in Lima, Mexico City, and Buenos Aires.

As the decade progressed, a trend developed that is likely to continue to be characteristic of Chinese relations in Latin America in the 1980s. By the late 1970s, economic factors became of greater importance than geopolitical ones in the emerging relationships. Although China maintains a high degree of interest in political issues in the region and encourages united front action against the Soviet Union and Cuba, the real strength in maintaining good ties lies in economic cooperation. China's ties with Chile survived the swing from a socialist regime to a right-wing military junta because of the relatively inoffensive political stand that China had taken before the coup and mutual desire to maintain trade afterward. Political changes in the 1970s in Guyana and Jamaica, where pro-Chinese leanings once were evident, did not destroy bilateral relations because of previous ties based on economic and technical exchanges. China's flexibility in dealing with regimes of greatly varying political leanings also helped it to retain ties that might have been easily severed in an earlier period.

While one can argue that China's motives in maintaining sound trade relations with Latin America are nothing less than geopolitical in nature, it remains true that China maintains stable relations through economic practices and not by political assurances alone. That this tactic is part of a long-range anti-Soviet and anti-Taiwan strategy, however, is obvious. It is also tacit in China's Latin America policy that it no longer supports opposition to regimes with which it has official relations and generally refrains from encouraging forces seeking to destabilize nonrecognized governments. Party-to-party relations are generally restricted to the parties in power or those tolerated by the party in power.

Exchanges of vice ministerial (and equivalent) and higher-level delegations have steadily increased since 1971. Except for the politically tumultuous year of 1976 and the first year of post-Mao readjustment (1977), two-way exchanges of cabinet- and higher-level officials (presidents, prime ministers, and deputy prime ministers) have averaged 17 visits per year since 1971. The exchanges, however, have been uneven, with considerably more Latin American government officials traveling to China (including some from nonrecognized countries) than Chinese traveling to the Latin American region. Argentine and Mexican leaders have been the most frequent visitors to China while Mexico and Peru are the countries visited the most by Chinese officials.

Among the highlights of Latin American visits to the People's Republic in the normalization period were those by the presidents of Argentina, Guyana (Arthur Chung, a man of Chinese descent), and Mexico (two presidents) and the prime ministers of Barbados, Guyana, and Trinidad and Tobago. Additionally, former presidents from Colombia, Mexico, and Peru have traveled to China as have numerous "first family" members. For their part, the Chinese have dispatched only three vice premiers — Chen Yonggui in 1975, Geng Biao in 1978, and Kang Shi'en in 1979. Additionally, three National People's Congress vice chairman — Li Suwen in 1975, Ji Pengfei (now a vice premier) in 1978, and Ngapoi Ngawang Jigme in 1981 — have taken tours in reciprocity for numerous Latin American congressional and parliamentary delegations that have visited China.

The vast majority of these government delegations have been economic related and usually were led by vice ministers of foreign trade or petroleum-related ministries. A small but significant number of military delegations have been exchanged between China and Latin America. Chinese People's Liberation Army deputy chiefs of General Staff have visited Mexico and Peru while Argentina, Mexico, and Peru have sent delegations specifically military in nature to China. Many other Latin American cabinet ministers who have visited China (particularly those from Argentina, Chile, and Peru) have been active-duty generals and admirals holding civilian portfolios. Not cited in any of the above-mentioned exchanges are the numerous visitations by subcabinet level officials from both sides of the Pacific. Delegations of party officials were relatively few in number in the 1970s but can be expected to increase in the 1980s.

Economic Interests

China favors a policy of "economic independence" for the Latin American nations. It was stated in a Chinese report in the early 1970s that economic independence was a "component part of the national liberation movement" in Latin America.[18] One of the major economic problems facing Latin America, according to the Xinhua News Agency, is the rapid accumulation of foreign debts "as a result of ruthless exploitation by the superpowers and international monopoly capital in their attempt to ease their own economic crises."[19]

The solution to Latin American economic problems and a key to achieving economic independence in the Chinese analysis, is the creation of a "new international economic order" through regional economic integration and cooperation against the superpowers and oppressing industrialized nations.

In its own economic dealings with Latin America, China claims to follow policies of mutual benefit and no political interference. Peking has expressed support for regional and subregional cooperative organizations since the beginning of the normalization period.

As mentioned earlier, Chinese relations with Latin American countries are heavily influenced by trade. Among the 14 countries having official ties with the People's Republic of China, trade was specifically mentioned as the key element in the two-way relationship announced in the joint communique establishing relations of two of them (Argentina and Guyana) and was implicit in the communiques with seven others (Jamaica, Trinidad and Tobago, Venezuela, Brazil, Surinam, Ecuador, and Colombia). Unlike earlier recognitions that were preceded by the exchanges of numerous "friendship" delegations and political overtures, the majority of later recognitions were achieved after trade relations had been established.

Chinese trade with Latin America was sparse and, until 1972, ranked in last place when compared with other regions of the world. In 1972, for the first time, China-Latin America two-way trade surpassed that between China and the Middle East and China and South Asia. It continued to increase almost every subsequent year and competed well with the Middle East trade and had far outstripped trade with South Asia through the end of the 1970s. China-Latin America two-way trade figures for 1980 — $1.5 billion — represented an increase of 100 times that reported for 1970 ($15 million). That placed China-Latin America trade second only to China-Southeast Asia trade and ahead of that with the Middle East ($1.4 billion) and Sub-Saharan Africa ($1.3 billion).[20]

In spite of the new competitiveness of China-Latin America trade with other third world regions, the 1980 trade represented only 4 percent of China's total world trade. The China-Latin America trade is also significantly imbalanced, as it is worldwide, with Chinese imports comprising 66 percent of the total.

In recent years, China has claimed to have established trade relations with 37 "countries and regions" in Latin America. This includes nine government trade agreements or long-term barter agreements and, obviously, numerous contracts with virtually every political jurisdiction, whether independent or not, throughout Latin America. Among the Chinese imports from the region, according to their own account, are copper, lead, zinc, sulphur, nitrate and other minerals, cereals, cotton, sugar, soy ·beans, edible oil, sisal, fish meal, cocoa, wheat seed, rubber, and farm animal husbandry and fishery products. Exports include textiles, light industrial products, arts and crafts, farm and sideline products, machinery, farm machines and tools, and nonferrous metals. These exports, according to a vice minister of foreign trade, "enjoy a popular market in Latin America."[21]

According to Chinese accounts, their trade with Latin America is widespread and seemingly well-balanced, involving raw materials imported and light industrial and consumer goods exported by the Chinese. U.S. government reports, however, indicate that China's main trading partners (Argentina, Brazil, Chile, Cuba, Mexico, and Peru) sell considerably more to China than they buy, with cotton, grain, sugar, copper, and iron ore being the major items of interest to the Chinese.[22] Interestingly, one item omitted from China's own list of exports is the crude oil and drilling exploration technology being sold to Brazil.[23] China also has expressed interest in Venezuelan and Trinidadian oil.

China's economic relations with Latin America also include financial and technical assistance. This aid is negligible on a world basis, and in a 22-year period beginning in 1956, China granted only $154 million in aid to the region, the primary recipients being Chile and Peru (loans with no or low interest) and Guyana and Jamaica (monetary and technical assistance in building textile and other plants). This represented only 3 percent of all aid given by China to developing countries in the same period (Africa was first with 56 percent). Similarly, the U.S. government has reported that in the 1955-78 period no military trainees were sent from Latin America to China although other sources indicate that some training did take place for left-wing insurgents in the 1950s and 1960s. China has sent a handful of civilian technicians — 160 in the most recent year for which statistics are available (1978). This was miniscule when compared with the number sent to Africa in the same year (over 19,000) and worldwide (22,000).[24]

A "LAST FRONTIER"

Latin America has traditionally been placed last in China's third world policy in terms of strategic objectives, diplomatic exchanges, economic contacts, and general interest. In the future, the "last" place of Latin America in Chinese foreign policy will no longer be last in the sense of "least." Instead, the region will be a "last frontier" — the one remaining part of the world where China can gain a significant number of new governmental, economic, and political ties and can still seek strategic influence.

There is mutual concern over this "last frontier" in the area of China-U.S. relations as well. In the past, China drew analogies between Cuba and other revolutionary regimes or budding liberation movements. In the early 1960s Chou En-lai himself expressed the desire that there be "a second and third Cuba."[25] The paraphrase "a second and third Vietnam" has likewise been seen in a positive light. As China transformed its views of Cuba from revolutionary model to Soviet satellite and mercenary proxy, so too did it modify its view of Vietnam. Since 1978, when the Peking-Hanoi rupture occurred and the Moscow-Hanoi alliance was formalized, China has frequently referred to Vietnam as "the Cuba of Southeast Asia" and the two countries as the "Soviet Twins." The charges have been made on several counts: Vietnam and Cuba as Soviet satellites and for their having waged Soviet-inspired wars against Kampuchea and in Africa, respectively.

This analogy can be drawn even further. If Vietnam is an Asian Cuba, and Cuba a Latin American Vietnam, where does that leave China and the United States in terms of mutual perceptions? Geographically, both Vietnam and Cuba are immediate "backyard" problems for China and the United States, respectively. Both are concerned about the other's proximate problem and, indeed, consider these problems strategically as their own. There is a convergence of interest between the United States and China on Cuba and Vietnam. Additionally, the long-range ramifications of Cuban actions throughout Latin America (and Africa) and Vietnamese activities in Southeast Asia, compounded by the leadership and complicity of the common Soviet enemy, give rise to further mutual concern. Chinese reports of Cuban activities in Vietnam and Kampuchea in support of the Vietnamese government and U.S. reports of Cuban shipments of Vietnamese-origin weapons into troubled El Salvador all bear further witness to the problems shared by China and the United States.

Thus, China is likely to heighten its concern and activities in the Latin American region in protection of its own interests and without U.S. objections (as long as there is not a radical change in Washington's China policy). It is likely to do so through the vehicle of economic relations, primarily, and expanded diplomatic ties, secondarily. Its success will be dependent on modifications in U.S.-China relations and the extent to which the two project that relationship — whether it improves or worsens — in the Latin American region.

NOTES

1. Mu Youlin, "China and the Third World," *Beijing Review* (hereinafter *BR*), April 27, 1981, p. 3.

2. A more detailed description of Chinese-Latin American relations in the 1949-77 period can be found in my chapter "China's Foreign Relations With Latin America," in *Dimensions of China's Foreign Relations*, ed. Chün-tu Hsüeh (New York: Praeger, 1977), pp. 191-231; second printing, with minor corrections, 1978.

3. Yan Jiu, "The Decline of the U.S. Position in Latin America," *Renmin Ribao*, October 9, 1980, p. 7, as reported in Foreign Broadcast Information Service, *Daily Report, People's Republic of China* (hereinafter FBIS/*China*), October 15, 1980, p. B2.

4. "Unrest in Latin America," *BR*, January 19, 1981, p. 15.

5. Ibid.; and the Xinhua News Agency, January 3, 1981, in FBIS/*China*, January 5, 1981, p. J1.

6. Ibid.

7. Xinhua News Agency, December 25, 1980, in FBIS/*China*, December 30, 1980, pp. J1-2.

8. Ibid., p. J2; and Guo Ji, "China and El Salvador," *BR*, March 9, 1981, p. 3.

9. Beijing Domestic Service, November 12, 1980, in FBIS/*China*, November 13, 1980, pp. J1-2; and Yao Chuntao, "The Situation in El Salvador," *BR*, January 26, 1981, pp. 14-15.

10. Xinhua News Agency, January 3, 1981, in FBIS/*China*, January 5, 1981, p. J1.

11. *Renmin Ribao*, February 3, 1981, as cited by Xinhua News Agency, February 3, 1981, in FBIS/*China*, February 4, 1981, p. J1.

12. Beijing Domestic Service, April 11, 1980, in FBIS/*China*, April 16, 1980, p. J1.

13. Xinhua News Agency, September 22, 1979, in FBIS/*China*, September 25, 1979, p. B1; and *Renmin Ribao*, September 4, 1979, p. 6, in FBIS/*China*, September 7, 1979, p. B1.

14. Xinhua News Agency, November 13, 1979, in FBIS/*China*, November 19, 1979, p. J1.

15. The 14, in order of recognition are Cuba (1960), Chile (1970), Peru (1971), Mexico (1972), Argentina (1972), Guyana (1972), Jamaica (1972), Trinidad and Tobago (1974), Venezuela (1974), Brazil (1974), Surinam (1976), Barbados (1977), Ecuador (1980), and Colombia (1980).

16. Those that still have relations with Taiwan are Bolivia, Costa Rica, Dominican Republic, El Salvador, Guatemala, Haiti, Honduras, Nicaragua, Panama, Paraguay, and Uruguay. The five nations that have relations with neither Peking nor Taipei are Bahamas, Dominica, Grenada, St. Lucia, and St. Vincent.

17. Voting in favor were Chile, Cuba, Ecuador, Guyana, Mexico, Peru, and Trinidad and Tobago (all of which have formal relations with the People's Republic); against were Bolivia, Brazil, Costa Rica, Dominican Republic, El Salvador, Guatemala, Haiti, Honduras, Nicaragua, Paraguay, Uruguay, and Venezuela (Brazil and Venezuela subsequently established relations with the PRC); and abstaining were Argentina, Barbados, Colombia, Jamaica, and Panama (all but the latter have established relations with the People's Republic of China).

18. "Latin American Countries Opposing Hegemonism: Struggle for National Economic Development," *Peking Review*, February 16, 1973, pp. 6-7, 12.

19. Xinhua News Agency, May 14, 1978, in FBIS/*China*, May 17, 1978, pp. A21-22.

20. Kathryn Dewenter, "China's Foreign Trade by Area and Country, 1970-79," *The China Business Review* (Washington), July-August 1980, p. 35; and U.S. Central Intelligence Agency, *China: International Trade, Fourth Quarter, 1980*, ER CIT 81-003, May 1981, pp. 2, 17, 19. Chinese-supplied trade figures, while not as specifically broken down as U.S.-supplied ones, are higher. For example, Dewenter indicates a 1979 two-way trade figure of $1.06 billion as compared with Chinese figures of $1.26 billion. There is a wider discrepancy between the two sources for earlier data. Chinese-supplied figures for the 1960s claim an average annual two-way trade of $200 million versus $15 million (1970 only) claimed by Dewenter. See Cheng Fei, "China's Trade with Latin America," *China's Foreign Trade* (Peking), January-February 1981, p. 62.

21. Chen Jie, "Trade Between China and Latin American Countries," *China Foreign Trade*, July-August 1980, p. 2. Also see "With Which Countries and Regions Has China Established Trade Relations?" Ibid., July-August 1979, pp. 10-11; and Cheng Fei, "China's Trade with Latin America," p. 62.

22. See various editions of CIA reports: *People's Republic of China: International Trade Handbook*; *China: International Trade*; and *Handbook of Economic Statistics*, Washington, 1974-80.

23. See CIA, *China: International Trade, Third Quarter, 1980*, ER CIT 81-002, March 1981, table 13, which lists Chinese crude oil exports to Brazil since 1978. Since

that time, exports have averaged about 18,000 bbl. per day. Also see "Brazil and China Act to Improve Trade," New York *Times*, June 12, 1980, p. D11.

24. See CIA reports cited in note 22.

25. "Premier Chou En-lai's Press Conference in Algiers (December 26, 1963)," *Afro-Asian Solidarity Against Imperialism* (Peking: Foreign Languages Press, 1964), p. 77.

INDEX

ABOUT THE EDITOR AND CONTRIBUTORS

CHÜN-TU HSÜEH (LL.B., Chaoyang University College of Law, China; M.A., Ph.D., Columbia University), professor of government and politics at the University of Maryland, College Park, was formerly visiting professor and acting director of the Research Unit for Chinese and East Asian Politics at the Free University of Berlin. He has taught at Harvard University, Columbia University, and the University of Hong Kong. His book *Huang Hsing and the Chinese Revolution* (Stanford University Press, 1961, reprinted 1968) was translated and jointly published by the Hunan People's Publishing House, China, and the Hong Kong Branch of the Joint Publishing Company of Peking in 1980. Dr. Hsüeh is the editor of and a contributor to *Revolutionary Leaders of Modern China* (New York: Oxford University Press, 1971, reprinted 1973; French edition, *Les dirigeants de la Chine révolutionnaire* (Paris: Calmann-Lévy, 1973), *Asian Political Scientists in North America: Professional and Ethnic Problems* (Baltimore: Occasional Papers Series in Contemporary Asian Studies, School of Law, University of Maryland, 1977), and *Dimensions of China's Foreign Relations* (New York: Praeger, 1977, reprinted 1978). He is the co-translator of *Traditional Government in Imperial China: A Critical Analysis* (New York: St. Martin's Press, and the Chinese University Press of Hong Kong, 1982).

JEAN-LUC DOMENACH received his French doctoral degree in political science. He is with the *Foundation nationale des sciences politiques* (Paris) and lectures at the *Institut national des langues et civilisations orientales* and the *Ecole Polytechnique*. He has contributed to *Regards froids sur la Chine* (Paris: le Seuil, 1976) and a number of scholarly journals, including *Les Annales* and *Revue francaise de science politique*. In 1976-78 he served as a cultural attaché at the French consulate in Hong Kong.

KAREL KOVANDA (Ph.D., Massachusetts Institute of Technology) received his undergraduate education in Prague, Czechoslovakia. He left his country for the United States in 1970, worked in the Soviet-East European Department of Radio Peking in 1977-79, and has taught at the University of California at Santa Barbara. He is the co-translator of *Dialectics of the Concrete* (Boston, 1976) and has published numerous articles in the United States and abroad.

ROBERT C. NORTH (Ph.D., Stanford University), formerly president of the International Studies Association, is professor of political science at Stanford University. He is the author of several books, including *The Foreign*

Relations of China, 3d ed. (North Scituate, Mass.: Duxbury Press, 1978); *Chinese Communism* (New York: McGraw-Hill, 1966); *Moscow and Communists*, 2d ed. (Stanford University Press, 1963); *The World That Could Be*, 2d ed. (New York: W. W. Norton, 1976); and coauthor of *Nations in Conflict* (San Francisco: W. H. Freeman, 1975) and *International Crisis* (Montreal: McGill-Queens University Press, 1976).

SHEE POON KIM (B.A., Nanyang University, Singapore; Ph.D., Indiana University) is a senior lecturer in political science at the National University of Singapore. He has taught at the University of Hull, United Kingdom. In 1981 Dr. Shee was a visiting professor of government and international studies at the University of South Carolina, the International Studies Association scholar in residence, and research associate at the Center for Chinese Studies, University of California, Berkeley. His publications include *Thailand's Relations with the People's Republic of China, 1949-1975* (Singapore, 1979) and other articles in scholarly journals.

ROBERT L. WORDEN (Ph.D., Georgetown University) has been a Chinese affairs specialist at the Library of Congress since 1973, currently serving as a senior research analyst. He has taught at Georgetown University Graduate School and has been a guest lecturer on Chinese leadership and foreign policy at the U.S. Department of State's Foreign Service Institute, American University, and the Johns Hopkins School of Advanced International Studies. His publications include a chapter on Latin America in Chün-tu Hsüeh, ed., *Dimensions of China's Foreign Relations* (New York: Praeger, 1977), and articles and chapters in other monographs and journals.

RAYMOND F. WYLIE (Ph.D., University of London) is associate professor of international relations and chairman of the Committee on East Asian Studies at Lehigh University. He is the author of *The Emergence of Maoism: Mao Tse-tung, Ch'en Po-ta, and the Search for Chinese Theory, 1935-1945* (Stanford University Press, 1980).

HERBERT S. YEE (Ph.D., University of Hawaii), assistant professor of international relations at International Christian University, Tokyo, Japan, has taught at the University of Maryland-Baltimore County. He was a research fellow at the Foreign Policy Research Center of Dalhousie University, Canada, for 1976-78. He has contributed articles on Asian politics to a number of scholarly journals.

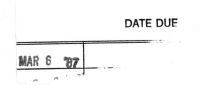